PRAISE FOR
THE LISTENING ROAD

"Neil Tomba's work *The Listening Road* will take you on a unique spiritual journey designed to encourage you to open up your ears and your heart to people who need to know about and respond to our great God and the good news of the gospel. This fine work will eradicate our excuses for not using every natural opportunity to share our faith."

—DR. TONY EVANS, SENIOR PASTOR OF OAK CLIFF BIBLE FELLOWSHIP AND PRESIDENT OF THE URBAN ALTERNATIVE

"*The Listening Road* is a soul-searching journey into the heart of American faith practices. Neil's conversations are gritty, real, authentic, and worshipful. You'll be challenged and encouraged on every page."

—LOUIE GIGLIO, PASTOR OF PASSION CITY CHURCH, VISIONARY FOR THE PASSION MOVEMENT, AND BESTSELLING AUTHOR OF *GOLIATH MUST FALL* AND *DON'T GIVE THE ENEMY A SEAT AT YOUR TABLE*

"A wise man named Denver once told me God gave us two ears and one mouth and that should be enough to convince us what is the most important. In *The Listening Road*, from coast to coast across America, with unrelenting determination, Pastor Neil perfected the art of listening without preaching. As you turn the pages of this wonderful journey, breathe the air and feel the wind and rain as you bike every mile, fix every flat, and listen on this ride of a lifetime. This remarkable tale of connecting with real people, total strangers, on a deep level may seem strange, but it is something we should all learn on our personal 'listening roads' as we quietly share the good news of Christ. If we are honest, most of us live in communities that are miles wide and only inches deep. People all around us, even strangers, are dying to share their stories. Pastor Neil found the time to listen without judging. Only then did he earn the right to tell them about the hope that lies within all believers. Now, let's ride."

—RON HALL, AUTHOR OF #1 *NEW YORK TIMES* BESTSELLER *SAME KIND OF DIFFERENT AS ME* AND THE SEQUEL *WORKIN' OUR WAY HOME*

"Pastor Neil Tomba and his bike trekked across America to have kind, curious, and respectful conversations about God. This book offers us amazing stories that open up the heart of the nation as Neil prompts people to ask—and answer—big questions about their faith. Read this book, then pass it along to your friends. You won't be disappointed."

—Dr. Wayne Cordeiro, founding pastor of New Hope
International Ministries and bestselling author of *The
Divine Mentor*, *Leading on Empty*, and *Jesus Pure & Simple*

"Our lives are so rushed we often have too little time to ask core questions of people and listen. Neil Tomba's *The Listening Road* does that while detailing a challenging cross-country bike ride. People of all stripes appear with their reflections on the possibilities of faith. It is putting an ear to the ground of our country and searching for its soul beat. I think you will find these conversations as fascinating as I did, learning in the process how questions sometimes open up doors to the hearts of people."

—Darrell Bock, senior research professor of New Testament
Studies and executive director for cultural engagement
at Hendricks Center, Dallas Theological Seminary

"Neil Tomba has done something totally amazing. Not only has he activated a life dream from his own gospel-centered bucket list, he's captured the story in a way that will fuel your own dreams and guide you into an everyday goldmine—the opportunity to talk about Jesus where you live, work, and play."

—Will Mancini, founder of the Future Church Co. and Younique

The LISTENING ROAD

The LISTENING ROAD

ONE MAN'S RIDE ACROSS AMERICA TO
START CONVERSATIONS ABOUT GOD

NEIL TOMBA

NELSON
BOOKS

An Imprint of Thomas Nelson

Published in Nashville, Tennessee, by Nelson Books, an imprint of Thomas Nelson. Nelson Books and Thomas Nelson are registered trademarks of HarperCollins Christian Publishing, Inc.

Thomas Nelson titles may be purchased in bulk for educational, business, fundraising, or sales promotional use. For information, please e-mail SpecialMarkets@ThomasNelson.com.

Unless otherwise noted, Scripture quotations are taken from The Holy Bible, New International Version®, NIV®. Copyright © 1973, 1978, 1984, 2011 by Biblica, Inc.® Used by permission of Zondervan. All rights reserved worldwide. www.Zondervan.com. The "NIV" and "New International Version" are trademarks registered in the United States Patent and Trademark Office by Biblica, Inc.®

Scripture quotations marked ESV are taken from the ESV® Bible (The Holy Bible, English Standard Version®). Copyright © 2001 by Crossway, a publishing ministry of Good News Publishers. Used by permission. All rights reserved.

Scripture quotations marked NKJV are taken from the New King James Version®. Copyright © 1982 by Thomas Nelson. Used by permission. All rights reserved.

Any internet addresses, phone numbers, or company or product information printed in this book are offered as a resource and are not intended in any way to be or to imply an endorsement by Thomas Nelson, nor does Thomas Nelson vouch for the existence, content, or services of these sites, phone numbers, companies, or products beyond the life of this book.

All conversations featured in this book took place. In some cases the wording has been altered slightly from the original for the sake of clarity or brevity.

ISBN 978-1-4002-2460-9 (eBook)
ISBN 978-1-4002-2459-3 (HC)

Library of Congress Cataloging-in-Publication Data

Names: Tomba, Neil, 1961- author.
Title: The listening road : one man's ride across America to start conversations about God / Neil Tomba.
Description: Nashville, Tennessee : Nelson Books, 2021. | Summary: "The true story of one man's remarkable journey biking across the United States, engaging with people from all walks of life in conversations about faith, disillusionment, purpose, and Jesus--and his hope-filled discovery that even in the most divisive climate, connection is possible"-- Provided by publisher.
Identifiers: LCCN 2020051057 (print) | LCCN 2020051058 (ebook) | ISBN 9781400224593 (hardcover) | ISBN 9781400224609 (eBook)
Subjects: LCSH: Tomba, Neil, 1961---Travel--United States. | Clergy--Travel--United States. | Spiritual life--Christianity. | Bicycle touring--United States. | United States--Description and travel. | United States--Social life and customs.
Classification: LCC BV4014 .T66 2021 (print) | LCC BV4014 (ebook) | DDC 277.30092 [B]--dc23
LC record available at https://lccn.loc.gov/2020051057
LC ebook record available at https://lccn.loc.gov/2020051058

Printed in the United States of America

21 22 23 24 25   LSC   10 9 8 7 6 5 4 3 2 1

For people everywhere who long for deeper conversations

CONTENTS

CONTENTS

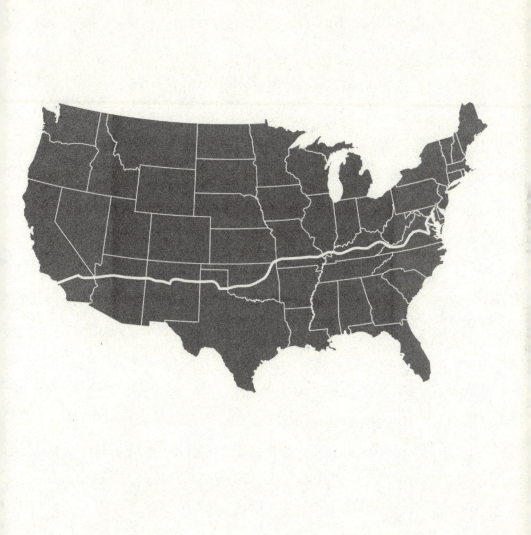

— 1 —

THE EIGHTEEN-YEAR DREAM

When people ask me today how long it took to ride my bicycle across America, I just grin and say, "eighteen years." That's how long it took me to work through the obstacles that kept me from taking time off work to make a long cross-country trip happen. The trip had sounded like an amazing adventure from the get-go, and I knew it would have purpose too. I dreamed of meeting people and having significant conversations with them about who they were and what mattered most in their lives. But something always got in the way.

See, when I was growing up, my dad taught me to keep my head down and be a hard charger. Riding a bicycle was play, and he was all about work, work, work. In my dad's worldview, there wasn't a lot of room for margins. Certainly not for taking time off work to go on long bike rides or to have deeper conversations with people, particularly folks you didn't even know. That mindset stuck with me long into my adulthood.

It was right about the time I became the senior pastor of Northwest Bible Church in Dallas in 2001 that my dream of riding a bike cross-country was born. Our church ran a two-week camp each summer in

Colorado, and part of my job was to lead it. It was a blast. We rode mountain bikes, and I led hikes. I felt like I was a kid who was working really hard . . . at *play*.

One afternoon I was riding my mountain bike on the epic Monarch Crest Trail when I rode through a beautiful section of woods that I'd ridden through more than once. It was a shortcut to get back to the cabin we were staying at. The trail was padded with pine straw, and after coasting through the trees I emerged onto a rough gravel road. There lay a pond and a fish hatchery, and a family was there with their fly rods out, catching fish. This dad and mom and a little boy and girl captured my attention. The area was so beautiful and so far off the main road that I wondered how they had found this place and if they came here often. That made me think more about their stories. I began to think about countless conversations I'd had at times like this, and I really wanted to stop and talk with them. I didn't even realize I was slowing down as I drew closer. I just felt the longing to talk with them—and not only that, but to go across the whole country having conversations with all kinds of people about who they are and what matters in their lives.

I never forgot that moment. That's when the dream was born. But I toyed with that dream for eighteen years because I didn't give myself permission to pursue it at first. See, in my mind riding a bike was still play.

And I needed to work.

Three things became catalysts for change in my dream. First, around seven years ago, when I was fifty-one, doctors discovered a tumor in my small intestine. They suspected cancer, so I had the tumor removed, along with my ileocecal valve, the one between the small and large intestine. Fortunately, the tumor wasn't cancerous, but a doctor told me, "Neil, you could have died from this." I'd felt a small brush with my own mortality then, and I thought, *Some things need to change. Maybe I could take time for play after all. Maybe I could take time for passions that aren't work.*

Second, I'd always wanted to do a Half Ironman, which involves swimming, biking, and running. But training for one had always felt like play, so it had never happened. After my surgery I set a goal: do a Half Ironman.

Thirteen months after the surgery, I finished the race.

My three daughters were grown by then, and for years I had been hearing about the Leadville 100. It's a long mountain bike race held each year on rugged trails and dirt roads through the heart of Colorado's Rocky Mountains. I'd always wanted to attempt that, but I'd felt too guilty about the time commitment required for training and travel. The race starts at 10,000 feet and ascends to 12,400 feet, and it requires more training than even a Half Ironman. But one of my daughters, Sheree, had trained for the race and asked me to be on her pit crew. I'd gone to support her, and while I was there, I'd looked around and said, "You know, I think I could do this." I was hooked.

I trained and soon set out on my first attempt. The race was so hard. The first two times I tried, I didn't make it to the finish line. But the third time I did. That became the second catalyst and got me thinking, *If I can ride a mountain bike over the Leadville 100, I bet I can ride a road bike across America.*

About then the leadership team at my church started working on a new vision in which we encouraged people in our congregation to get outside the walls of the church, have more conversations about Jesus with neighbors, and seek more opportunities to serve people of our city. This became the third catalyst. America seemed so divided over people's opinions about everything. We wanted to learn to talk about the most important things in a way that made people feel respected, heard, and valued.

Too often I'd seen—or been a part of—conversations where neither person was truly listening to the other, and I suspected we were all suffering from a chronic lack of genuine listening. It seemed increasingly important to figure out how to do this, how to invite people in instead of shutting the door in their faces. And maybe this idea that wouldn't go away was more than an irresponsible dream.

One of the leaders in our church is a young attorney and entrepreneur named Reece. In talking to him and the team about our church's vision, I mentioned my dream of riding my bike across the country and how it might relate to our church's overall vision. Reece got really excited.

"You need to do this, Neil," he said. "Do it now. And do it in a big way."

Reece encouraged me to think far bigger than I had before. I'd imagined doing this ride in a small way, with just me on my bike following my wife in a van. But Reece insisted I ride with a team of people to help me go faster, farther. He also said that lots of other people should hear about our trip. That meant we needed to document with a film crew every conversation I had, which he could arrange for me.

With Reece's help, my dream of a coast-to-coast ride grew some wings. A team came together very quickly, almost miraculously.

One longtime friend in his midfifties, Paul, was heading toward early retirement and insisted he come along as support staff.

Another friend in his fifties, Jeff, grew so excited about the trip that he actually quit his job so he could help.

A mountain-biking buddy of mine, Wes, was an experienced cyclist and immediately volunteered to become part of my riding team.

I talked to my daughter Sheree about coaching me and designing a training plan.

A woman in her early thirties, Caroline, worked in our sports-and-recreation ministry at the church. Her story of losing fifty pounds while preparing for a Half Ironman impressed us all and proved her drive. She was a novice biker, but she agreed to train with Sheree so she could be one of the three cyclists who would ride all the way cross-country.

Two missionaries who had been supported by our church for more than forty years, Glenn and Judy, offered to drive a support vehicle.

Reece's colleague Jon, a professional videographer and director, was eager to come and film the project, and Jon had an assistant, James, who could help for two weeks.

A Chinese seminary student, Christine, could assist for the remainder of the trip, and another student, Joy, from India, agreed to be a driver for a few weeks.

Una, a Tongan American, would also be a driver, along with Sarah, an administrator at our church.

My wife, Vela, rounded out the team.

We started to have monthly meetings to pray about the trip and work out the logistics of traveling and everyone being away from home for more than a month. One of the biggest questions I had privately was whether anybody on the road would actually talk to me, particularly on camera. I wasn't a professional journalist. I'd never interviewed people other than our church members. I was worried about my lack of experience, but I eventually decided that I had to put anxiety out of my mind. I wanted the conversations to be real, not staged or fake; they had to be authentic dialogues. What else could I do except go ask people if they wanted to talk—and then just do it?

I started to train for the trip in earnest. I was eating healthy. I didn't have any nagging injuries. I began riding anywhere from 150 to 200 miles each week, doing 20-mile rides several times throughout the week and 75 to 100 miles each Saturday. After I'd finish a ride, I'd climb off my bike and immediately do a set of fifty push-ups. Plenty of days I'd tack on two additional sets of twenty-five. I used a power meter and a computer program on my bike to measure something called functional threshold power (FTP) so I could analyze my workouts and my endurance performance ability. One day I did a 210-mile ride to raise awareness about our trip. The more I trained, the stronger I became.

One by one, every component of our trip came together. Team members. Finances. Physical ability. Transportation. Everything. The momentum was gaining. This dream was actually going to happen.

Two weeks before the start date of our trip, I decided to do an evening ride with a group of fifty people from a local bike shop, despite the fact that my daughter who had been coaching me didn't want me to do a group ride this close to start time.

It was a beautiful Dallas evening, eighty-five degrees out, sunny and still light. We were set to ride loops around White Rock Lake. Normally on rides like these I rode as hard as I could near the front of the pack, but that evening I told myself to go more slowly. I hung near the back of the lead group, with about eight riders ahead of me. A larger bunch of riders followed us.

The ride started perfectly. We rode to the lake and started to make the loops. I felt stronger than I'd ever felt. Indestructible. But as we rounded a corner and went into a slight downhill, at the bottom of the dip, I hit a bump. We were flying along at about thirty miles per hour, and when I hit the bump, the chain popped off my front sprocket. We were heading uphill by then, and in that exact moment, when I pressed hard on my pedal, I encountered no resistance thanks to my unattached chain.

My foot slipped off my pedal. The bike wobbled, and my back wheel slid out from underneath me. Suddenly I was going down. *Hard.*

My bike slid out to the left. The entire right side of my body aimed toward the pavement. I felt one leg scrape the ground first. Then my arm slammed against the road. Then my hip.

For a moment everything was confusion and chaos. I sensed tumbling. Grinding. Skin ripping. An incredibly sharp pain.

When my bike finally stopped moving, all I could do was lie on the pavement, trying to suck in enough air to breathe. I saw blood. Lots of blood. *My* blood, coming from at least five brand-new ragged openings on my body. Huge sections of my skin were badly road burned. The rush of pain to my brain was so unbearable I thought I was going to pass out. The screaming started once I could suck in enough air to make a sustained sound.

That's when the truth of what had just happened hit me hard. All along in the training I'd been asking myself if I had what it would take to make this trip. A huge challenge lay before me, and I wondered if I could make it the whole way across the country. I'd been wondering how the trip would change me in the process. Now we were two weeks away from the date we were set to leave, and this challenge had already defeated me. The challenge was already over.

I wasn't even going to be able to start.

— 2 —

DESPERATE DEPENDENCE

I did not want to be defeated.

Certainly not yet.

I lay on the road for a few split seconds, tangled in the mess of my bicycle. Other bicyclists screeched to a stop around me, shouting their concerns. Was I okay? Did I want an ambulance? Was I dead?

Slowly I untangled myself, sat upright, and took stock of my wounds. My elbow dripped blood. A fist-sized hole had been ripped from the fabric of my jersey near my shoulder, and my skin showed through, raw and bleeding. I had large swaths of road rash on my right hip, quadricep, knee, and ankle, with dirt and bits of black asphalt imbedded in what remained of my skin. The middle of each gash was mostly red, like uncooked hamburger, while the circumference of several gashes was gray, indicating that the friction of the crash had actually burned my skin.

A buddy straightened out my handlebars and popped the chain back on the sprocket while I shook off the group's concern. Calling an ambulance was out of the question. As a kid, when I got hurt playing sports, I tended to get in trouble because I was always supposed to be working, not playing—and old habits die hard. From the crash site I called Vela and asked her to stop by the pharmacy and get me a ton of bandages. Over the years I've worn her down, and I knew she wouldn't push me to go to the doctor unless I already had one foot through death's door. My head wasn't cracked open, so in my thinking I only had my *hand* on death's doorknob.

Truly, I was in sorry shape. As I rode home I felt blood pooling in my shorts. It seeped through the fabric and dripped down my right leg. With each pedal stroke my skin stretched and tore.

Once home, I turned on the shower and grabbed two washcloths— one to scrub my skin, the other to bite down on to stop the screaming. Vela was home from the pharmacy in a flash and bandaged my wounds after I emerged from the shower. She was heading out of town to see one of our daughters, and I nodded at her to go. She didn't need to be around to hear my agony.

Early the next morning I changed the bandages and drove to work. I felt horrible all day, the pain almost unmanageable. The next two nights I coped by lying on a large towel on the floor of our bedroom and hollering in pain. Sleep fled. I wanted to let my wounds dry out, yet so much seepage was coming from them that I didn't want to risk ruining our bed. On the third day I went to the doctor, who told me to go to a wound-care facility for specialized treatment. I didn't like the sound of that, so I decided the best way forward would be to just take my mind off things and pack for the trip.

Several more days passed in a blur of aching. I still couldn't sleep. I had been in the best shape of my life before the crash, but now I felt my fitness level heading downhill. I couldn't train. I couldn't even ride my bike.

To top it off, I realized that a cross-country bike trip was an unusual thing for a pastor to do. I'd tried to carefully cast the vision of this trip to our leadership team, elder board, and congregation, yet there were still some folks who thought I was crazy. In their minds, senior pastors just didn't do this sort of thing. Plenty of people, including elders, were worried about all the things that could go wrong.

After several tough meetings, I slumped to my lowest point in fifteen months. Physically I was in agony. Emotionally I was spent. Even spiritually I felt down. God knew I'd had my heart set on taking this trip. Why had he allowed this crash and this questioning?

So many things had already come together to make this trip a reality. Ten team members had taken time off work. The other cyclists had trained hard for months on end. Money had been raised. Websites had been created. Supplies had been gathered. Vans had been painted.

I felt the weight of responsibility on my shoulders. This was my trip to lead, and there was no way I could back out now.

I simply *had* to do this.

Three days before the trip was set to begin, I was on my knees at 5:30 a.m. on the floor of my bedroom, pleading for God to help me. Jesus' bold yet loving words from John 15:5 came to mind: "Apart from me you can do nothing." I leaned into those words and kept praying for him to make a way for us to move forward.

I recalled our church's mission statement: *To invite people into the unexpected joy of desperate dependence on Jesus.* Years earlier, when that statement was created, the word *desperate* had been carefully chosen because whenever God calls us to do something for his sake, there's a good chance it won't be easy.

Surely God was now calling me to a greater sense of dependence on *his* strength, not my own. The whole point of this trip was for me to see if I could talk with strangers about deeper things. It wasn't about caution. It was about taking risks. Now, thanks to the crash and the criticism, I'd been put in a place where I'd already reached the end of myself. Surely this was what desperate dependence felt like.

Only God could make this trip happen now.

Surely God would come through for us. Holding onto that hope became my unexpected joy.

I decided to go ahead with the plan. We had raised the money. People had planned extensively for this trip. I didn't see *not* to start as an option.

As the time arrived for the trip to begin, the team prepared to fly from Texas to California, while I caught a quick flight to New York to make a TV publicity appearance. The producers had asked me to bring a bike, so after I got off the plane, I rented one from a shop and rode to the studio. It was the first time I'd been on a bike since the crash, and as I rode I felt a twinge of peace come over me for the first time in two weeks. The streets and storefronts of New York had been freshly washed with rain. The morning air felt cool and bright, beckoning me to greater adventure.

The show went well. Then I hopped another plane and flew back across the country to Los Angeles, arriving in time for dinner with the team. As I looked around the table of friends and supporters, I was aware of how large this dream had already grown. It had gained momentum, and now we were set to launch something that held the potential to spark a movement.

We were in search of no specific outcome. We were simply prepared to ride bikes and have conversations—and to do it in a way that made people feel heard. That was the spark I hoped would be fanned into flames. The purity of the dream was just to go out and be curious about people's stories. To open doors, not close them.

I felt so happy to be at that dinner table at the trip's start. Yet after two long flights in two days—on top of my injuries and emotional turmoil—I had to admit I was already exhausted.

The next day was May 27, 2019, the official start of our trip. I was up at 4:30 a.m., running on adrenaline. My hip and knee were still tight from the crash. Scabs on my shoulder and arm were cracking and bleeding.

As the sun rose, I wheeled my bike onto the wooden slats of the Santa Monica Pier. The day felt cool and misty, about fifty degrees Fahrenheit. Palm trees dotted the streak of land behind me where the beach ended and the city began. A seagull flew far off to my right, and the breakers of the Pacific rolled and crashed beneath me. To the west the multihued blue of the ocean stretched as far as I could see.

Dressed in biking shorts, bright red jerseys, and helmets, Caroline and Wes were already puttering around on the pier, checking their bikes and supplies with the rest of the team. Another rider, John, was set to ride with us for the first week only, and immediately I sensed him bringing a steady calm to the team. Vela was there with a big grin and a sign she'd made to cheer me on. She would drive one of the support vehicles.

While I looked at the excitement and optimism on each team member's face, thousands of questions still plagued my mind. Would complete strangers actually talk with me—and would they truly open up? Could my team and I really ride 3,000 miles to the other side of the country— especially when I was starting out injured and exhausted? How would I change and grow during the trip? What would we all see and experience? Would I learn the lessons I needed to learn?

We talked among ourselves briefly and posed for a few pictures, but I knew the clock was ticking. We needed to hit the road. Even though we'd planned to set aside generous portions of each day for conversations, we still needed to ride hard—about 100 miles each day—to accomplish the trip in the thirty-three days we had off work (with two days allotted for rest). We simply needed to begin.

I said a silent prayer, turned my bike around to head east, and then suddenly stopped.

In front of me were a middle-aged man and woman dressed in red and black biking jerseys, getting ready to head out on their own ride. They saw I was on a bike, and I caught their eye, so I grinned and walked over.

"Hey there, I'm getting ready to go across the country today!" I said in my friendliest voice.

The woman laughed, motioned to the man, and said, "You know, he's making me ride to Mount Wilson today. Climbing 15,000 feet. We had just looked at your team and made a guess that you were riding cross-country."

I shook their hands and introduced myself, and they said their names were John and Melissa. We talked about biking and where they were going and the best kinds of handlebars for longer rides. Then I explained how I'd been dreaming about our trip for eighteen years, just riding across the country and having conversations with people, hopefully about deeper things. "Our country is so crazy right now, and people are afraid to talk to anybody," I said. "I'm going to go out and ask people what's on their hearts. I'm curious—do you ever talk about spiritual matters?"

"Well, we've just been watching *The Handmaid's Tale* on TV," Melissa said. "It's a little spiritual. And we've been watching *The Kindness Diaries*, about the guy who travels the world being kind to people."

"Oh, I love that show," I said.

We talked about the shows, and I asked a few more casual questions. I tried to listen to them far more than I talked. They described how they weren't really into faith or God, although they were into seeking spiritual things. John had grown up going to church but had hated it as a kid because he'd wanted to hang out with his friends instead. As an adult he went to church once in a while, mostly on Easter and Christmas.

Melissa folded her arms across her chest and said she was a cultural Jew but not practicing in any way. She said she was "working her way through life," although I wasn't sure what that meant. When I asked for clarification, she said that for her, spiritual seeking meant being out in nature or on her bike.

We talked some more about this and that—maybe ten minutes total.

I just tried to affirm their stories and show that I appreciated them talking so openly. It was cool to hear them be honest about where they were spiritually. When they were ready to depart, I thanked them for talking with me. They gave me hugs as fellow bikers, and both said, "Thank you for talking with us." And boom, that was it. They pedaled away, and I thought, *Okay, then*.

It hadn't been a long conversation, but we'd talked about more than the weather. We hadn't argued, even though our worldviews didn't totally mesh. I had listened. We had ended our talk in a friendly way. I was sure that if I ever saw John or Melissa again, the door would be open to another conversation.

Our trip had truly begun.

— 3 —

STRANGERS OPENING UP

We were heading east toward San Bernardino, but first we had to navigate the busy traffic of Los Angeles and get out of the city. We pedaled through the traffic of the side streets and hit lots of stoplights. Thanks to the traffic, it was hard for our support vehicles to keep pace with us, and I lost sight of them several times.

All my senses felt heightened. I had never ridden a bike in Los Angeles, and I quickly noticed how all the people drive fast, like they mean business. I was already looking for people to talk with, too, and I wasn't sure exactly how that would play out. If I stopped, that meant the entire team would also stop, and I didn't want to spook the people I stopped to talk with. I could only imagine the looks on their faces when ten strangers and two support vehicles pulled over and asked them to bare their souls.

I decided my best-case scenario would be to initiate conversations whenever the team stopped for natural breaks, like for lunch or gasoline. I still kept my eyes open, though, always looking for natural openings, even on the fly, wondering exactly how a conversation like that might take place.

We pedaled through Santa Monica and Culver City and headed north, then east. We traversed the stately neighborhoods of Beverly Hills and saw the huge homes and mansions of Hollywood stars. We passed through the palm-treed city streets of West Hollywood and saw the iconic white-lettered Hollywood sign perched on the hilltop of Burbank's Griffith Park. A slew of names for the smaller city-suburbs in the greater Los Angeles metroplex passed us by: Alhambra. West Covina. San Dimas. Claremont. Sometimes I saw city names on the sides of buildings and businesses. Often I didn't know quite where I was. We hit the famous old Route 66, which roughly parallels first Interstate 210, then State Route 210, and we pedaled on through Rancho Cucamonga and Fontana.

I still wondered if I could just stop whenever I saw somebody who looked interesting and strike up a conversation. Availability was the key for me. Someone who was walking along the road or just sitting somewhere, who seemed to be taking a break or have a few minutes to spare—that's who I wanted to talk with. I was also hoping to talk with a diversity of people. Not only in terms of how they looked, but in how they thought.

As the day progressed, the temperature climbed. We were out in the middle of nowhere now. The green and brown hills of the San Gabriel Mountains were at our left. Traffic whizzed past us. We sweated and pedaled and drank water and kept pedaling.

We were somewhere on Route 66 when I spotted two sport motor-cyclists stopped by the side of the road, adjusting their gear. It was time for a snack break, so I decided to try my luck. I pulled over and stopped near them. The team followed. I grabbed an energy bar and some water from one of our support vehicles and headed over to talk to the guys.

Chris and Shawn were their names. They were both middle-aged and physically fit, with sandy-gray hair and affable faces, dressed in full rider gear. They'd taken their helmets off. I explained about my trip and asked if they wanted to talk. They both shrugged and said why not.

I asked a few starter questions, mostly about motorcycle riding and how they knew each other. Chris explained that they were distantly related and had known each other for years.

"Let me ask you this," I said casually, taking the last bite of my energy bar and stowing the wrapper in a pocket. "Y'all ever think about deeper things? Or do you have anybody in your life who you talk to about spiritual matters?"

"Yeah," Chris said and pointed to his bike. "We're doing it right now." He grinned and described how he loved to go for long rides on his motorcycle, sometimes for days at a time. "Not to be religious," he added, "but when I'm on the bike for a long time, just cranking and banking for hour after hour, I feel like I become one with my bike, one with the road, one with the environment. It's an incredibly spiritual feeling."

I smiled and motioned to my teammates. "I was just telling these guys about a similar feeling when we're all riding together, all connected in our pace line. I feel connected to the bike, to the road, to nature, and even to God." I turned to the other motorcyclist. "How about you, bro?"

"Well, Chris and I have known each other a long time," Shawn said. "We've always had a kind of kindred-spirit connection. When he's riding ahead of me, we don't have intercoms, but I still feel a strong connection with him. Like I'm riding with somebody I really care about. I love that feeling."

Shawn went on to describe how he'd married a Catholic woman and converted to Catholicism about ten years earlier. He enjoyed going to mass with his wife. He'd been in the Marine Corps, and he felt there were similarities between the rituals of the Corps and the rituals of the Catholic Church. He saw how such rituals helped bring people together.

I nodded and asked them how Jesus fit into the mix for their lives.

Shawn spoke first. "As I get older, I find Christ's life so interesting.

What he did. Who he was. I have this vision of Jesus, when he made his point to the money changers in the temple, flipping their tables so hard." He took a step back with a grin, became animated, and kinda pumped his fist in the air. "Put that in your head for a minute."

"Jesus wasn't a wimp, that's for sure," I said.

"No way," Shawn added. "Think about the courage that took. And knowing all the while that he was God in the form of a man and that he'd eventually need to take on all that horrible discomfort—that he'd be nearly flogged to death, then pounded to a piece of wood and hung up to die. That really strikes me. The story of Christ is well-documented, and whether or not you believe he rose from the dead, it's amazing to think that he knew all about his death, yet willingly went to the cross anyway. I find it fascinating. That resurrection part—there's more I need to understand. I try to learn a bit more each year about that, and I didn't do as well as I should have this year in learning. But that was a good question to ask me, to ask about Jesus."

"Nice." I turned to Chris and asked, "How about you? What does Jesus mean to you?"

"I grew up in a religious household," Chris said. "I have uncles and grandfathers who are pastors and missionaries. There's a lot of my family in the church. It was something that was very important to me while growing up. I went to Augsburg, a Christian college in Minnesota, and still live a Christian life today, but I don't observe the Christian faith anymore. To be honest, I'm a little ashamed to talk about that because I usually keep that to myself."

"There's no judgment here," I said, with a genuine smile.

Chris nodded. "As I learned more about the Bible, I started to doubt it. So my faith has been a sort of struggle for me since about my sophomore year of college. The Bible's a historical document, but it seems more human written than written by God. What turned me off most was the turmoil I saw in my particular church. I've seen similar turmoil going on in lots of churches too."

I stifled a groan in solidarity. I've experienced turmoil in churches myself.

Chris kept going. "I understand why it's important for people to go to church, because it's a way for a community to get together and share a common faith and common interests. But there's so many things going on there, and of course we all know what's happened in the Catholic Church. In the church I went to, a Lutheran church, there was backbiting and gossiping. We had a pastor who turned out to be a predator on children too. So all that turmoil combined with itself and caused me to question my faith."

I felt heartbroken. "As a pastor, when I hear that, it's painful," I said. "But I appreciate your honesty. And I don't know if I can say this quite the way I want to, but sometimes I feel like God is a big gambler. He takes the huge risk of building a church that's a living, visible expression of Jesus on earth. Yet that church is made of imperfect people who need a savior—and sometimes those people are going to really mess up. Can I just say, as a pastor, I'm sorry that was your experience with church?"

"Thank you," Chris said. "I appreciate your honesty. I don't look down on people who do believe. Faith is important in people's lives. It's just lost its importance for me. Yet I'm a big believer in supporting people in their faith, no matter if they go to church or not, no matter if they observe Jesus or not." He shrugged. "You know, I haven't talked like this in a long time. I don't even talk to my wife about this kind of stuff because I find it so very, very personal."

Shawn turned to me, gestured to Chris, and said, "I've known this guy for thirty years, and I've never heard any of this."

I liked that statement. It felt to me that we were facilitating conversations not only between new acquaintances but between friends as well. I could only imagine the dialogue that would ensue between Chris and Shawn later that day.

The conversation seemed to be nearing a conclusion. I thanked them for taking time in the middle of their ride to talk with me.

Chris asked if he could say one more thing. It was the day after Memorial Day, and he talked about the sense of spirituality he felt when observing this holiday of remembrance. His father had died in service to our country when his F-14 Tomcat went down, and Chris kept a photograph of him seated in his plane, taken days before his death. We talked a bit more about people who perform incredible feats of sacrifice, and then the motorcyclists both said thanks for stopping by.

I asked them if I could pray for them.

"Yeah," Chris said immediately. "I want you to pray for my struggles with faith and Christianity and also pray for our safety today as we ride. This is a dangerous road we're on. I'll be thinking about you guys as well."

Shawn asked if I could pray for his family.

Right then and there I invited them to pray with me, and both men nodded yes. I led a short prayer from the seat of my bike, thanking God for these guys' openness and all we had talked about, praying for their families and their safety and for Chris's faith to become clear, however God wanted to work that out in his life.

When the prayer ended, the guys both hugged me. And then my team and I were off, pedaling up the road.

We were far from the city by then, away from heavy traffic. After experiencing a lot of discomfort in her saddle, my graduate-student friend Caroline made the difficult decision to ride in the van until we reached our destination for the night. The heat of the day beat down on the rest of us on our bikes, and I had to consciously remind myself to keep drinking water. We kept pedaling for miles.

The road we were on was a two-lane highway, with cars whizzing past us every so often. We started riding up the slope of a long hill. The incline looked gentle at first, but the longer we rode, the harder it became. The air was stifling.

I wanted to remain in the moment, staying close with the thoughts that were still running through my mind about the conversation with the motorcyclists. That conversation had been all I'd hoped for—a taste of exactly what I wanted to accomplish on the trip. Who knew what those two men would think about on the rest of their ride this afternoon—or what those thoughts would lead to in the coming days. I was leaving that up to God.

Meanwhile, the hill wasn't giving way. My thighs ached. Sweat poured off me. I glanced at the other riders. Everybody was struggling. But still, stroke after stroke, we kept moving up the hill.

I've always been thankful for the times in the past when I've wanted to quit but have kept going anyway. Sometimes I would tell myself just to ride another hundred feet. To keep going another five minutes. When that little goal was reached, I'd set another small goal and accomplish that. That's what I kept telling myself on the hill—to just keep going. To just make it one more minute. Then another. Then another.

Sure enough, in another two hundred yards or so, the hill gave way and leveled out. I started to breathe easier, and we rode on flat country for a long way after that.

We eventually reached San Bernardino and our stopping place for the night—the famous layover on Route 66 known as the Wigwam Motel, where travelers sleep in teepees. It's a bit kitschy and a bit historic at the same time. We had only gone 77 miles, a shorter ride than most days were scheduled to be. Yet the day had seemed so full.

When we checked in, I had a good conversation with Samir, the manager of the Wigwam. He and his family were from India originally, and I had been to Bangalore several times, so we talked about his home country and his family for a while. His father was a deeply devout Hindu, and

Samir said he shared the same faith, although he added that Hinduism wasn't as important to him as it was to his father. Samir enjoyed working at the motel and liked meeting travelers most of all. It was a fun conversation, and he was very talkative.

When everything was done for the day and I lay down in my bed, I couldn't help but feel encouraged that the conversations were going well so far on the trip. I concluded that there are plenty of people who are open to talking as long as others are willing to listen. Sometimes, as with the motorcyclists, a nonthreatening conversation can get people to open up not only to me, a stranger, but to one another.

When I closed my eyes, I fell instantly into a deep and dreamless sleep, the best rest I'd had in more than two weeks. Another full day, filled with unknowns, lay ahead.

— 4 —

RIDING WITH PAIN

The next day we were on the road by 5:30 a.m. The plan was to make it to Barstow, which was 88 miles away. Caroline was again quite sore but wearing a brave face for the rest of us. She pulled her dark, shoulder-length hair into a ponytail, hopped on her bike, and gave me a thumbs-up. The team was off, riding in the cool of the morning, hoping to put in some distance before the day's heat hit with its intensity. But I was still concerned as I watched Caroline ride. I was acutely aware of what she was struggling with.

Although less experienced than some of the other riders on the team, Caroline had been a warrior all through training. Sheree had worked with her extensively to get her up to speed on her bike. Caroline was extremely smart, athletic, and fit. She had competed well in a Half Ironman. But she still had some catching up to do, so for nearly a year she'd followed a robust training schedule. She'd worked out with weights and ridden her bike an hour and a half each weekday, three hours on Saturdays, and again on Sundays.

All had been going well until six months before our trip began.

Caroline developed a four-inch saddle sore—an abrasion on her inner leg from the friction against her bicycle seat. She had struggled in her training from that point onward.

Saddle sores sound like a cowboy injury, but they're no laughing matter. Nearly every long-distance bicyclist battles them at some point. I've had them, and they're a bear. Imagine an intense blister on your foot while hiking. Pain grinds with every step. Caroline would later describe it to me as feeling like "a bunch of sharp pencils jabbing into your skin."

But Caroline didn't tell any of us about the sore at first, not even Sheree. She was so excited about riding cross-country that she didn't want to jeopardize her chances of going. She figured she'd just push through the pain and everything would turn out fine.

But three months before the trip began, it became too painful for Caroline even to sit in her chair at work. She cut way back on training and started visiting doctors, and that's when she began talking to us in depth about what was happening. We were all quite concerned. The sore simply wasn't healing.

Doctors told her to spend a good long while off her bike, but Caroline didn't want to do that. It wasn't her stubbornness talking; it was her bigheartedness. She'd caught the vision and purpose of what the trip was all about, and she wanted to participate fully. Besides, she told us, she had a high tolerance for pain. She figured she'd get used to the sore.

Caroline tried various fixes in an attempt to heal, but nothing was doing the trick. A month before the trip began, a doctor gave her a steroid shot to hasten healing. By then she was in sorry shape. Essentially she was riding on an open wound.

She and I met and talked about several scenarios. I knew how much she wanted to be on the trip and complete the ride, but I wondered if perhaps she could serve the team in a different way. It's helpful, for instance, to have a team member in a van who knows something about being a long-distance cyclist. Maybe Caroline could act as a liaison between the riders and the support staff. She was open to that idea, but she still wanted to ride if possible. Caroline is an athlete at heart and wanted to be on her bike so badly.

We discussed in depth the idea of suffering, especially the tendency to want to suffer alone. I encouraged her to keep opening up to team members, to communicate how she was truly doing. It's okay to look weak, I said. In the end you're actually stronger when you let others know you need help. She said thanks, she was learning that lesson. But she didn't want Wes and me trying to be her parents, either. She didn't want us to be constantly asking her how she was doing.

"All right," I finally said. "You can do this. I believe in you—and I know your presence will benefit others on the trip."

"Thanks," she said. "That means a lot. I'm going to give it my all."

I couldn't help smiling. As difficult as it was going to be for her, I respected her drive. There was no way this young woman was going to miss out.

Now, as we pedaled toward Barstow in the early morning hours, I watched Caroline from the corner of my eye. At times she rode with her hands higher on the bars, more upright than normal, undoubtedly trying to change her position to alleviate her pain. Other times she didn't look completely aligned with her bike, probably riding slightly sideways on her seat. Occasionally she rode standing up for short distances. (It's not feasible to ride longer that way.) I knew she must be hurting.

I fought the urge to say something. As her pastor and someone more than two and a half decades older, I couldn't help feeling responsible for her. I didn't want her to push herself too hard or too long. But I didn't want to step in and parent her either. It felt like a delicate balance between caring and not overstepping boundaries. My encouragement to her always was to do the wisest thing.

Meanwhile the sun rose and grew hot. The road shimmered ahead of us, and the landscape was dry and brown, with sandy patches of short, stubbly grass and weeds alongside the road. When we stopped for snacks, I poured water on my head, trying to cool off.

Once we were rehydrated and back on the ride, I spotted three men working in the yard of a house. We rode right by them, but then I thought about it again, made a U-turn in the middle of the highway, and went back to talk to them. The sheer presence of these guys intrigued me. The house was out in the middle of nowhere, far away from other residences or buildings. I wondered what these guys did. Why would they live here? Why would anyone live here?

Joe, age seventy-one, was part Native American. His friend, who had served in Vietnam and went by the name Sergeant Major, said he was seventy-two. The third man was Hanson, age fifty-nine. Hanson soon left, but I talked with the other two.

They both cracked jokes, one right after another, and we all laughed together. But then they became serious, and both of these older men voiced concerns about the state of affairs in America, worrying about the well-being of the next generation. As they described bits and pieces of their lives, it was clear they'd had some hard experiences.

When I asked if they wanted to talk about deeper things, Joe started talking about abortion. He said a lot, quite passionately, although it was hard to follow his exact train of thought. Sergeant Major talked about Vietnam, and I asked him what had been the most difficult thing about being there.

He gave a little laugh. "Staying alive." Then he told me a story about a buddy of his who had fallen asleep at his post and taken an enemy's bullet in his head.

Sergeant Major had clearly seen some horrific things, and I felt like we could have talked for hours. But our conversation wasn't long. The men had work to do. They thanked me for stopping, picked up rakes and shovels, and went at it. I returned to the road.

Later, over a hamburger and fries at a diner, I struck up a conversation with Kelly and Victor, a young Hispanic couple with a beautiful baby, Olivia. Victor set his tattooed arms on the table and told me he was the middle child of twelve and his mother had died when he was only twelve years old. His oldest brother and sister had taken custody of all the children. They'd moved from California to Ohio. In his grief and loneliness as a boy, he'd prayed every evening with his older sister. During those times he had felt the presence of God in the room, he said.

Victor spoke quickly and without inhibitions, and a longer story poured out about his growing-up years, how he'd always known there was something more to life than the here and now. But as a young adult, he'd wandered away from his childhood faith and spent years living in what he described as "distance from God" and "disobedience"—drinking too much, womanizing, and "doing his own thing."

"I was definitely searching for something," Victor said at the table. He stopped talking for a moment and looked directly at me, perhaps gauging my reaction. Maybe he wanted to see if he sensed any judgment from me, because he soon added, "After a time, I felt like I had strayed from God too far. Like I had disappointed God so much that I could not ever come back."

It was a strong statement, and I murmured for him to continue with his story, while wondering if I should jump in and protest. I knew lots of people felt the same way, but the conclusion doesn't reflect Scripture. I thought about the story Jesus told of a father whose son leaves home to live a sinful life. The father, who represents God in the biblical story, waits and waits for the wayward son to return home. When he finally sees the son from a far way off, he runs down the road toward him, welcoming him with open arms.[1]

I decided to just keep listening, though, because Victor was going on to explain how his older sister had kept praying for him, always gently urging him to return to his faith. Within the season of his ups and downs, Victor believed he'd heard the voice of God inviting him back. Eventually, he had rededicated his life to God and never looked back. And then, after a number of years, he'd met Kelly, a single mother with a daughter from a previous relationship.

At this point Victor stopped talking and looked to Kelly across the lunch table. She poured out her story quick-fire, like her husband. She'd experienced many struggles in her early adulthood and had been by herself a lot, quite lonely. She'd become frustrated after she dated several guys who hadn't come through for her. At age thirty-one, tired of being single and desperate, she'd asked God to give her a sign. Strangely, she said, the number thirty-four had come to mind and stuck. She hadn't known what the number meant, but it stayed strong in her mind. She'd even written down the number.

A few years later, when she turned thirty-four, Kelly had met Victor. She described how she'd felt a big shift in her life, like God was showing her love by providing a stand-up guy for her, a man who sought to care for her and love her with all his heart. She believed the Lord had showed her through a dream the husband she was meant to marry: Victor. She hadn't known what to do with the dream. But a few weeks later, Victor proposed.

I turned to Victor, gave him a high five, and said, "Good job!" We all laughed.

They both talked a bit more. Then, to my surprise, they asked if they could pray for me. When I said yes, they immediately grasped my hands and held tight. Victor prayed for me right there in the restaurant, asking for God's favor and strength on our trip. His words flowed freely, the prayer pouring out of the man with the tattooed arms like cool water for a hot and weary traveler.

The meal was over, although I hadn't eaten much. I'd found it hard to stuff my face while listening to such an important conversation. We said our good-byes, then headed outside and continued riding.

Caroline was in a lot of pain and again made the difficult decision to ride in the van for much of the afternoon. I knew she didn't want to be there, but I was glad to know that at least for a while she wouldn't be suffering so much.

As the sun began to inch toward the horizon, my back tire went flat. I was using tubeless tires, which make for a smoother and faster ride compared to tires with tubes, but they are harder to fix. The team pulled over to a parking lot, and I found the repair kit that contained the plugger and tire plugs. I fixed my tire in the shade of the van. My stomach growled. The air was still hot.

That evening we finally reached Barstow, our destination for the day. We'd ridden 88 miles, farther than the day before, although not as far as we planned to go other days later in the trip. Since we needed to average 100 miles per day, we had a few 110-milers coming up to make up for these shorter rides.

Our team had worked hard that day—Caroline in particular. She'd ridden through pain, and I'd spoken with people who had experienced pain and overcome. I wondered if overcoming pain was going to become a recurring theme of this journey.

I couldn't help but remind myself that we had more than a month of riding and listening still to go. I hoped we could all go the distance.

— 5 —

A LISTENING PRESENCE

We were up early again, breakfasted, and on the road before the sun was barely in the sky. Our destination was Needles, California, near the Arizona border. We'd be riding across the Mojave Desert, and even though it was still spring, we knew the day would get hot.

Judy and Glenn, who would be driving one van, did everything to help us get on our way that morning, as did Vela, with her consistent good nature, who would be in the other support vehicle. Caroline felt better enough to ride again, and soon we were off in our pace line, with Wes's large frame in front and the rest of us aligned behind him, pedaling at a good clip.

This is what cyclists call drafting—when you ride behind another cyclist and benefit from less wind resistance. You can save 25 to 30 percent of your energy if you're behind someone, and the closer behind you ride, the better drafting works. But if you're not careful, this can create a dangerous situation of high-speed bumper bikes. You have to learn how to keep a steady pace as a team and adjust whenever a cyclist in front of you slows down.

I took the lead for a while, then Caroline took the lead. Then John. Then Wes again. We had some fun on our bikes, each picking a roadside target ahead—a lone pine tree perhaps, or a speed limit sign—then all racing to be first to get there.

The landscape around us was dotted with sagebrush. Brown flat-top hills rose in the distance. Long, straight, flat stretches of roadway pointed ahead over the desert. The sun baked down on us, and at the first stop I drank water and ate an energy bar and poured water over my head to cool off. We would need to be particularly careful in such intense heat.

Of all quirky random things, we passed an old La-Z-Boy recliner discarded by the roadside. Then another. Then a third. Surely that was a new record for the most dumped-chair sightings in one day.

To avoid heavy automobile traffic, we often traveled down smaller, older roads that roughly paralleled the main route. The strategy worked well for riding our bicycles, but it made it more difficult to spot people to potentially talk with. We were on such a road this morning, riding in the middle of nowhere.

By 10:30 a.m. I hadn't seen anyone, so I prayed, *Okay, Lord, if you want this to happen, you're going to need to supply somebody. Could we just see somebody out walking by the side of the road?*

It felt like a bold prayer. Audacious. Because clearly there was no reason for anybody to be out on this road.

But then, no more than ten minutes later, I spotted a large-framed man dressed in black workout shorts and a blue T-shirt walking along the side of the road. He seemed to be out getting his morning exercise. This seemed like a bizarre place to do it, and I immediately had a thousand questions for him.

I slowed and sidled up to the man, told him about our trip, and asked if he'd like to talk.

He said his name was James, and he explained that he was a long-haul trucker from Arlington, Texas, who liked to park his truck every so often and walk to get some exercise. He stopped in a specific place every time he drove through this desert region. He liked to walk a mile out on the road, turn around, and walk the mile back.

I could only grin.

James kept walking, very relaxed, while I rode slowly alongside. I asked about being a trucker, and he said he got into it because he liked being out on the open road. "I don't do well in an office," he said with a smile.

"Hey, I don't either." I smiled back. "That's why I'm out here right now."

Back in Arlington, James told me, he had a wife, four sons, and twenty grandkids. So we talked about grandkids for a while. Then I asked if he ever talked with anyone about spiritual matters. He explained that he and his wife had both been raised as Catholics. He still went to mass regularly when he was home, although his wife now attended a different church, nondenominational. And most days on the road he lived by a spiritual routine. He got up early (sometimes as early as 2:00 a.m.), went through morning prayers, drove his shift, then said the rosary at the end of the day. The practice of his faith had become part of his life.

"Where does Jesus fit into the mix for you?" I asked. Our conversation felt like it was flowing well.

"He's supposed to be number one," James said. "He's the goalpost at the end of the field. I admit I tend to zigzag as I run, but I try to keep my eyes on the Lord."

We talked about how faith can seem like a race to be run, and at the core of the race is the assurance that Jesus died for all people, even those who don't think they live good enough lives. We talked about grace, how being saved and going to heaven is not a reward for doing good things but a gift from God that he gives freely, because of his mercy, to all who ask.

Our discussion turned to the afterlife, and James said he believed he'd go to heaven after he died. "When you pass away, you go to judgment," he said. "I'd like the Lord to be able to look at me and say, 'Good job. Welcome home.' If you believe in Jesus as your Lord and Savior, that's how you know you're going to heaven."

"Here's a question," I said. "If you could have Jesus do one thing to help the world, what would it be?"

"Well, I guess I'd like him to help people be more tolerant of each other," James said. "Few people really talk to strangers like we're doing now because people have their opinions and take sides. It's like 'my way or no way.' But I'd say if everybody relaxed and became more tolerant of each other, that would be a good thing."

"Man, that's cool," I said. "If you could say anything to people about how to make the world better, what would you say?"

"It starts at home. Love your wife. Love your kids. Respect your neighbor."

Wow, I thought. *He's said it all right there.*

James walked with an easy gait, like it was perfectly normal to have deep conversations with strangers on bicycles out in the middle of nowhere. He checked his pedometer. He'd walked his mile, and it was time to turn around and head the other way. I thanked him and gave him a hug. Then we said our good-byes and went our separate ways.

I couldn't help but think how easy it is to assume that people won't want to talk about deeper things. Here was this trucker walking down the road for his morning exercise. Why would he want to talk with me? It was easy to give a thousand reasons why a conversation like the one I'd just had wasn't supposed to happen. Yet it did happen.

I could only smile.

We regrouped as riders and rode until lunchtime, then stopped at a roadside pullout and made sandwiches from fixings that Glenn and

Judy laid out for us. A train creaked and clacked down its tracks maybe a hundred yards away. No shade anywhere. Impossible to get out of the sun.

Lunch wrapped up, and we hopped back on our bikes and headed out. The farther we rode, the hotter it became.

As part of my rider's gear, I wore specially made sunshades over my arms and legs so my skin wouldn't get fried. The shades looked like clingy sleeves someone had cut off a long-sleeved shirt and a pair of tight leggings. Designed to help block the sun's intensity and cool the body temperature, they definitely helped. But we were still riding across the desert during the hottest part of the day, and I felt it. At one point we passed a parched-looking sign from the US Department of Interior that read "Welcome to the Heart of the Mojave."

We stopped at a convenience store for snacks and a bathroom break. The place was empty except for us, and the woman behind the counter wouldn't meet my gaze. She was maybe in her midsixties, and her gray hair was pulled back into a bun.

I gave her a friendly greeting, commented on the weather, and asked her how she was doing. She admitted she was having a hard day. When I asked a few simple questions, her story poured out.

Her grandfather had been a preacher, and she'd grown up in church. She'd married and raised a family. When her son was a young man, he'd been out working a late-night shift one evening. On his way home his vehicle had collided with an eighteen-wheeler and he'd died. The woman's grief was still fresh, and while the store was empty, she'd been lost in thought, remembering her beloved son.

"Frankly, I'm mad at Jesus," she said.

That was a tough one.

I simply stood with her in that moment, sharing her grief, offering my listening presence, and letting her speak. When she came to the end of her story, I asked if she would like me to pray with her and she said yes, so I prayed for God to meet her in her pain and to show her his heart for her. Then we both said amen.

"Hey, do you remember the story of Jesus with his good friend Lazarus?" I asked, and she nodded for me to continue. "It's a pretty familiar one if you've grown up in church. But there's something about that story we tend to miss." She nodded again, and I continued. "Lazarus died, and his sisters Mary and Martha met Jesus at their brother's tomb. Twice the Bible says that Jesus was 'deeply moved' about his friend's death.[1] But that's a soft translation. The original language actually conveys anger. Jesus got mad when his friend died. Anger and grief can be closely intertwined, and that's okay."

For the first time since I'd walked into the store, the woman looked directly at me, her expression almost incredulous. Then her eyes brightened. "I never thought of Jesus that way."

It felt like we were making a real connection—to each other, yet also to Jesus. Not a plastic Jesus who never showed any emotion but a real Jesus who hated death and grieved for his lost loved ones. A Jesus who didn't hide his anger. A Jesus who wept.[2]

We said our good-byes, and my team and I left the store to continue our journey. The sun was merciless now. I was supposed to have eaten a snack when we stopped, but the conversation with the woman had preempted my eating. I should have been more intentional about taking care of myself, but I felt okay, albeit a little hungry.

Caroline said she was starting to ache, so she got into the van. The rest of us kept going. The bottom of my feet began to hurt, and I didn't know what that was about. We kept pedaling, mile after mile after mile across the desert.

At mile 92 for the day, I wanted to stop. My feet ached. My stomach felt terrible. My head pounded. I slowed and grew very quiet. My whole body began to cramp.

"Neil! What's wrong?" Wes called. But his voice sounded hollow, far away.

"Neil!" came his voice again.

I didn't answer. I wasn't saying a word.

"Neil!"

In the bicycling world, they call this "bonking" or "hitting a wall." It's a sudden serious loss of energy caused by abnormally low blood-sugar levels. Essentially it means you haven't taken in enough carbohydrates. Wes kept hollering at me and finally convinced me to stop. I hadn't been hydrating and eating properly for the conditions of the day, and now my lack of self-care had caught up to me.

I ate an energy bar and guzzled water, then coconut water, then an energy drink, but it felt like I couldn't get enough liquid into me. Still feeling miserable, I climbed back on my bike and kept going, barely noticing the concern on the other riders' faces. We were hardly making any headway. I was setting the pace, and we moved at a snail's crawl.

By mile 95 I was in agony. By mile 98 I was barely moving. At mile 100 I pulled over and stopped. The road we were on was merging into Interstate 40, and I wasn't sure which way to go from here. The last eight miles had been the hardest of the trip so far. Maybe of my lifetime.

"We can't go any farther," Wes said. "We're not going to ride on that freeway."

I began to look around for someone with a GPS.

"He's right," John said. "We're all going to have to ride inside the vans for a while."

My brow lowered. "I'm not riding in a van."

"You're going to have to, hon." Vela placed her hand on my shoulder and gave me a little pat. She pulled out her smartphone and showed me the map. "There are no other roads to get where we need to go."

We hadn't established a policy about freeway riding before the trip began, but now we realized we needed one. You can legally ride a bicycle on only a select few interstates in America; bikes are forbidden on most of them. Arizona does allow freeway riding, but we weren't in Arizona yet. California prohibits most freeway riding, although I couldn't see any signage, so I wasn't positive about this stretch. More than anything I was concerned about the integrity of the trip. I wanted to ride every single mile, but the GPS wasn't lying. A ten-mile stretch loomed ahead of us with nothing but freeway.

"Come on, guys," I said with a frown. "There's got to be another road. Are you sure we can't ride on this section of the freeway? We'll be careful."

"No." Wes's voice was firm. "We're not going to ride on the freeway. And neither are you."

I didn't know who had died and made him boss. He wasn't the boss. I was the boss—or at least I was supposed to be. I stared at Wes. John. Caroline. Vela. The rest of the team. My frown was nearing a snarl. *That's the problem with traveling with a bunch of people*, I thought. *They only slow you down, and you've got to make all these compromises.*

With a huff I strapped my bike onto the carrier and climbed into the air-conditioned van. In truth, my body needed the break from activity. All the food and liquid from earlier hadn't brought relief. My stomach still felt terrible. My entire body was one big cramp. Even so, I was determined to get back on the bike as soon as possible. I glanced at the odometer and made a mental note.

The van started moving.

Five miles. Seven miles. Ten miles. Side roads started appearing again.

"This'll do," I called. "We can ride from here."

The van pulled over, and we opened the doors. The heat hit us like a blast from a huge hairdryer. Wes and John and I climbed on our bikes again. I felt the lowest I'd felt in months.

We rode another 17 miserable miles and reached our destination, a KOA campground. We were hot and sweaty. No one spoke much.

A branch of the Colorado River flowed through the campground. A few team members began to set up camp while others hit the showers. The worst of my pain and cramping had subsided in the last hour, but I still wasn't in good shape. I stood for a moment near my bike, feeling such a strange mix of emotions. Relief that the day's physical challenges were over. Annoyance that I'd been pushed into riding in the van. Guilt for how I'd snapped at the team.

"C'mon, Neil," Wes said, and motioned me toward the river. I stared at him for a moment, then nodded.

The two of us walked to the water, neither saying a word. He took off his shoes, and I took off mine. The sandy ground felt holy under our bare feet.

We waded into the river, which in late spring ran icy cold. We waded forward until the bottom of our shorts touched the water. Then, as if on cue, both of us collapsed backward into the frigid water.

It was a baptism of sorts. A renewal. Instantly we were both up and whooping.

"Man, that's cold!" Wes exclaimed. He laughed.

"Wow, that feels good!" I let out another whoop.

Wes extended his right arm toward me, and we fist-bumped in solidarity. "Good job today," he said. "That was a tough one."

"Yeah." Slowly I shook my head. "I hate being the guy who struggles." Wes chuckled.

I looked at him closely, carefully, and added, "I mean, as much as I've ever preached about it, as much as I've ever said we need help from others, as much as we say God's power is perfected in weakness . . . man, when a hard spot comes up, I don't want to be that guy everybody's looking at, wondering if he's going to be okay."

Wes didn't say a word. He stood alongside me, being the listening presence I needed, both of us dripping in the middle of the river.

I clasped my hands in front of me, chest level, almost like I was praying. Maybe I was, with words I didn't know how to articulate. Because at that moment the biggest emotion welling up in me was gratitude.

I'd been humbled by this day. Slowed. Chastened. But I was so thankful we were taking this trip. And I was so thankful for this team. Things were happening that would only happen with this particular parade of people.

When you are doing life together with others, you do go slower. But you also go farther. And you go places you would have never gone without them.

— 6 —

FRIENDSHIP DESPITE DIFFERENCES

After Wes and I plunged into the river and came up renewed, the sun didn't have far to go before it set. We dried and changed and ate dinner, then I went looking for a conversation. It wasn't hard to find. The campground was full of people.

Near the river's edge I met Harry and Yolanda, a couple in their forties. Harry had short, graying hair and a quick smile, and Yolanda's hair was tied back in a bun. They were drinking beers and smoking cigarettes, just hanging out. I learned they weren't actually staying at the campground but had come to the river to cool off after the day's heat. Harry had lived near Needles for the past thirty years, and Yolanda, originally from New York, had lived there the past ten.

The conversation turned to deeper matters, and Harry, who tended bar at a tavern just down the road, said that God was a frequent subject of conversation where he worked. "When people are hanging out in a bar, they talk about God all the time," he said. He wasn't kidding.

"Yeah," Yolanda answered. "Everybody feels safe around Harry. He won't admit to it, but he's the best bartender in town."

Harry grinned.

"I get that," I said. "People tend to be real when they're just hanging out. When people talk to you about spirituality, do you feel open to talking about deeper things in return?"

"Sure," Harry said. "That's the best way to be, really."

I thought a moment. "So when somebody in your bar says the name *Jesus*, what's the first thing that comes to mind? Good, bad, or indifferent?"

"He's my Savior," Yolanda said.

"Mine too," Harry said. "Definitely good."

Neither of them went to church at present, but Yolanda had gone to Catholic school when she was young and had mostly good memories from there. Harry had grown up in a Methodist church. He said he used to go with his mother.

"So how does Jesus make a difference in your life today?" I asked.

"He helps me daily," Yolanda said. "Jesus wants to help people. He gives me what I need, and I believe he is listening." The statement felt like it came from a place of great substance for her.

"I'd hope that Jesus would help people have freedom and happiness," Harry said. He seemed sincere too.

We talked a bit more about this and that, nothing terribly deep, then said our good-byes for the evening. I was struck with how relaxed Harry and Yolanda seemed about their faith, yet how genuine too. They weren't necessarily the types who come to mind when "religious people" are portrayed in popular culture. But they were living in an authentic space.

What I found most memorable about our conversation was how gently and naturally it had unfolded. I'm a type A personality, an achiever, and when I'm talking about spiritual matters, I usually feel a pressure to cram everything into a conversation all at once. Yet I was learning there was real freedom in taking my time and letting people be themselves.

As I wandered back to our campsite, the good smell of barbecue in the air, I thought about how relaxed Jesus often was in his timing, never pushed around by a clock. He didn't even begin his formal ministry until he was thirty years old. And even when he was teaching and healing, he never seemed to be rushed. Luke 8:40–56 tells about how Jesus could have helped a child in distress if only he'd picked up his pace, but he deliberately chose to slow down, turn aside, and help a woman in need first. Everybody thought he had ruined things for the child by not being speedy. But Jesus reached the child later and helped her in a far better way than was first hoped.

Good things can happen when we simply let people be themselves, trusting that God is working in their lives in his time and way, and we don't try to push them in any direction.

The next morning dawned bright and hot. As the day began, I purposely tried to slow down and take deeper breaths. The memory of when I'd hit the wall yesterday was still fresh, and I wanted to stay on top of my hydration and nutrition today. I didn't want to drive the team too hard or be irritable with anybody, and I knew I needed to face my personal limitations.

I might be able to get up at 5:30 a.m. and ride hard until 10:30 p.m. every day. I might be okay to ride 100 miles in a day. I might be up for lots of conversations along the way. But I didn't have the bandwidth to set up routes, ensure we were going where we should, or manage the team. I needed to let other people handle these tasks. My goal for the day was to stay comfortable with myself, do the ride, and let God bring to me more natural, relaxed conversations like I'd had the evening before with Harry and Yolanda.

We left the campground and headed out toward Peach Springs,

Arizona. For the first hour and a half, the route went straight up through the desert hills. John wasn't riding this leg because he hadn't trained for hills as much. Wes was pacing Caroline, which I was glad for, and they were speeding up and slowing down with the rise and fall of specific inclines on the climb. But I made the choice to let go of the pressure of staying with them for a while. For now, I simply needed to ride at my own pace and make it up this long hill.

When I do long climbs, I watch the power meter on my bike so I put out a consistent amount of effort. So I simply dialed in my meter and kept going, just me and the road.

We reached the tiny historic gold-mining town of Oatman, Arizona. To my surprise, wild donkeys were roaming here, there, and everywhere throughout the town—rubbing up against our bikes, begging for food, doing their business in the middle of the road. It was hilarious. Apparently their forebears had been brought to the town more than a century earlier as pack animals for miners. The miners had long since left, but the burros had stayed. They slept up in the hills each night, then wandered down to town each morning to nibble carrots offered by tourists.

Outside a store I struck up a conversation with Brandon, a thirty-something bicyclist with a bushy blond beard. He was headed to California, where we'd just come from. Thickly built, he looked like a modern Viking. He'd traveled the world and worked for an organization in Nepal called the Khumbu Climbing Center. It used to be that wealthy climbers would go to Mount Everest and hire locals to help them up the mountain. But many of those locals weren't properly outfitted or trained for high-altitude climbing, and a ridiculous number of indigenous climbers had died on the mountain. Thanks to the work of the climbing center, that trend had changed.

"It's my mission in life to focus on small places where I can make a difference in the world," he told me.

I was totally impressed. "Brandon, you strike me as a person who really cares about people. Where does that sense of mission come from?"

He shrugged. "I grew up on a small farm in rural North Carolina with a tight-knit extended family. My parents and grandparents on both sides of the family were kind and generous, always helping people, and I decided back then that's a really great way to approach life. Pick the venues where you can be kind and generous, and hopefully those venues will match things you enjoy and feel rewarded doing."

He was speaking my language. "That's what we want to do on this trip," I said. "In a world where it seems everybody wants to get at everybody else's throats, we want to go out and be curious and have conversations about things that matter, hopefully with kindness, even when people don't agree. I'm wondering if there was faith in the mix for your family, if that was what drove your parents and grandparents."

"Interesting question," he said. "I grew up in a Christian tradition, both the hellfire and damnation side and also the grace and mercy side. I saw how we all have choices every day in how we approach people. Our personal behavior can either harken back to hellfire and damnation or to grace and mercy. In our country these days, we've reached the place where a lot of people feel it's more acceptable to voice their negative thoughts. None of us get it right every time, but we can all do our best to be kind, generous, and gracious. We can let our angels come out or our demons. We don't have to share our negative thoughts with other people or act on those thoughts. The grace and mercy side of my upbringing, for me, found a lot of commonalities in Buddhist, Hindu, and Islamic traditions. I saw how there are universalities to the world's spiritual and religious traditions."

He was speaking gently yet firmly, and I couldn't help but blurt, "You know, Brandon, I just met you, but I see the grace and mercy side coming out, and I appreciate that." He chuckled and said thanks, and I added, "I'm curious. You've been on a journey literally all around the world and interacted with people from so many different religions. What do you do with Jesus?"

He scratched his beard. "I grew up Southern Baptist, but these days I consider myself more spiritual than religious. I've found very good people from all religious traditions. So I gravitate toward people who embrace the positive side of their faith. Likewise, I often try not to embrace the folks who are less kind with those parts of their tradition, who choose to be negative toward others because of their faith."

I nodded. "That's a good way of saying it." I thought a moment. "In the Southern Baptist tradition, you undoubtedly learned that Jesus said he was the way, the truth, and the life and that no one could get to the Father except through him.[1] What do you do with that? Can someone hold to the exclusivity of that teaching and still be kind?"

"Hmm," he said. "When I hear that statement, I don't think Jesus was saying 'through me personally.' Jesus wasn't selfish. I think the statement was meant to convey, 'You come to the Father by these things I'm teaching about.' People come to God by kindness. By generosity. By forgiveness. Like, Jesus and his disciples, as far as I remember, traveled with former prostitutes as part of their cohort. And when Jesus was on the cross, there were two men crucified on either side of him. Both thieves. To the one thief who asked for forgiveness, Jesus said he could find it by believing in him. Did Jesus mean believe in him personally or believe in the message that he brought—a message about grace and mercy? That's how I think of it. Billions of people in this world are raised without hearing about Jesus. Yet they're raised in traditions where they hear about kindness, mercy, generosity—traits, actions, and mindsets that are remarkably similar to the story we hear in the Bible."

"You've obviously thought about this," I said. "It's easy for people, if they don't want to deal with something they can't see, to write it off or to be superficial. I wish we could ride together in the same direction for a couple of days and talk some more."

He smiled. We both knew he was headed the other direction on his bike. But he added, "When I part ways with anybody I meet, I always say, 'Till next time.' You never know when our paths will cross again."

We said our good-byes, and Brandon started cycling west.

This trip was definitely changing my mind about a number of things. Brandon wasn't a churchgoer anymore, and as a pastor I had often assumed that people who didn't go to church hadn't thought about God as much as I had. But Brandon had clearly been doing a lot of thinking. I didn't agree with all his conclusions, yet I respected his approach. I still held to Jesus as the unique and only way to the Father, but I also appreciated this man who was on his spiritual journey, hopefully toward Jesus' truth.

The town was rich with people milling about, shopping, eating and drinking, and feeding the burros, and I soon began talking with an older, whiskered motorcyclist named Mike. He was dressed in black, wearing sunglasses and a leather skullcap. We talked about how far each of us had ridden that day, and we chatted about motorcycles and bicycles for a bit. Then I asked him if he ever talked about God or faith, and unexpectedly he blurted out, "Badabook, badaboom."

I stood there perplexed. "You got me. What's that mean?"

Mike shrugged, his countenance hardening. "Well, I think it's self-explanatory. I think about religion, but I never engage in it."

"Why not?"

"Because any conversation about God immediately begins to peel away after a few questions and starts to diverge into politics—and nobody wants to get into that. I'm a nontheology kind of guy, so if you started me on that path, we'd be here until the cows come home. The universe is huge. It's incomprehensible. We're all running around like little ants, doing our own things. You're out riding a bicycle in ninety-degree weather. But the bigger picture of things . . . that's infinite. So to imagine there's a single God that built this one little place, this one spiral galaxy, this infinite thing known as space—that's tough to swallow."

I nodded. "That's the exact thing I want to talk about."

"Religion can be so divisive." He was heating up even further. "That bothers me. Like, I study quantum physics. That's what I've dug into to explain the universe. I'm entitled to do that. So why is my nontheological view any less relevant than your theological view? Yet religious people impose their view everywhere they go, with their 'God bless you' statements and stuff like that. After a while an atheist might start to take offense."

He was definitely heated now—almost hostile. I wasn't sure if he was going to roll up his sleeves to fight or walk away in a huff. But I wasn't going to argue with him. I said simply, "Tell me if I'm wrong, but it sounds like you haven't felt respected."

"Yeah. Or represented. The kind of people who think similarly to me are few and far between. Atheists are something like 25 percent of the population.[2] That's certainly not the majority in this country. Most people say they believe in some kind of supreme being. Hey, I respect that. It's great for you because that's the choice you've made. I've evolved to a different place, and that should be my choice. It's hard being an atheist in America. The minute you say you're an atheist, you get rocks thrown at you."

I chuckled. "I'm not going to throw any rocks."

"Well, keep an open mind," Mike said. "That's all I ask of anybody. I keep an open mind, and I'm not in any position to say God doesn't exist. I'm not arrogant. But I don't see proof of God." He paused, like he was thinking. "And I don't see the 'not proof' either. I say if the universe is infinite and time can be warped and changed, then once we start down the path of studying quantum physics, where does that all end?"

I nodded and drew a big circle in the air with my finger. "So if we say that everything in this circle is everything my puny mind understands about the infiniteness of the universe, then is it possible there's something outside the circle that we don't know about yet?"

"Sure," Mike said with a roar. "Embrace the multiverse!"

We both laughed. His hardened countenance was relaxing into something more open. We talked more about physics and the universe and what it means for something to go on forever. Our conversation was winding to a close.

"I think we found common ground," I said. "You hadn't been heard. You hadn't felt treated fairly by religious America. I want you to know your opinion is heard."

"That's right." Mike laughed, took a step forward, and gave me a hug. We talked a bit more, and he shook my hand. We talked still more, and he patted me on the shoulder. We took a couple of pictures together, and he threw his arm around me and smiled. His eyes were twinkling. His countenance had completely changed. It was incredible how he had switched from closed-off anger to open friendliness.

I kept thinking about that after we parted ways and I was back on my bike. I could have ruined our conversation in so many ways. I could have tried to debate. I could have argued with him or been dismissive. The whole time we were talking, my struggle had been to stay present with him, to keep the relationship open and not allow it to be closed. And it had worked. When we parted, we weren't angry at each other. If we saw each other again, we'd start up another conversation easily. And when Mike meets another follower of Jesus, he may be more amenable to another conversation, another link in the chain that's reaching into his life to draw him to God.

Mike and I were now far from enemies.

I guess you could say we had even become friends.

— 7 —

DIVINE APPOINTMENTS

After we pulled out of Oatman, we faced another long, winding climb through a rocky gorge up to Sitgreaves Pass, elevation 3,550 feet. Back home in Dallas I spend much of my biking time riding around a flat lake, but the ride up the pass was like a little taste of glory.

My body was feeling pretty good, like I was firing on all eight cylinders, but Caroline was still limping along, putting on a brave face. I could see she was wiped out. I tried to say something kind, but she grimaced and told me to stop worrying about her, that she had this. She didn't exactly snap at me. But her tone was sterner than usual, like she was a warrior in her own right and it wasn't my place to barge in on her personal battle. She rode in front for a while, maybe just to show she could do it.

At the top, we reached a lookout and stopped, caught our breath, and gazed over miles of brown and blue desert hills, mostly treeless. Caroline gave me a kinder look then, and I returned it. There's a fine line between caring for someone and trying to make decisions on their behalf. I hoped I was doing the former, not the latter.

Coming down the other side, we were really flying, whizzing along as fast as forty miles per hour. Suddenly I heard a short, loud buzz and felt my head get smacked. Instantly a sharp, burning jolt hit my scalp. I slammed on the brakes, skidded to the side of the road, and whipped off my helmet. Some kind of bee or wasp had rammed its way under my helmet and stung me. At least I hoped that's all it was. Vela looked at my scalp closely and doctored me up. I shook off the lingering pain, and we kept riding.

That night we stayed at a hotel in Peach Springs owned by the Hualapai Tribe. The tiny Hualapai Baptist Church building was near the hotel, and I met a man named Joe who attended the church. We spoke for about half an hour, and I asked him for more information about the tribe and about how the church had come to be built. Joe spoke carefully and respectfully. He was deeply devoted to both his Hualapai heritage and his Baptist faith and said that he always tried to speak to others about spiritual matters with gentleness and tact.

He explained that the railroad had been built through the area in the late 1800s, a trading post had been established next to the tracks, and the town of Peach Springs had sprung up around the trading post. The famed Chicago evangelist Harry Ironside often traveled through the region and noticed that when the train stopped, railway workers loaded up with water, supplies, and apparently other things because back then the town had several saloons but no churches. Ironside asked about starting a church, and folks agreed it would be a helpful influence.

Joe said his family had lived in the area for generations. His parents had been Christians but had strayed from their faith. When Joe had become serious about his own faith in 2005, he'd read in Hebrews 10:24–25 that people of faith are encouraged to gather together regularly and not give up that habit. Hesitantly and respectfully, he'd showed his dad the passage of Scripture, and he'd been surprised—and pleased—when his dad started going to church again. To me, this was a helpful and beautiful reminder that spiritual conversations can do a world of good.

The next day I woke up at about 3:30 a.m. My knees and quads hurt. I was really feeling the ride in my muscles. When I looked outside the window, I saw branches bending. A tumbleweed scuttled by. The wind was blowing hard. We had 105 miles scheduled for the day, and I knew it was going to be tough.

Glenn was becoming a pro at packing and unpacking the van, constantly tweaking his system so he could fit everything inside in the shortest amount of time. He fit a bunch of smaller boxes inside a larger box and attached it to the front of the van, so we each had our own individual lockers when we needed to quickly reach for snacks or sunscreen. His system spoke to me. He was really trying to care for the team.

After Glenn had packed the van that morning, Wes needed something from a green suitcase at the very bottom of the load. Glenn pulled six other suitcases out to reach the green one, then he repacked the van again. Wes and Glenn normally got along well, fortunately, and Glenn just grinned at the extra work.

The wind plagued us all morning. It rushed at us head-on, buffeting and pushing us around. We rode through long, straight stretches of flatland without much vegetation. We could see for miles, and there were no windbreaks anywhere. The road roughly paralleled the railroad tracks, so we listened to the whistles and clacks of trains for hours as the sun beat down on us.

I was really hurting now. My knees and quads were screaming, and my shoulders were aching too. The adrenaline from the start of the trip had worn off, and we were all digging into our reserves. Plus, I was beginning to feel the toll that my accident back home had taken on me. Wes was a champ on the bike and took the lead, not letting up, blocking as much wind as he could, mile after mile on those flat straight roads full of nothing.

At last we pulled into the town of Seligman, Arizona, and stopped at a diner for lunch. Already I felt exhausted, and the day's ride was only half over. I wanted to lie down in the back of the van and take a nap. But a thought came to mind—one I couldn't shake.

For nearly a year before the trip began, several of us team members had met at my house monthly and prayed that God would give us "divine appointments" on this trip. That was the specific wording we used, over and over again. We wanted to meet the people that God wanted us to meet, for whatever purposes he had in mind.

I was still thinking about the phrase "divine appointments" when a tour bus pulled up and a bunch of people climbed out. The driver came around the front of the van and immediately called to us, "Man! Blessings on y'all for what you're doing!"

He was bearded, large and muscled, and smiling broadly. I decided not to reply at first. I wanted to know why he had greeted us that way, if it was simply the way he greeted all people or if it meant something more. He approached Caroline, Wes, John, and me, introduced himself as Carlito, then extended his hand and shook ours, saying: "Now, you guys probably don't believe in Jesus, but I gotta tell you about the Lord."

Inwardly I smiled, and I introduced myself in return, but again I didn't say much. The team followed my lead and kept quiet. We wanted to hear what Carlito had to say. Here was someone trying to engage us— complete strangers to him—in a conversation about faith. That certainly was a reversal.

Carlito told us a summarized version of why he was so excited about God. He'd been born in Puerto Rico and eventually came to live in Las Vegas. He'd been through a divorce several years back. Through many circumstances he'd found himself in an extremely rough place in life. At his lowest point he'd written a note to God, basically giving an ultimatum: "If you don't show me what needs to change, then I'm going to kill myself."

At nine thirty that night, Carlito had grabbed his gun and gone for a walk, intending to take his life if nothing happened. Seemingly at random, he'd walked by a church. At that late hour the building looked empty. But just then a man walked out of the church, met Carlito, gave him a huge hug, and told him about the hope of a new life that could be found in Christ. Carlito dedicated his life to God that very night. Since then, his life had completely changed.

At that point I broke my silence, mentioned I was a pastor, and told Carlito about what we were doing with the ride.

"Hoo, man," Carlito said. "This is a *divine appointment*."

My eyes opened wide. That was it—the exact phrase we had used in our prayers. Before I could say anything, Carlito fished in his pocket, pulled out a tiny manila envelope, and handed it to me.

"I have a gift for y'all," he said.

Inside was twenty dollars.

I wanted to object. I may have even said so out loud. It wasn't like he was making a ton of cash as a bus driver, and besides, we weren't asking for money. But he explained he always carried an envelope containing twenty dollars. Whenever he met somebody and the encounter seemed like a divine appointment, he gave that person the money. It might be someone in need, and the money could buy a meal or two. Or it might simply be someone who was doing a good work. In that case, Carlito explained, the gift showed solidarity. He wanted to partner with people doing purposeful things. His graciousness, boldness, and generosity blew me away.

We said our good-byes to Carlito, and our team went inside the diner and ate lunch. I tried to talk with the owner, but he declined my invitation, saying he was too busy. I tried talking to a few customers, but they turned us down too. I felt okay about that. God was arranging the conversations he wanted me to have. I was sure of it.

With lunch over, I wandered outside and struck up a conversation with a guy named Bill, who was seated next to a three-wheeler motorbike. He told me he was seventy-one. We talked about motorcycles for a good while, as I used to ride a Suzuki 500 sport bike. He said he had drag-raced back in the 1960s and now liked to fix up old trucks for fun. An affable, relaxed fellow, he told me about his two kids and four grandkids, and I told him about mine. We could have talked all day.

"What do you value most in life, Bill?" I asked.

Without missing a beat he said, "I love talking with real people. Honest people. That's something we need more of these days. I tell ya, the entertainment industry isn't honest anymore. Look how far they've gone downhill. Politicians aren't honest anymore. The news media doesn't tell the truth. And churches too. There's good and bad churches out there, but what we really need in America these days is honesty and religion."

I asked if he was a religious man himself, and Bill said no, not really, although he used to be. He didn't go to church anymore because he felt there were too many hypocrites in church. He'd been raised Southern Baptist and had attended church until he left both home and church at the end of his teen years. He'd returned to church when he was raising children of his own. Now he was away again.

I asked him if he'd personally experienced difficulty in a church, if that was what kept him away.

"Nah, I didn't have too hard of a time in church," Bill said. "There's good people there, just like there's people who aren't, just like everywhere you go. But I'd say you can talk to God anywhere. Sometimes you have more meaningful talks with God when you're alone in a field. In the church I went to as a kid, everything was a sin there. Even dancing was a sin, and I said to myself, 'Well, God will have to judge me, because I like to dance.' I like honest churches today—cowboy churches, motorcycle churches. I like honest folks, and that's what you find there. I tell ya, people gotta get back to being honest with themselves and everybody else."

"I agree," I said. "Too many churches focus on the wrong thing." I paused before adding, "I'm curious—since you grew up Southern Baptist, what do you think about Jesus today?"

"I talk to him all the time," Bill said with a smile. "There's so many things in life that are so simple. I was called some bad things when I was young, and I wasn't treated really good. I'll just leave it at that. But I tell you what, with my kids and my grandkids today, I never get off the phone without telling them I love them. That's very important. I remember a pastor I knew when I was young—he was married with four kids and used to work for us sometimes, just for extra money. He had a good sense of humor both in and out of the pulpit. He loved people and always treated them right, and he was always there to help anybody in need. There was nobody in the church who didn't like him. I hold people like that in a lot of respect. That's what a belief in Jesus is about, I'd say. You gotta believe, sure, but you gotta be honest and treat people right. Now, I hate a fire-and-brimstone preacher. They can't hold my attention. But somebody who gets up there and talks honestly—that's somebody I'll listen to."

"Man, I like that," I said. It felt like Bill had opened his heart just a bit there. "We're talking about a Savior who hangs naked on a cross for our sins. If we can't come honestly before him, we're missing out."

Bill chuckled. "I've had people ask me if I think I'm going to heaven. And I say, 'Well, I've done good stuff in my life, and I've done bad stuff too. I'm a sinner like everybody else. When the time comes and God taps me on the shoulder, he'll tell me then. I'm not going to guess before that.'"

We talked more about faith, and he mentioned that for the past three years he'd been making sandwiches for people—anybody who needed a free meal. He and some buddies started a program, and so far they'd given away more than 120,000 sandwiches.

Nothing was rushed about Bill, and in his unique way he was doing the work of Jesus, helping people in need. At times I was looking for places in the conversation to interject truth that naturally connected to the story he was telling. I didn't agree with all his beliefs or practices, but I didn't feel pressure to debate with him about it. That wasn't what our conversation was about. The focus was connection, leaving the conversation open to having another one, or just being part of a stream of people who are helping him on his journey and letting God do the real work.

We shook hands, and I told him how much I'd enjoyed talking with him.

When our team got back on the road, I felt encouraged by meeting Carlito and Bill but also very tired. The wind blew hard against our faces again, and I was running on fumes. After we hit the town of Williams, the road started climbing again and seemed only to go up. Absolutely brutal. We rode to 5,000 feet, the most serious climbing of the trip so far. I felt finished, done for, when I reached the summit.

Coming down on the other side, I got another flat tire. I kept a spare bike on one of the support vans, so I rode that bike for another five miles. But it was a stiffer bike, and every bump in the road jarred me.

That evening we reached our destination, the town of Belmont. Wes and Jeff took care of me; they found a bicycle shop and swapped the tubeless tires on my main bike for tires with tubes. They'd be easier to patch on the fly the next time I got a flat.

After supper the woman behind the motel counter introduced herself as Sasha. When she found out who we were and what we were doing, she said she had some hard questions about God. Could she talk with us?

It was late, and I was beat. This was only our fifth full day of riding, and it had been a long, hard day, a real grind. I needed to hit the sheets and get some rest. So I asked if we could talk in the morning. She said yes, and I promised to meet her bright and early.

It didn't take long for me to fall asleep, but before I drifted off, I thought about the day's conversations. I was thrilled to see how God was creating moments for me to invite people to open up and connect, to have the privilege of hearing about their journeys and loving them by listening.

His divine appointments were showing up.

— 8 —

PURSUING TRUTH
AND BEAUTY

The calendar told me it was June 1. To be honest, I wasn't looking forward to the day.

Glenn pulled out at 5:00 a.m. to drive Paul and John, who had joined the trip for only the first few days, to the Flagstaff airport. It had been great to ride with them so far, and I hated to see them go, though I understood their scheduling limitations. But saying good-bye to friends wasn't my only frustration—and I wasn't the only one who felt that way.

Thanks to wind and hard climbing and flat tires, we hadn't made the distance we'd planned on yesterday, so now we were stuck in an unplanned hotel. We were off pace, off our charted route, and finding it difficult to stick to any sort of schedule.

There'd been several days with these sorts of problems. Getting up so early in the morning, day after day, was hard for several people on the team. We couldn't agree on restaurants. Even when we had a route planned, we often took wrong turns, particularly first thing in the morning. Each night the film crew stayed up until all hours to download the reams of footage they'd shot for the documentary. Everybody seemed cranky. Short-tempered. Irritable. Particularly me.

Paul had spoken to the team the night before, when I was so tired, and he'd basically told us we needed to work harder, figure out better systems, and tighten down loose strings. It had been a difficult conversation, though I knew it was a needful rebuke. The trip was still young, and we had a long way to go. Paul is a longtime friend and an incredibly generous person. He'd been a key organizer for the trip, taking care of the entire accounting process besides driving a support vehicle. I knew he loved the team and simply wanted to help us continue the ride. But not everyone was convinced.

"It's a weird dynamic here, isn't it?" Caroline said to me after Paul's talk. The color had returned to her face after the day's ride, but I could see she was feeling conflicted. "We're on these roads that are almost empty, and we see wide open spaces as we ride. But it doesn't feel like that with the team yet. It's like we're in a closet with ten other exhausted people. Like we're all in this tiny enclosed room together. Everybody's out of their comfort zone. We're all bumping into each other."

"That's for sure," I said. "We just didn't know what we were getting into with this ride, did we?"

She nodded.

I thought back to something I'd said to the team earlier, about how, when Jesus told his disciples "Follow me," they hadn't had a clue what he truly meant.[1] Jesus calls us to adventure, not to safety, but the disciples didn't know that at first. They figured he would overthrow Rome and give them all prominent places in an earthly kingdom. But Jesus was calling them to places of service, purpose, and even discomfort. He was offering them a spiritual kingdom.

Could people really trust Jesus when life became uncomfortable? That's what I asked myself right then. I was pushing my body and mind to the limit, along with the rest of our team. Could I really trust Jesus on this adventure, even when life wasn't comfortable?

In spite of Paul's hard conversation, I was feeling tremendously proud of the team. True, we still had a way to go before we gelled completely, and I knew what Caroline meant about feeling like we were all in a tiny room together. Paul's talk hadn't bothered me that much, but other things did.

At breakfast, Wes told the team his theory on pancakes—that you should eat either syrup or butter on pancakes, but definitely not both. It seemed like such an insignificant thing to take a hard stance on, but he was serious—and I found myself disproportionately annoyed. Normally I eat very healthy when I'm home, but on this trip I was eating anything and everything. Cheeseburgers by the pound. Convenience store soft-serve ice cream. Pancakes loaded with everything on the table. I was so calorie starved at the end of each day that everything I saw looked good. I loved Wes enormously, and he was a huge help on this trip, but I couldn't believe he was insisting there was only one way to eat pancakes—his way.

Fortunately, after the loss of Paul and John, we received an extra support person, Una, and she was as easygoing as they come. Una was a thirty-year-old real estate agent who was originally from Tonga and now lived in Dallas. Dark-skinned, with long, wavy hair, she had a huge smile. Una bounded into our group with lots of energy and got us all smiling right away. She had taught herself medical massage, so she worked on my shoulder, which had been hurting since the crash. Her hands worked wonders on my shoulder and my disposition. I considered asking her how she liked her pancakes but stopped short. Some questions are better left unasked.

We had our route planned for the day—more than 100 miles, much of it through Navajo land. Though mostly downhill, it would include a lot of riding on gravel roads, which made me nervous. The weather was predicted to be hot, hot, hot. The shop we'd taken my bike to the day before had broken the stem—the component that connects the handlebars to the steering tube of the front forks—so I'd had it replaced. I was learning that bikes, as well as dispositions, could be fragile things, particularly over gravel roads.

Before we left for the morning, I made good on my promise and met with Sasha, the woman from the motel who'd asked to speak with me the night before. An older woman with a warm smile, she was twenty minutes late because, as she explained with a chuckle, she was fixing her hair for the camera. We sat on a bench by a window in the conference room of the inn.

Sasha had lived in Arizona for thirty years, and we talked about the region a bit. Then I asked her to describe her belief system and faith—or lack of it.

"First thing I'd like to say is I'm agnostic," she said. "I need proof, and I have not seen anything that's convinced me God exists. There's so much ugliness in the church that I've seen and heard. It's appalling to me."

"Did you grow up in church?" Something about her tone alerted me to listen closely.

"No," she said. "That's not part of my history."

"So tell me about the kind of exposure you've had with people who've gone to church."

"Well, I've been to church. My family were Protestants. When I was growing up, I went faithfully . . . from time to time. My mother was a hard worker, so we never set churchgoing as a regular part of what we did. It never seemed that important."

I nodded and asked her specifically about Jesus. What did she believe about him, from what she had heard and understood?

"I've never seen the man, never heard the man," Sasha said. "So he doesn't seem real. Someone might meet Jesus and have a spiritual awakening, but another person might call it standing in a positive vibration. That's where I differ from others. I help people if I can help people, and it's not like I have anything against God. It's just that I've never met the man." Her voice rose at the end as if in question, and she smiled.

I chuckled. "I want to come back to that in a minute, but I really want to hear you about these positive vibrations that you mentioned. I'm curious where you learned about that."

"I guess from all my comings and goings and from reading things and then feeling things," she said with a forthright smile. "I am spiritual. Vibrations let you know you're on the right path. Like if you go right and feel something or go left and feel something else, or something tells you not to go that way. It doesn't mean that it's God. If somebody's guiding me, it's myself."

"Sasha, I can tell you're a positive person," I said. "From the moment I walked in yesterday, you greeted me warmly, and I just want to tell you I appreciated it."

"Thank you."

"Let's talk about what you said a minute ago—that you 'haven't met the man,'" I said. "I bet if others were honest, they'd say the same thing. I wonder, what would it take for God to convince you he exists?"

Sasha didn't hesitate. "To see him. To actually know he's there. This is somebody who's supposed to know the number of hairs on my head.[2] So why does he not present himself?"

"I love your question, 'Why does he not present himself?'" I said. "I'm not trying to force anything on anybody. I'm just trying to start the conversation and create some places for people to think. If you'd like, I'll leave you with a copy of the gospel of Mark. I think you'll find it interesting."

She inhaled sharply, seemingly exasperated, and I asked her why.

"Honestly," she said. "I probably wouldn't read it. My beliefs are pretty solid already. When it comes to Christians, I don't see too many people who aren't critical." She paused, then blurted, "And the churches have pedophiles. I mean, what kind of God is that? I know he allows free will and all, but please." Her tone held disgust and something more. Something intensely personal and painful.

"Thanks for your honesty," I said carefully, searching for the right response. "I told you last night I was a pastor, right?"

She nodded.

"So I just want you to hear from me, as a pastor, that it is wrong for any clergy to abuse their power, especially over children. I want you to hear that because it makes me so sad. Hear this too: I am sorry, and I want to apologize on behalf of all those people who have obviously failed you. Your reaction makes me wonder if childhood trauma is part of your story. If that is true, I want to ask you for your forgiveness. I'm so sorry if someone like me created this kind of pain and confusion in your life."

Her tone softened. "I thank you for that, and you're right, it is close to my story. That part of me is hidden, and the only thing I can say is what happened to me is sad and it's cruel. That's why it's hard to trust. I can't go into a church if I know that a guy over there, or some usher or whoever, has hurt people. Because you never know."

My eyes were wet. I felt for this woman and what she'd gone through. She'd obviously been hurt deeply, and the trauma she'd experienced had built walls between her and God. We talked a little about how Jesus always respected and cared for women and children. Women were among his followers, and when other people pushed children away, Jesus let the children come near to be blessed. I was trying to strip away all religious accoutrements from the discussion and just focus on a God who cared for Sasha.

She asked me a few questions of her own—like whether I believed in aliens. She had read about ancient aliens who had come to earth long ago in spaceships, looking for gold.

"I want it to make sense," she said. "I want it to be true. Because I want to find the truth and know the truth."

"I agree with you there," I said. "Let's pursue truth. Did you know that Jesus said we can know truth and that truth will set us free?"[3]

"Well, I'm sixty-one." Sasha chuckled. "If Jesus hasn't shown me truth by now, where's he been?"

I chuckled too. "I wonder if he's been pursuing you in ways you haven't seen yet. I've been dreaming of taking this trip for eighteen years, and I don't even know how we wound up at your hotel. We had a schedule, but we couldn't always follow it, so stopping at this hotel wasn't part of our original plan. Maybe me being here, talking to you about these things, is part of Jesus in your life."

She laughed good-naturedly.

The conversation had made my day—it had felt so genuine—and I told her so. I asked her if I could pray for her, and she said sure, why not. So I thanked the Lord for Sasha's hospitality, openness, and honesty. I prayed that God would bless her as she continued to be a blessing to others. I prayed for the pain and hurt in her heart, that healing and comfort would come. And I prayed that God would make himself real to her.

We said our good-byes, and I went out to find my bike.

The roads were rough. The sun was unbearable. We pedaled our way through the vast Navajo Nation, the largest American Indian reservation in the country. We came to a flea market in a small town, where I started talking with a Navajo man named Emmerson, who wore a large, cheerful, wide-brimmed hat. He pointed out the various mountains in the region that his people considered sacred and mentioned that two of his grandfathers had been World War II veterans—one had fought in the Pacific and the other in Europe. He taught me how to say a few words in his native language, including the word for White man, *bilagáana*.[4]

I asked what he would want a bilagáana to know about the Navajo people.

He thought a moment. "We're just regular people, like everybody else. Sometimes we like to keep to ourselves, but once you get to know us, we're just regular people."

We talked about faith, and Emmerson said he'd been raised to respect traditional Navajo religion. He still practiced it today, although his wife was Catholic.

"Back in the 1960s they used to take you away from your parents and put you in a boarding school," he said. "Some schools were Catholic. Some were Latter-day Saints. Some were Baptist. So there are a lot of mixtures of faith around here. But I'm traditional. I believe in the Navajo way."

"I'm so sorry so much sorrow happened to the Navajo people," I said.

He made a gesture, almost as if shrugging it off, and I sensed he wanted me to continue, so I asked, "What are some of your Navajo faith traditions?"

"The biggest way to look at the Navajo faith is that it's a walk in beauty," he said. "If you walk in beauty, you won't go mess with stuff you shouldn't. Remember I told you about our sacred mountains. See, there are ways and directions for praying. Each area—north, south, east, and west—has different prayers and different ways to get yourself right if you screw up."

"Oh, wow," I said. "How very interesting. When you are praying in these directions, can I ask who you are praying to?"

"Well, there are variants—and certain things we keep quiet on. The prayers are more a traditional thing that you don't speak about to outsiders. Once you get inside with the Navajo people, they will explain it to you. But it's very personal. To me the biggest thing I was always taught is that you walk in beauty. And if you screw up, that's when you start praying, begging for forgiveness."

I was fascinated. I asked him how to say "walk in beauty" in Navajo, and he told me. "I want to do that," I said.

We talked about seeking forgiveness and what that looked like in his faith. He mentioned there were certain shamans on the reservation that a person could seek help from.

I asked if he and his wife, being Catholic, had ever conversed about Jesus and who he was.

He nodded. "I was always taught to respect other people's beliefs. I understand there are things we don't know about. I've read the Bible, and it's basically the same thing as what many faiths say. It's important as human beings to treat each other properly. Respect others. That's the biggest thing."

"Emmerson, I respect you. I want you to know that. And I'm thankful to be here today and to meet you. It's a real privilege."

"Thank you," he said and looked around him at the sky and the hills. "You are welcome here. You are invited to enjoy the Navajo land."

We shook hands, and I asked if I could give him a hug. He said yes. He had welcomed me onto his land, his home turf. I didn't take that lightly. We hugged and parted ways.

I wandered around the flea market a little more and spoke to a Navajo husband and wife. The man had served two tours in Iraq. I talked with another Navajo man whose son was a serviceman. Neither conversation went very far, although it intrigued me that so many of the Navajo people I'd spoken with that day had been involved in the United States military.

Caroline, Wes, and I continued riding. We spent most of the day in a beautiful area with brown and red mountains, pine trees, and rolling hills. At last, after pedaling 102 miles, we reached our destination, Holbrook, Arizona. My repaired bike had held up well over the rougher roads.

I ate until I was stuffed and flopped into bed, windblown and exhausted, knowing something larger was happening than a bike ride. We'd talked about truth today. Deeper truth. We'd taken steps along with people in their search for truth and the pursuit of beauty. And people had welcomed us into their lives.

I hoped I had welcomed them into my life too.

— 9 —

SPARKING A NEW DIALOGUE

Early in the morning I woke and glanced over at Vela. It was so great to have her on this trip. We were staying in a cabin at a campground. The bed was comfortable, and I had slept well.

Carefully I got out of bed so as not to wake her. I read my Bible and did some push-ups. It was Sunday, so I was thinking of home and our church. I made a note to call a few key staff members to check in.

I glanced at Vela again. She looked so peaceful, so beautiful. And I was so grateful to have her here with me.

When I had dreamed about taking this trip, I'd always imagined a small enterprise—just me and a bike with Vela driving our SUV. But we had both known there were limitations to such a trip. We could only imagine how tedious it would be for her to drive a car at fifteen miles per hour over a long distance. Sure, she'd be watching out for the safety of the cyclist—me—and looking at the landscape. But I wasn't sure if I wanted to inflict that on my dear wife, hour after hour, day after day. It wasn't her idea of a vacation.

Vela is a highly sociable person with a quick mind and a great sense of humor. She's also very wise. And she's a firm believer that each of us needs to do what God has called us to do within our own circles of influence. She and I are definitely a team, but we each also have our own distinct roles and ministries within the church and the community. When the trip started coming together in a larger way, with an entire team of people, I wasn't even sure she'd want to come along. The bike trip had always been more my dream than our dream. But I had asked her, and she'd said with a chuckle, "Sure I'll go. I wouldn't want to miss the party."

Now that we were on the trip, I couldn't imagine taking this journey without her. When you've been married for so many years, you know each other through and through. You sense each other's emotions. If one is feeling tired or down or exhausted, the other knows how to help. And Vela's help was invaluable to me.

On the team's very first night, when we'd stopped at the famed Wigwam Motel, Vela and I had been informed that we wouldn't be sharing a room. In fact, we'd be in separate rooms for the duration of the trip. To cut costs, all the guys would share one room and all the women another. Glenn and Judy, the only other couple on the trip, would share a room because they were seniors, but that was it.

I hadn't organized the lodgings, so this was the first time either of us had heard about this plan. But Vela put her foot down. We would find the extra money somewhere, she insisted. There was no way she and I were going to be apart for that long.

Vela knew that at the end of each day I'd be beat. I'd have ridden 100 miles. Had intense conversations. Had my mind on the church back home. Interacted with the team. Processed everything. Plus, I'd already be wondering how to communicate to folks later on. So I would need some absolute downtime. Vela could offer me that. She was my safe place. So we'd stayed together in the same room every night of our journey.

Today promised to be another difficult day. Our plan called for 105 miles of riding with more than 5,000 feet of elevation gain. The whole team was up and packing the vans early, getting ready. Caroline said she felt the best she'd felt in weeks. She hadn't ridden an entire day yet, but she vowed to go the full distance today.

We were all set to leave the campground when I spotted an intriguing-looking couple seated at a picnic table. I wandered over to see if I could strike up a conversation.

Jeff and Christine were middle-aged and instantly friendly. Christine wore a black and red flannel shirt and her hair in two braids. Jeff had a scraggly white goatee that came down at least a hand's breadth past his chin. They explained that their new truck had problems with the transmission module. They were drinking coffee and waiting for a tow truck.

We talked about the difficulty of car problems on the road and about family. Jeff and Christine had been married for thirty-six years. They were on their way from California to Wisconsin to visit relatives—a trip they took every June. Jeff had been raised in a small town and was used to walking up to strangers in stores or restaurants and talking with anybody he met, while Christine was more guarded.

The conversation soon turned to matters of faith. Jeff had grown up Catholic, and Christine was an atheist. They'd worked out the differences between them, never argued or fought about religion, and had raised their children to pick whatever religion they wanted. Two of their three grown sons now identified as Christian.

I asked Jeff if his faith was still important to him, and he said it was. "I believe in the God I know *now*," he said, "maybe even more than the God I grew up learning about. I believe there's something more than just this life. But I don't believe all the Catholic things anymore." He motioned to his wife. "They didn't believe that we should get married unless she got baptized first. The Catholic Church wouldn't even marry us, and I was like 'What?'"

"I'd had catechism as a child in the Lutheran church," Christine explained. "They married us there."

"Oh, okay. You grew up going to church," I said with a nod toward Christine. "So when did you look at your faith and say, 'This isn't for me'? Did something precipitate that?"

"I couldn't quite rationalize why there were so many churches," she said. "Or maybe I just couldn't find one that fit. My decision to walk away from the church wasn't an epiphany or anything. I just went a different direction. I don't know." She shrugged, chuckled, and looked directly at me. "These are the sorts of conversations I never get into. I always told the children, 'Don't talk about religion, sex, or politics.'"

Jeff chuckled along with her. "And I would always say to them, 'Don't ever condemn the Lord, because if there is a God, you're going to have a lot of answering to do.'"

I noticed that when Jeff said that, Christine gave Jeff a look that was hard to pinpoint, so I asked her to explain.

"Well, I went to my son's church when he got baptized," Christine said. "But I always had a hard time with the idea of judgment. So many churches seem to be all about judgment. I believe we're all going to be somewhere after we die. But I don't make a judgment on people, on who they are or what they do. I think everybody needs kindness, and judgment stands in the way of kindness."

"Yeah, I'd say the both of us just take religion for what it is today," Jeff said.

"When I was growing up, we always *had* to go to church," Christine said. "I wanted to find my own way. And that was important to me when we were raising our kids too—that they decide for themselves."

"Very interesting," I said. "It sounds like both of you grew up hearing about Jesus. I'm curious what you believe about him now."

"Well, I believe Jesus existed," Christine said, "because there's a book, and that's history. Jesus was a real man. He was on this earth, and he was a good and moral man. I don't believe there's a deity in the sky looking down on us, or whatever. But sure, Jesus died on the cross. We have that as history. Today Jesus is gone. The Bible is still here. But there ain't nothing else left."

Jeff smiled. "I spend twice as much time being good so that she gets into heaven too. When I get to the pearly gates, I'll point at her and say, 'Yep, I got this nonbeliever I'm bringing in with me. She's been a good woman all her life.'"

We all chuckled. Here was a point where I had my reservations, but I kept them to myself. I don't believe that anyone's salvation is a result of being good. The Bible indicates it's a matter of God's mercy—that he extends salvation to anyone who believes.[1] But I didn't want to interrupt the flow of the conversation by contradicting Jeff. Instead I said, "Wow, it's encouraging to see y'all's relationship. I want to encourage you in that. Y'all get along so well."

There was a pause in the conversation. Then Jeff turned on the seat of the picnic table to face Christine and addressed his wife directly. "What would it take for you to believe anyway?"

That shocked me. It was a great question to ask, and it held much more power coming from him than from me. I was so glad I hadn't jumped in too soon or interrupted him to talk about being saved by mercy. Because I waited and allowed ten seconds of silence, Jeff had the chance to ask the question I wanted to ask.

Christine looked directly at her husband and thought a moment. "He'd have to come down and talk to me." She turned her focus back to me. "Now do I talk to God sometimes? Sure. At least I talk to someone . . . or something. With raising three kids—oh sure, I talked to someone."

We all laughed. They were terrific folks who had learned to work together as a couple despite their differences in beliefs. We shook hands all around, and then we hugged. I was particularly happy that my conversation with Jeff and Christine had prompted a deeper conversation between the two of them. I was fairly certain they'd do more talking between themselves later on.

Team members were set to go, but a lot of people in the campground were just hanging out in the early morning sunshine. I couldn't let this opportunity pass by. Quickly I approached a young couple, perhaps in their late twenties, who were drinking dark, hot tea from tall glass mugs. Vela meandered over and sat down to join us. Lizzie, a hairstylist and art teacher, had pink hair and wore a stylish green sweater. Miguel, a cardiovascular researcher with a PhD in neuroscience, sported a mustache and sideburns, tattoos, a black T-shirt, and a trucker hat. They were cool and edgy and lots of fun. Miguel was from Portugal and Lizzie from San Diego, where they both lived currently. We talked about our respective road trips and what was most important in life.

Lizzie talked about having fun. She also said she loved the creativity and flexibility of her work and enjoyed how her hair clients often discussed deeper matters when they sat in her chair. She saw her role as helping make people beautiful on the outside while also encouraging their hearts inside.

Miguel loved riding bicycles. He'd been in the States for three years and would soon head back to Europe.

"I'd say the social and political climate in the United States is pretty divided right now," Miguel said. "So it's nice to talk to people and actually hear what they have to say. We live in California and hang out with a lot of like-minded people. It's good to hang out with people who don't always think the same way, even though it's sometimes a struggle for me, honestly, to hear that certain people believe certain things."

"Wow," I said. "That's exactly why we're taking this trip. In fact, you just used some of the very words I use when describing this trip. The climate in America is so divided right now, and people are afraid to talk about anything that's important because they fear getting stomped on. So we decided to go out; be curious, kind, and respectful; and try to hear people's stories. You mentioned that sometimes it's a struggle to hear certain people. What have you heard that's surprised you?"

"The things a person believes in can be very complex," Miguel said. "Many people are a result of their environment. Like, I'm from a big city, so that's how I see the world. But not everybody is that way."

"I agree," Lizzie said. "People who live in bigger cities can definitely be exposed to different things than people from smaller towns."

We talked about their faith backgrounds. Lizzie had been raised in the Catholic Church until she was eight or nine, but her family hadn't gone to church much after that. She didn't classify herself as having any religion today, although she had siblings she described as "very religious" and "borderline racist" because they didn't agree with their neighbors who had different skin colors and practiced different religions.

Miguel's mother was Protestant and his father was Jewish, and Miguel had grown up going to both church and synagogue. Today he considered himself an atheist.

"My parents never pushed anything on us," Miguel said. "They gave us a choice. We would go to church to get educated and have experiences."

"All right, so we have Catholic, Protestant, and Jewish represented here." I motioned to the young couple. "We've got it all covered." Everybody laughed. "I'm curious—when I say 'Jesus,' what do you think?"

"Most times when people say 'Jesus,' they're speaking of him in a religious sense," Lizzie said. "Me, I'd say he was probably a real man, although maybe the information was documented incorrectly. Honestly, I don't know. I don't think about it. I'm not really interested."

"I don't believe in any higher being," Miguel said. "I don't believe that there's any mission, any plan. I'm sure Jesus is a historical figure, like Moses or whatever, and I see value in religion because it can give people a purpose. Definitely there are religious charities that help people. In San Diego we have some good charities run by the church that help the homeless, and that's great. But for me, I don't agree with doctrine, and I don't practice it."

I paused a moment. "I'm wondering if either of you know people of faith who you respect, and if you could have a fruitful, meaningful conversation about faith with them—the kind of conversation that wouldn't lead to an argument."

"Yes," Miguel said. "In the scientific community, I work with people who are Christians, Muslims, and Jews. They all do the same job I do, and we're all very objective and hypothesis driven. These are people I respect and have talked to about religion, and it's interesting. The conversations are healthy."

"I definitely do," Lizzie said. "Last Friday night I was bartending at my girlfriend's music and sound studio. From the very first time I met her, we've always gotten along well. It wasn't until I had known her a bit that I realized she's a devout Catholic. So I've gone with her and her family to church, to support her and her beliefs. Also, one of my clients is a pastor for a United Methodist church, and we've talked about religion in a healthy way."

The conversation was winding to a close. Miguel and Lizzie's tea was getting cold, and I needed to get on the road. We talked about the environment and recycling, about paying attention to things that matter, and about being fully present. I mentioned a few examples of how Jesus was present in each moment. It was a good conversation. It felt like enough for now.

Before the trip began, I had wondered if I should bring along anything to give out to people. We had brought T-shirts and business cards, so people could follow our trip online, along with a few Bibles and books.

But I had made a conscious decision never to force anything on anybody. If the moment felt right to offer a gift, I would.

It didn't feel right to offer anything to Lizzie and Miguel. We'd had a good conversation, and now we were done; they were ready to move on. I wanted to honor that. This was one of those conversations where I was leaving the follow-up to them—to further conversations they might have. And to the Holy Spirit. God could arrange the next step in their spiritual growth far better than I could.

At last Wes, Caroline, and I started riding. We climbed for quite a while, then the road leveled out at the top of a ridge. Caroline mentioned she was feeling good. Wes was feeling good, too, and we'd all hit a strong pace. I turned to Wes as we descended the next grade, the wind at our backs, and I said, "You know, we're really living the dream."

He gave me a funny look for a moment, probably wondering if I was being sarcastic. If someone asks you on a Monday how you're doing and you're having a hard morning, you might roll your eyes and say, "Living the dream."

But I was serious. I loved what we were doing on this trip. Our conversations could be leading people to bigger conversations, maybe even transformative ones. We were throwing ourselves into the effort of actively listening, spreading kindness, and sparking a new kind of dialogue in our country. It was what I'd been dreaming of doing for eighteen years.

Wes must have sensed my sincerity because he soon turned back to me and said, "You know, we truly are."

— 10 —

GENTLENESS AND RESPECT

The scenery was beautiful as we descended from the ridge later that Sunday morning. Rugged brown mountains jutted up over the landscape. We rode into a little town right at lunchtime and started looking for a place to eat. Only one restaurant appeared open, and as we approached it I saw a man walking down the street who looked to be homeless. He carried a backpack and wore a tank top, baggy sweatpants, and flip-flops. His arms were sporadically tattooed, and his neck tattoo read: "In Loving Memory of Mikey."

He glanced at us on our bikes as we rode by and called out, "It looks like you guys are living the dream!"

This was a divine appointment; I was sure of it. I pulled over and said, "Yeah, we were just talking about that. What's your dream?"

"My dream is to travel the country," he said, "just like you guys are doing. To express myself as a person and let people know who I am. I'm no different than anybody else. I'm no better than anybody else. We're all just put in this world, and we're all just trying to survive and make it. That's my thing."

He was so open to talking that I couldn't pass up the opportunity. He introduced himself as Mike, and I asked him to tell me a bit about himself, right there by the side of the road. His story poured out in a rush.

"My parents abandoned me when I was six years old," Mike said. "They left me on the corner of St. Louis and Missouri in the snow, and I've been on my own since then. They had two other kids, my baby brother and little sister. My parents figured they couldn't provide for us all, and I was the oldest and didn't need as much attention, so I was the one who got left behind. I'm forty-three today. I have three kids, ages twenty-seven, nineteen, and sixteen, who I love very much. That's why I stay in this town. I'm not going to leave them like I was left behind. I want to show them that I'm a survivor, that I can do it, that I can be there for them. I was with their mom for twenty-two years, since I was sixteen and she was twenty. We were opposites, and opposites attract, okay? She didn't like anything I liked, and I didn't like anything she liked. We tried to make it work for the kids. But we were always yelling at each other, so there comes a time when you gotta go. That's the reality of life. Don't take nothing for granted. I'm on the streets now, and I have nowhere to go. So I walk around with my backpack, my sleeping bag, and a pillow."

He paused to take a breath, and I took advantage of that moment.

"Mike, here's what impresses me about you," I said. "You were abandoned by your own parents, yet you stay here because of your kids." He nodded, and his face twisted up with emotion. "Where did you learn to stick around, Mike? Because that's amazing."

"I can't take off on my kids." Mike tapped the side of his forehead with two fingers. "That's where my mentality is. It makes me sad to think about it, and it makes me want to cry. I'm never going to let my kids go. I'll die right here on the sidewalk for my kids if I have to. But I won't leave them."

A tear rolled down his face. I was misting up too.

"How long you been on the streets, Mike?"

"Past three years."

"Three years. Wow. Are you hoping to get off the streets?"

"Yeah. I want to find a life and show everybody that I can be some-body. But it's rough. I've struggled in my head some, you know, with mental issues. I'm not perfect in my head. It's not extreme, but sometimes it feels like the walls are closing in. I have nowhere to go."

"Mike, I'm going to ask you a favor, and you're free to say no," I said. "Jesus often ate meals with people because it was good just to hang out—"

"Just to be a friend," Mike added.

"Yeah. So I was wondering if you'd let us buy you lunch. Would you eat lunch with our group today?"

"Yes, sir," he said. "I'd love that."

The team stowed our bikes, then we followed Mike inside the café and sat at a booth. I ordered the prime rib special with mashed potatoes and corn. Mike ordered a philly cheesesteak. He explained more about his tattoos, saying he'd gotten several of them in prison. He'd broken into a house while looking for shelter, and that had gotten him in trouble with the law. I wanted to ask him about his neck tattoo, the one that read "In loving memory of Mikey," but something held me back. I sensed that was a story of deep loss that he would tell only if he was ready.

After talking some about baseball, which he loved, he brought up the subject of prison again, stressing the necessity of showing respect to everyone. Then he turned back to his childhood.

"What did I do so wrong, to be abandoned by my folks?" he asked into the air, almost rhetorically.

"You were just a six-year-old kid," I said. "I'm curious—if you could meet up with your parents today, what would you want from them? Would you want to know why?"

"Yes, I would. All those years of being by myself. That's a dark, lonely place to be. I always wanted to ask them, 'Why me?' I heard they're both deceased now. So I have a lot of unanswered questions like, was it my fault? I was a kid. How could you not love me? But they brought me into this world, so I can't hate them."

One of his tattoos was a cross, and I asked about that. He said he gave it to himself with a sewing needle when he was eight years old because he never wanted to lose faith in himself. He described how he now went to church sometimes because it made him feel free and maybe loved.

"You know, Mike," I said. "This just came to mind. You might have heard in church that God is like a father. He's a good father. Sometimes that's hard to believe because of what our own fathers have done to us. I'm a father of three kids, and I make mistakes."

"None of us are perfect," Mike said.

"Here's what I'm thinking. I can't speak for your father or mother, but I know this truth about God your Father in heaven: He'd love to sit down and have a meal with you. And I think this is what he would say to you: 'Mike, I can't wait to go to a park and throw a baseball around with you.' And he'd say, 'I think you're the most awesome son in the whole world.'"

"That'd be nice," Mike said slowly, thoughtfully. "I would love that." He looked away a moment and wiped the wetness from his eyes. "Yeah. A father who'd come home from work and say, 'I thought about you all day today. You're always on my mind.'"

"Can you imagine that?"

"I yearn for that attention." Mike wiped his eyes again.

We talked about Jesus, how John 1:12 says, "To all who did receive him, to those who believed in his name, he gave the right to become children of God." And I asked Mike what he thought about Jesus.

"I believe Jesus gives unconditional love," Mike said. "I believe if you sin, you can ask for forgiveness, and he will forgive you. He gives you wisdom, knowledge, patience. That's real love. Yeah, you gotta believe in the Lord. You gotta walk that path. He will help you. Like, even me seeing you guys on your bikes—and now here we are. Everything happens for a reason."

"I'm not going to forget you, Mike," I said.

"I'm not going to forget you either."

We finished our meal together, then wrapped up the conversation and said our good-byes. Just as we were leaving, a man entered the café, waved at Mike, and came over to me. He introduced himself as a pastor in town. He explained that he'd talked to Mike several times and that Mike was getting some help. It felt good to know that somebody else was watching out for him.

Mike was rough around the edges and had definitely gone through some painful experiences in his life, but he was so surprisingly clear about the truth. As the team left the café and we climbed back on our bikes, I couldn't help but think of what Jesus said about people who are poor in spirit. He said they're blessed because the kingdom of heaven is theirs.[1]

Mile after mile passed on wide-open roads, and we rode all that afternoon without talking to anybody else. My mind was still focused on Mike. I thought about how many people are asking themselves the same questions: Does anybody love me? Have I been abandoned? Am I alone? The lesson for me in talking with Mike was that everybody has a story. When we ask people to tell their stories, we help answer the questions they have. We let people know they're not alone or abandoned. We help people know they are listened to and loved. That their stories matter.

When we finished the day, we had ridden 103 miles. We all cheered because Caroline had ridden the entire way for the first time, and the whole team was ecstatic about her determination and progress.

Overnight we stayed in a campground of cabins run by Native Americans. They operated the campground on a donation-only basis. The cabins were rustic yet clean and comfortable. The sky overhead was full of stars, and the people who ran the camp were kind and friendly. They fed us dinner and sang for us in their native language. It was a peaceful evening.

In the morning we were on the road early, headed for New Mexico. I hadn't slept well, and I wasn't sure why. The day before had gone so well, but I woke up exhausted, and this day was already hot. We had more than 100 miles to go, and the temptation to be grumpy and irritable sprang up in me.

I remembered a short manifesto I had created while training for the ride, a series of statements to help me remember that the road ahead wasn't going to be easy. I had written it on a poster and shared it with our church:

I do not train to avoid suffering.
I do not prepare to avoid challenge.
I train and prepare to effectively engage
in suffering and challenge.

That's what this day would be about. I had trained for days like this, days when I didn't want to get out of bed, days when I didn't want to ride the distance. The challenge was upon me, and part of this whole cross-country ride was about God working on me to become more thankful, less irritable, and more content to effectively engage in discomfort and challenge when it was wrapped around a good purpose.

We stopped for breakfast at a café in the small town of Ramah, New Mexico, where the team dined on hot, flavorful oatmeal, biscuits and gravy, steak and eggs, pancakes and bacon, and broiled ham and hash browns. A feast. I sat down with a group of guys who said they ate there every morning, and talk drifted to the economy and divisions in the country. I could tell that each man around the table really cared about his country and town. By the stories they told, I knew they were kind, solid, and hardworking.

But a hesitation lay under the conversation. They were friendly yet guarded. I couldn't quite put my finger on why. About halfway through our talk, they told me they were Latter-day Saints and that the area was a Mormon community. A lightbulb went on. I'd been experiencing something from them that I'd felt with the atheists, agnostics, and perhaps some of the Native Americans I'd talked to. They feared that if they talked about their beliefs, they'd be judged. Ridiculed. Rejected.

I thanked the men for their hospitality, and I praised them for their service to their community. We talked about faith some, and they expressed that they simply wanted to be thought of as Christians.

When I left and started riding again, I found I really needed to think through what it meant to be the presence of Jesus in such situations. My own desire, always, is that people hear the full truth of the gospel and what it means to live in grace.[2] But I realized that I sometimes needed to fight my desire to do so because people weren't always ready to hear that message from me. My relationship with them wasn't established enough for me to speak the fuller truth in a way it could be heard. I needed to be gentle first, and they needed to know I was committed to loving and respecting them.[3] If I had come in with the ammunition of arguments, the guys around the table would have shut down.

I had often been reminded in Christian circles that if I didn't share the gospel in a given conversation, then the person I was talking with might die without ever hearing the truth. If I didn't share the plan of salvation, then maybe the person would spend eternity without God. But on this trip I had been learning to have more faith in God than ever before, to trust that he would do what was necessary to bring people to him.

For much of my evangelistic life, I had been trying to tell people what I believed. But on this trip, I was learning that conversations went better when I asked people to tell me what they believed. As they were prompted to articulate their beliefs, then the deeper conversation could begin. Once they expressed their beliefs, they started to process those beliefs. They were invested in the conversation. That clarified where they were so they could take steps to where they needed to be.

I was still mulling over these thoughts when I started to feel physically lousy. The terrain was hilly, and my legs lost energy. My stomach complained. My head ached. The sun was broiling, and I'd been exhausted since I got up. We crossed the Continental Divide, and a sign indicated an elevation of 7,882 feet. The team pulled over at a roadside attraction, and while they toured some ice caves, I hopped into the van, cracked open a window, and slept.

Half an hour later I woke and still didn't feel great, although I felt better enough to keep going. For the rest of the day we rode slowly through amazing rock formations and around craggy tableland and buttes. Late in the afternoon we pulled into Grants, New Mexico. We hadn't reached our daily 100-mile goal yet, not even close. We had ridden only 56 miles. But my stomach, head, and legs were aching badly, so we decided to grab some dinner and stop for the evening. The altitude, heat, and exhaustion were really affecting me.

After we ate, I felt a bit better. As nighttime fell I struck up a conversation with the owner-manager of the hotel, a seventy-four-year-old Korean man named Kim. I asked him about his faith too soon, and he quickly changed the subject to his personal history.

Kim had grown up in South Korea during the era we call the Korean War or the Korean Conflict. His parents had both died, and as a boy he'd done whatever he could to survive—shined shoes, sold newspapers. He'd often gone hungry. But he'd worked his way through school, come to America at age thirty-four, and gone into business for himself. We talked about his family, which included three grown children and grandchildren. Then I asked the faith question again.

This time he was ready to talk, and he said he identified as a Buddhist.

"Well, it's always a genuine privilege for me to meet someone of a different faith," I replied. "I have some Buddhist friends, and they've told me about some of the expressions of their faith." Kim and I talked about going to temple and about Buddhist prayer practices. He admitted he didn't have much time to go to temple himself.

"So I'm curious," I said, "what do you know about Jesus? Have you ever learned about him?"

Kim smiled. "That's a good question. During high school I went to a Baptist church with my friends in South Korea. I liked to sing, so I joined their choir." He smiled broadly. "You know, it was fun. I don't remember any of the songs. If I have a hard time today, I ask my god for help. The Buddha."

We talked more about Buddhism, and Kim explained that statues of the Buddha weren't considered gods in themselves but representations of the deity. He believed Jesus was one god of many, and he respected Jesus, although he didn't see him as the only God. We talked about forgiveness, happiness, purpose in life, and what happens to us when we die.

Kim and I didn't believe all the same things, but we found common ground and were respectful of each other. I sensed a genuine warmth between us as we shook hands and hugged before we parted.

When I went to bed that night, I meditated on how I could trust that God was ultimately in control of what was happening on this journey. His job was to save people when and where he chooses. My job was to establish a conversation with another person and to keep that conversation real, seasoned with gentleness and respect.

God would work the rest out in his own time.

— 11 —

THE ART OF LISTENING

Tension was mounting again. Team members were consistently getting up late, and Wes was one of the worst culprits. I loved Wes like a brother, but I was also getting ticked at him again. Before the trip began we'd all agreed on start times. Everybody needed to get up at 5:30 a.m., eat breakfast, have their luggage at the curb so the vans could be packed, and be ready to go so the bikers could be on the road by 7:00. But that simply wasn't happening.

It wasn't entirely Wes's fault. The routes had to be changed almost every day, and each night Wes and Jeff stayed up late to map out the next day's ride. Once we got going, Wes was pulling the most, positioning himself as the guy in front of the pace line who blocked the wind. I knew he was working hard. But I couldn't help but scowl this morning when he was late again and held us all back.

"Hey," he snapped in my direction. "You're the one going to bed at nine o'clock each night."

I wasn't. I was going to bed at ten thirty most nights, some nights even later. I was exhausted like everybody else. But the discrepancy didn't seem worth arguing about.

It was June 4, the ninth day of the trip, and our first stop was McDonald's for breakfast. Normally I wasn't a McDonald's guy. I preferred to eat at local mom-and-pop diners. They were full of soul, ripe for good conversations. But mom-and-pop diners weren't known for their quickness. McDonald's restaurants were everywhere, efficient, and inexpensive. I wolfed down scrambled eggs, pancakes (loaded with both butter *and* syrup!), sausage, and a biscuit, then went back to the counter and ordered a breakfast sandwich.

We headed out of Grants on one of the service roads that followed Route 66. The daily goal was to put in at least 50 miles before lunch, but we must have taken a wrong turn somewhere because the first stretch of road was a washboard and slowed us down miserably. We jostled along, hitting bump after bump. Fortunately by the sixth mile the road smoothed out again, and we sped up.

We passed a lot of adobe houses and tilled fields. The sky was a sheet of blue, and the smell of sagebrush filled the air. We spotted a field full of horses running free in the sunshine. A dog meandered along the roadside and gave us a playful yap as we rode by. Then for a long time everything was quiet except for the constant whiz of our chains through our derailleurs and the passing of the occasional car.

By midmorning we'd ridden 25 miles, and the day was heating up. I spotted a man working on his car in his driveway. A large shade tree in his yard near the road looked cool and inviting, so I pulled over near the tree and asked if he wanted to talk. He said no, he was too busy. I asked if we could stay under the shade tree just until we filled our water bottles, and he said sure, no problem.

We filled our bottles from the cooler in the support vehicle, and I grabbed an energy bar and downed a container of coconut water. I was stalling a bit because I had a hunch a conversation might be imminent.

When a cadre of bicyclists and two support vehicles pulls up in front of your house, it's hard not to become curious.

Sure enough, the man who'd just told us he was too busy to talk soon walked over and introduced himself as Jeffrey. I asked him a few questions about the area, and he told me the land we were standing on had once belonged to his grandparents. Train tracks ran nearby, and his grandparents had operated a bed-and-breakfast for travelers. Jeffrey had worked as a lab tech in Albuquerque, but he'd quit his job four years ago to move back to his grandparents' land.

Jeffrey spoke with a kind, gentle voice. He explained he was from the Laguna Pueblo tribe, the Little Bear clan, and talked about his four grown children.

"What do you hope to pass along to them?" I asked.

"The language of our tribe," he answered. "It's been dying out. I'd love to be able to pass that on to them." He told me some Laguna words and seemed pleased that I made the effort to learn them.

I asked about his faith, and Jeffrey told me that when people in his tribe sit to eat, they place spirit bowls on the table and serve portions of food in the bowls to feed spirit people. We talked about spiritual dances and dress and the famous kachina dolls, which represent the spirits of things in the natural world. Historically the Lagunas farmed corn, and in each farming season they prayed to the spirits for rain and good crops.

I nodded as I listened and then asked, "Do the Lagunas believe in one God over all the spirits—a creator God?"

"Yes," Jeffrey said. "Just like people believe in 'Jesus' and 'Lord,' we pray to a creator God. Different tribes have different gods that they pray to, like the sun god or Mother Earth. People around here often get up before dawn and pray to the sun as it comes up. They pray for blessing and pray for everybody to be well. But almost everybody I know believes in the Creator."

"That's interesting," I said. "And you mentioned Jesus. What do you think of him?"

"Well, I go to a Baptist church nearby," Jeffrey said, "so I believe in Jesus. I pray to him every day. I used to drink quite badly, and then I quit drinking three years ago. If I had kept drinking, I would not have everything that I have now. That's why I pray to Jesus, to give me strength for every day."

"Fascinating," I said. "I'm curious—do you pray to both Jesus and your traditional gods or just to Jesus alone?"

"Both," he said. "Our traditional gods are spirits, and sometimes people will say things like, 'Ghosts, spirits—they're just myths.' But I have actually seen things like that—spirits, or maybe ghosts. People say, 'Oh that's just hocus-pocus.' But no, spirits are real."

I asked him if his Baptist church friends ever had a problem with him praying both to Jesus and to spirits, and he said no, the majority of folks in the church were Native Americans, so the pastor had respect for that kind of duality. He quickly shifted the conversation and described the truck traffic through the area, but I wanted to ask him one more question about exclusive worship.

"So, going back to what we were just talking about, another question came to mind," I said. "In Luke 4:8, Jesus quoted the Old Testament and described how God alone should be worshiped and served. What do you think about that?"

Jeffrey shook his head. "Some people say they'd believe Jesus if they could see him face-to-face. And other people say there's only one way to believe. You gotta be careful. For me, it's kinda hard to explain how I can pray to both Jesus and other gods. My beliefs are sort of encompassing. This is a corrupt world, and I don't like to watch much news. Everybody needs to love one another. Like, I don't even know you guys, but already we're sort of bonded. A little bit of kindness can always help somebody.

We're all human. We're all on the planet for the same reasons. That's what my beliefs are about."

He smiled, and I smiled back. He didn't seem to realize that his last answer was no answer at all to the question of whether we should worship God alone, or that he'd gently changed the subject. But it wasn't my intention to debate him. Instead I said, "I've totally appreciated talking with you today. Thank you so much for your kindness."

Jeffrey smiled again. It was a cool moment. We had talked about some fairly weighty theology, and the conversation could have turned on a dime to become confrontational, with me trying to sort out his beliefs. But our interaction had stayed polite and relational, just as I'd hoped. And because I'd asked him questions and then listened to him talk, he'd gone to a deep place quite quickly. That was a good step in anyone's life. The questions themselves were valuable. I could see that he felt challenged just by wrestling with questions about what he believed.

I needed to use the restroom, so I very carefully asked Jeffrey if I could use his. He said sure, he understood. He walked me inside his house and introduced me to his girlfriend, Marcella, who was cooking tortillas in the kitchen. The oven was open, and the aroma of freshly baked corn filled their home. Jeffrey and I had been talking for probably forty-five minutes, so some of the team members stood near the doorway and asked if they could use the restroom too. Poor Jeffrey and Marcella hadn't known what kind of lineup they were in for when they said yes.

When I was outside again, Marcella came out to the front lawn with a platter of freshly made tortillas. She asked our team if anybody wanted some, and soon everybody was chowing down. Marcella started talking to Vela and Caroline, and there was lots of laughing and chatter.

Jeffrey had disappeared somewhere. Soon he reappeared with a handmade piece of Laguna pottery. It was beautiful and colorful. He handed it to me and said it was a present. I was speechless. Forty-five minutes ago we had been complete strangers. He'd been too busy even to talk to me. But now I found myself choked up by his gesture of kindness.

We hugged, I thanked him, and he thanked me back. I asked why he'd given me the gift, and he said, "Well, you let me tell my story." We took pictures together, and everybody shook hands. We gave them some T-shirts, and our team was soon headed down the road again.

We rode for another 20 miles. The wind picked up, and rain clouds began to gather. We stopped for lunch, and Vela gestured for me to come over to the van to see something. She had looked up the pottery on her phone. She showed me the web page.

My eyes grew wide. A piece of pottery almost identical to the piece Jeffrey had given me was selling for sixteen hundred dollars!

A tear slid down my face. It wasn't the monetary value of the gift that got to me. We would never sell it, after all. It was that the gift was so exorbitant, so lavish. We had given Jeffrey and Marcella T-shirts, and they'd given us a costly piece of handcrafted earthenware. Their kindness and generosity were overwhelming.

After we finished eating lunch, we climbed on our bikes and started to ride again. Just outside of Albuquerque we left the main drag and rode through the side streets of a suburban neighborhood. I spotted a bushy-bearded man and his young son near a motor home parked in front of a house. The man was dressed like any other average American in blue jeans and a T-shirt, but his black head covering announced that there was something different about him—at least different from me. The man's son also wore a head covering, a bright red one.

Vela and I had traveled to India and seen similar head coverings, so I guessed that this man and his son were Sikhs. When we were first married, we'd lived next door to a Sikh family, so I had an inkling of the man's worldview.

I stopped, introduced myself, and explained why we were taking this ride.

"So you're just riding across the country . . . *meeting people?*" the man asked. He squinted in my direction, and I sensed incredulity in his voice, a definite note of suspicion.

"Yep, that's right," I confirmed. "I'm wondering if you might want to talk."

He turned his back, squatted down, and returned to working on his motor home. The boy, maybe eight or nine years old, kept quiet. The moment felt unsettled and tense. The easiest thing would have been for me to wish them well and keep riding. But I wanted to stay in this moment to see if we could make a connection.

The bearded man didn't make a sound. Not even a grunt. A generator was making a ruckus toward the back of the motor home. A dog barked from across the street. The boy handed his father wrenches and screwdrivers and kept silent, watching me.

I knew that not everybody we met on this trip would want to talk to us—at least not at first, as Jeffrey had indicated. But I was willing to be patient and wait for the man to think things through. I wiped sweat from my forehead and looked at the traffic moving close by us. I hoped he would stand up again and get out of the street, maybe move to the front of the motor home, because I feared that we might get hit by an oncoming car where we were.

"Hang on a sec," the man muttered at last. He stood, eyed me again, walked to the back of the motor home, and flipped a switch. The ruckus of the generator died down. The hushed heat of the New Mexico summer settled over us like a blanket, although the dog across the street kept barking.

The man motioned for me to follow as he ambled to the front of his motor home. I climbed off my bike and wheeled it to where he stood out of harm's way. He adjusted his wire-rimmed glasses, introduced himself as Kiki, and looked like he was prepared to be asked some questions.

"So tell me how you got this Wanderlodge, man." I drawled out my words with a grin and my Texan chuckle. I hoped he'd relax from the get-go and talk about something he enjoyed. Plus, his rig was truly impressive, and I genuinely wanted to know. I'd long ago learned you can't fake interest if something bores you.

His eyes brightened. "We have traveled a lot." He nodded toward his young son. "As you guys undoubtedly understand, seeing the country on the ground and on the road—stopping to meet people—is the real way to experience America. It's a beautiful country, which you see when you actually slow down and get off the interstates to appreciate it. Traveling has always been a dream of mine, ever since I was in college. So now I'm taking my son around, showing him different places."

I turned to the boy. "You like riding in this big truck?"

"Yes," the boy said simply. He sat on the cement curb. "But what I really want is my own cell phone."

We all chuckled, and the tension I'd felt earlier vanished from the conversation. Now we were just two dads talking about things that interested us. Our children. Traveling. America. I decided to go deeper.

"You're Sikh, aren't you? Tell me some basic tenets of your Sikh faith."

"Well, it's really about embracing all faiths," Kiki said. "It's about being a good person and doing service to your community, helping one another and living an honest and hardworking life. At the end of the day, it's about relying on God."

"Do you actively practice your faith?"

"Every day," he said. "You try not to get down because of what you see. New Mexico is the second poorest state in America, and there are lots of problems that come with poverty. Crime. Opioid addiction. Problems that can really destroy families. You look around at people's houses in this neighborhood and see bars on windows. You see big gaps throughout the country between the rich and the poor. All we want here is what people want all across America. We want education, opportunity, jobs. We want to see our children do better than us." He shivered slightly, perhaps still thinking about the problems he had mentioned, but then he grinned. "People in Albuquerque say, 'Thank God for Mississippi, because otherwise we'd be on the bottom.'"

I grinned at his joke and said, "I think a lot of people can relate to what you're saying. Everybody wants opportunities. Health. Hope."

We talked about his family, about how his parents had come from northern India and settled in Chicago. He'd been born in America and loved his family's new country. He considered it the land of opportunity, although he had his concerns. We talked about some of the potential solutions to America's problems, and I said, "I'm a Christian, and I'm curious—from a Sikh perspective, what do you think of Jesus?"

"I know a lot of Christians." Kiki scratched his beard. "I went to Catholic school as a kid, and it's good when people dedicate their lives to God. I think Jesus' message was all about loving one another. The whole Jesus dying thing, God sending his Son—that's the message of the Bible, and it's a message of love. The message of love is found in all faiths, and it's one we should embrace. Jesus helped all people—lepers, blind people, the poor. That's love."

I nodded. "Another of Jesus' messages is forgiveness. What does the Sikh faith say about forgiveness?"

Kiki shrugged. "That's a tougher one. When you feel someone's wronged you, the call is to look inside yourself."

"How about if you personally mess up? Is there a need in the Sikh faith to seek forgiveness?"

He shook his head. "Not so much. We believe you're on a path to an understanding of God and life. Some people reach a higher level of this understanding. When we say our prayers, we start with 'There is one God.' See, our God is more like the Holy Ghost, a spirit without a physical form—an energy, a force. We believe we are all one at the end when we move on from this life. When we die, we go back into that energy. So as far as forgiveness goes, it's about bettering yourself, bettering your community. There's a tithe in the Sikh faith that involves giving back to charitable organizations. That's important."

We talked more about the origins of the Sikh faith, about the spiritual and secular parts of life—maybe half an hour in all. The wind was blowing harder now, pushing the heat out of the air. Kiki described more of his values and beliefs to me and concluded by saying with a smile, "Ultimately everybody wants peace."

When I heard him say that, it was my turn to smile.

I said, "Over the years people have tried to force others to believe or convert, and much of that was harmful. But the Bible talks about Jesus as the Prince of Peace. So when we say, 'Come, Lord Jesus,' we're really saying, 'Jesus, come and bring your peace.' I love the way the early followers of Jesus brought peace in really tangible ways.

"When ancient Rome fell and so many people were fleeing the city, the believers in Jesus stayed behind at the risk of their own lives and cared for the sick. People had abandoned babies, and the Christians picked up those forsaken children and took care of them. I think those are the same kinds of values you're talking about, right?" I paused, sensing our conversation was drawing to a close. "Anyway, brother, I just want to say peace to you."

He grinned. "Well, peace to you too."

I thought quickly. I knew there was a fine line between talking to a person about the things that matter and pressing a point too far, yet I decided to go one step deeper. "I wonder . . ." I said. "I'm a person of prayer. May I say a blessing over you? If you want to say one over me, you're more than welcome."

Kiki nodded.

"May the Lord bless you and keep you," I prayed. "May he make his face shine upon you. And may God bless you, that you might be a blessing to many."

"Thank you," he said. "And we say *sarbat da bhala*, which means 'the spirit of greatness.' It's a prayer that you would feel the spirit of greatness inside of you, the joy of God."

We shook hands. Then, after a short hesitation, we embraced. In the space of half an hour, we'd gone from being complete strangers to having a respectful conversation about deeper issues. While we still didn't see eye to eye on everything, we had found lots of common ground and common respect. For now that was good enough. Certainly we weren't angry with each other, outraged, or at odds. I had listened to him. I'm pretty sure he'd listened to me. Two strangers with different backgrounds and perspectives had found connection. The moment felt sacred.

Kiki and I said our good-byes. I climbed back on my bike, clipped into my pedals, and headed up the road toward the highway. As we had talked, the clouds overhead had darkened, and the air had turned noticeably cooler. Now a raindrop splashed against my cheek. Another. Then another. The skies opened up, and it started to pour.

We pulled over to get out rain gear. Wes and Caroline and I put on our rain jackets, and I pulled on the yellow cap that fits over my helmet. It wasn't something a cyclist who was trying to look cool would wear, and I was the only cyclist who'd brought one. Wes smirked at me, and Caroline called it a shower cap. But my head wasn't cold or wet, and after another hour of riding in the rain, everybody wanted one.

We turned off the highway and onto a trail through a wilderness park. The support vehicles left us with the promise that they'd meet us on the other side of the park. Our trail was muddy and dirty, and we started climbing in elevation. The first ten minutes were a long, slow grind uphill.

Wes's bike has a tighter frame than mine, and he was having a harder time on the trail, so I moved to the lead position and worked to find a pace we could all be happy with. Caroline, always a true competitor, looked like she was charging up the hill.

As we kept slogging upward, I thought about how often on this trip I had wanted to say something more to people I was talking with. I had felt a pastoral urge to point out how people's beliefs didn't reflect Scripture or to explain more in depth what the Bible teaches. That's part of my job back home, and I had trained at a graduate level to know the truth and help people find freedom within truth. Yet I'd been learning on this trip that giving people freedom to talk with authenticity can become part of how God uses us and speaks through us. It was okay that my conversations with Kiki and Jeffrey had ended where they had. God was in control of what happened next with them. My job was to be kind, curious, and respectful to people, their faiths, and who they were. My job was to listen. To hear them. To see them.

The trail kept climbing. I glanced back at Wes and Caroline. Each of us seemed to have found our groove. Wes was breathing easier. Caroline looked focused and confident. The rain kept falling, but for once I wasn't worried about anything. In that moment all that mattered was the road and the climb and all of us reaching the top together. I found myself embracing the rain, and the tiniest grin began to tug at the corners of my mouth. As I continued to crack open my own struggles, I knew I was being genuine. That honesty began to ease my worries about my conversations being inadequate and even my frustrations with team logistics.

The longer we traveled, the more I understood my purpose on this trip. My mission was sharpening. My job was to ask people to tell their stories and to listen. And then to be at peace with how God would finish the story of their faith.

As the top of the hill finally came into view, I thought—or perhaps I prayed silently—*Okay then, God, let it rain. Cover me with these droplets of conversation that people will give me. Send me into the streams of lessons that I might catch. Let me—and all who might one day hear about this journey—be saturated in the art of listening.*

— 12 —

THE GREATER WIN

We all were getting a little ragged around the edges, and the next morning a dribble of small inconveniences irritated us.

A support vehicle had a nail in a tire and had to be fixed.

Jeff's right arm was hurting badly. He often rode with the film crew and kept that arm out the passenger-side window with a camera, shooting the landscape. It was sunburned red as a lobster.

Wes had lost his riding gloves, and we all looked for them but couldn't find them anywhere. Wes shrugged it off and said he'd be okay.

Glenn couldn't find one of the bungee cords he used to secure equipment to the front of the support vehicles, so he made do without it.

Vela was feeling a little out of sorts after days of riding in the support vehicle with Glenn and Judy. The two of them rode in the front seats, and she had the back seat to herself. She liked them a lot, but it can be hard to talk with the same people hour after hour, day after day. Since Glenn and Judy had been married for so long, they often talked between themselves, and sometimes Vela just wanted to be quiet. She'd found a new hobby as she rode in the van: making videos about the trip and posting them on Instagram.

But this morning Vela faced a real problem. After we were under-way, she realized she'd lost her wallet. Frantically she looked everywhere around her in the van, without any luck. Meanwhile I was dealing with a flat bike tire—only twenty minutes into the morning's ride. No sooner had we gotten that fixed and were on the road again than our last motel manager called. Fortunately they'd found Vela's wallet. One of the support vehicles turned around and returned to the motel, then sped back to catch up with us.

Our problems weren't over yet. As Glenn drove, an eighteen-wheeler whooshed by, going in the opposite direction. As it passed Glenn saw something fly up, hit the windshield, and bounce off. He immediately stopped and walked back along the highway, scanning the roadside dirt. There were Wes's gloves! Evidently Wes had left them on top of the box on the front bumper, and the draft from the semi had dislodged them.

No sooner did Glenn start driving again than he felt something else hit the windshield. He stopped again to find a problem with a plastic box he'd hooked to the van's front, the one we used as our locker system. The lid had flown off the box, so he had to steal a bungee cord from Jeff's sleeping bag to secure it.

It was definitely a morning of little niggles. But in spite of the irri-tations, we were loving life out on the open road. The wind blew hard from behind us that morning—maybe a thirty-mile-per-hour tailwind—and continued throughout the afternoon. Thanks to the tailwind and the smooth road, we rode all the way to Santa Rosa, New Mexico—124 miles, our longest ride of the trip yet—and reached our destination by 4:00 p.m., earlier than usual. Caroline rode the entire way, and everybody cheered.

As we rode through town, we noticed a pavilion in the town square with people gathered around it. Two middle-aged Hispanic guys were grilling burgers, so I approached them and asked what was going on. They joked that I'd showed up just in time for a feast and that if they happened to drop a burger, it was mine. We all laughed.

These two good-natured guys introduced themselves as Fermin and Jimmy. Fermin wore a jaunty red San Francisco 49ers apron, a red shirt, and a red 49ers chef's hat. Jimmy was dressed in all blue. They said they were barbecuing burgers as part of a summer school food service initiative for neighborhood kids and families. I asked if we could talk while they continued to cook, and they said yes. Jimmy got busy at another table, so Fermin did most of the talking at first. He turned serious and launched into the deep end of his life immediately.

Fermin explained that he'd had two sons, seven and eleven years old, who had both been killed in a car accident four years before. A texting driver had wandered onto the wrong side of the road. While Fermin didn't have any children of his own in the local school anymore, he continued to show up at his job as a school cook and help out anywhere he could, in honor of his sons. He'd had a commemorative marker installed by the road near the place where the accident happened.

Fermin's story poured out of him in a rush. Then he stopped and looked at me significantly, as if he feared he'd said too much.

"That's so hard," I said. "I can't imagine it. Thank you for being so open and honest right away. And thanks for showing up and loving on kids." I extended my arm, and he gave me a fist bump.

He explained that his wife was the 911 dispatcher who had taken the call, and after four years, she'd only recently gone back to work. "The pain's always going to be there," Fermin said. "But if you work it relieves the pain a bit."

"You're here serving people," I said. "I gotta ask: What got you through?"

"My belief in God," Fermin said. "Taking one day at a time and believing that things are going to get better. My grandmother had always taught me about the Bible. She was a Jehovah's Witness, but I'm Catholic today. It's so strange . . . my kids might be gone, but I'm still here for a reason. I believe that. I don't know exactly what that reason is, other than

I'm here at this park cooking for a bunch of kids. You know, at Christmas I dress up as Santa Claus for the kids too. I'm still doing my thing."

As Fermin talked, his friend Jimmy approached the grill and started working side by side with him. I asked Jimmy what he'd seen take place in Fermin over the past four years.

"He's a survivor," Jimmy said. "He hit rock bottom and came back up. Accidents can affect a whole community, that's for sure, and everybody knows everybody around here. My niece was right behind the accident and saw it happen. It shook up the whole town."

Fermin nodded. "When a tragedy happens, everybody comes together. That's what happened here in Santa Rosa."

I asked Fermin where Jesus had been for him during all this, and Fermin didn't give a direct answer at first. He talked about how he hoped his children hadn't suffered in the accident and how for him it had felt like living through a real-life horror movie. For two months after the accident he hadn't been able to sleep. And then, eleven months later, his father died of colon cancer. It had been a rough year.

At that point, Fermin grew quiet and focused on the grill. I was okay with his silence. I just stood quietly, too, and reflected on something I was learning in my talks. When people are telling you the story of their life and talking about their spiritual journey, if they don't answer a question directly and go on a tangent instead, there's probably a lot more to their original story, sitting there, waiting inside them. Maybe they'll share it with you. Maybe they won't. It's okay either way, and you just have to be patient and let people say what they want to say, when they say it. With some people, it's like you're only seeing the tip of the iceberg. There's plenty more underneath the waterline, and they'll tell you about what's below only when they are ready, only when the relationship allows it.

I let a few moments pass, then asked Fermin what he might say to people going through a time of grieving.

"I'll tell them, 'Come with me. We'll go cry together.'" He looked away from the grill, and I wondered if smoke had gotten in his eyes. It was a beautiful answer he'd given me. A short answer, but one that contained layers of depth.

A woman in our church makes reusable stickers with verses printed on one side. I showed Fermin one with Romans 15:13 on it, and he thought it was cool, so I asked him if he'd like twenty of them to give out when he met with grieving people, to encourage them with hope. The verse reads: "May the God of hope fill you with all joy and peace as you trust in him, so that you may overflow with hope by the power of the Holy Spirit."

He accepted the stickers, paused a moment while he looked me in the eye, then added, "God sent you here for a reason. Thank you."

We hugged and said our good-byes. It felt like our conversation had helped him process his loss a bit more. That felt good. The questions and the listening were working.

Hungry from all the good smells, I bought several burgers from my two new friends, then walked around the park meeting other people.

Vela and Caroline were talking with a young woman named Sarah-Kate. I sat next to them, polished off my first burger, and listened to Sarah-Kate talk. She was the liaison for the summer food program, and she explained that it was a federal nutrition program for children run by the USDA. The program helped provide meals for children from lower-income families during the summer. All program meals were free for kids, and each meal included a main course, milk, fruit, and veggies.

"During the school year some kids eat lunch at school but then go home and don't get dinner," Sarah-Kate said. "In the United States one in five children are what's called 'food insecure,' which means they don't know where their next meal is coming from. In New Mexico that statistic is unfortunately one in four. So we want to provide nutrition for those children, and this summer program is a really good resource for them."

Sarah-Kate had a pixie haircut, looked trim and athletic, and was perhaps in her late twenties. She spoke with such passion about the program that I had to ask her where her enthusiasm came from. She smiled broadly and said she'd love to tell her story. It was a long one, she admitted, but she'd tell the short version.

"I grew up in a middle-class family," she said. "We were neither rich nor poor, and we always had enough to eat. Unfortunately I grew up with poor eating habits. It wasn't my parents' fault. They were good parents, but they just didn't know much about nutrition. By my sophomore year of high school, I weighed over two hundred pounds. I realized I wasn't healthy and something needed to change. I saw a dietitian, and she taught me about nutrition. By my senior year I'd lost seventy pounds, and I've more or less kept that off ever since. That's why my passion today is making sure children eat healthy."

"Wow, cool story," I said. "Your mission was born from your experience, and now it's produced this incredible compassion within you. At the church that I pastor back in Dallas, we often talk about how there's something powerful in each person's story. We call this the person's divine platform. The term means we recognize that our stories matter, and this powerful thing is the springboard for God to use our stories. That's certainly what I hear in your story."

"I agree," she said. "I certainly have a story, and I'm happy to share it when it's appropriate. I was baptized twice, the first time when I was nine years old. It was a sincere decision, but I was so young. I was baptized a second time when I was eighteen, after I'd rededicated my life to God as a senior in high school."

Caroline jumped into the conversation again and spoke directly to Sarah-Kate. "I love your story. I recently lost fifty pounds. I see that God has given us bodies, and it's up to us to learn to steward our bodies well. That's my heart as well. Your story is so beautiful. I love how you've developed this compassion for kids as a result of what you've been through."

Sarah-Kate gave Caroline a high five. "Props to you as well. Eating nutritionally was always the main thing for me. Eventually I joined my soccer team in high school and was on the bowling team, but I can definitely see now how I was abusing my body through food as a teenager by constantly eating. For years I was putting all this energy into my body but doing nothing with it. And that led not only to weight gain but to sadness, depression, and hating who I was. I didn't appreciate the person I was then. But I do now, and I take much better care of her now."

Sarah-Kate had a tattoo on her arm, a line from a song that ended in a semicolon. I didn't notice the semicolon at first, but Vela picked up on its significance and asked Sarah-Kate if she wanted to talk about it. A semicolon tattoo is often worn by people who have contemplated or attempted suicide. The semicolon conveys that a person's narrative is not over yet.[1]

"You're familiar with Project Semicolon?" Sarah-Kate asked our group. "I've had my own struggles with depression, and I know my story is not over. My situation is not my destination."

"One of our daughters was born with OCD tendencies," Vela said. "She struggled for years and attempted suicide. She has a tattoo of a semicolon."

It was an affirming moment between us all. We'd only just met Sarah-Kate, but here we were talking about life's most difficult moments and how we can triumph on the other side of them. Our conversation was another indication to me that none of us is alone. We are all interconnected through a greater community, and when we look closely, we see it's filled with resources, encouragement, and support. Just as Fermin's community had been there for him when he experienced the loss of his sons, a greater connectedness had been there for Sarah-Kate during her lowest times. Both of these people had emerged from their respective hardships more resilient and more compassionate. They were stronger in those places where they'd been broken, ready and willing to help people and serve.

Wes overheard both conversations that day. And later at our hotel, as we were getting our bags out of the van, he pulled me aside and said,

"Neil, today was a great day. Did I thank you yet for inviting me to come on this ride with you?"

Wes was a big asset to our project in so many ways. Mostly I was just so happy we all could share these days. The hassles and irritations of being on the road together were real and probably unavoidable. But the greater win was in view when we listened to people's stories and saw what God was doing all across the country in people's lives.

I looked Wes in the eye and said, "Have I thanked *you* yet for coming on this ride with me?"

— 13 —

OPENNESS AND HOPE

That night when I slept, I didn't feel right. A persistent pain growled in a tender area. In the morning I stumbled to the bathroom, grabbed a hand mirror, and looked more closely.

Saddle sores.

This was not good. It was only the eleventh day of the ride. We'd only gone a thousand miles, with more than two thousand still to go.

I called a buddy back in Dallas and asked him to order two pairs of high-quality riding bibs—long padded shorts with nylon suspenders. They have no waistband, which means the chamois pad that cushions your rear stays in place better. I already had some with me, but I needed the extra-soft kind. He said he'd have them overnighted to me at our next location.

I hobbled back to the bathroom, sat on the toilet, and soon encountered another painful problem, which coincidentally was not far from my saddle sores—a ruptured hemorrhoid. We'd been riding at high altitudes lately, which can cause your blood to thin. And we were eating so many calories, the extra intake was causing us to go to the bathroom more often than normal.

This was not good at all.

Overall my body was a wreck. In the year and a half I'd been training before the trip, I'd had absolutely zero problems. But ever since the accident at White Rock Lake, I'd been battling lingering soreness in many areas of my body. My neck. My shoulders. My legs, hip, and elbow from the scabs. Now the saddle sores and the blood. I had a feeling the next day's ride would not be fun.

Sure enough, once I got outside and climbed on my bike, all I wanted to do was lie down and ice my nether regions. We rode anyway. The day grew hotter than ever. My shirt and riding bibs were soon soaked in sweat. My body was in agony. After a few miles I pulled off at a roadside gas station, grabbed some Chamois Butt'r from the support van, and hit the restroom.

Chamois Butt'r is every long-distance bicyclist's best friend. It's a medicinal skin lubricant that comes in a tube. You slather it on your rear. But it's not easy to apply Chamois Butt'r in a public restroom. Another guy was in the stall next to me, and as I awkwardly applied the cream to unseen places, I fumbled and dropped the tube. It hit the ground with momentum and rolled under the partition near the other guy's foot. Desperate times called for desperate measures. I stuck my hand under the stall and pointed to the tube. He uttered a confused sort of laugh and handed it back.

Nothing seemed to be going well that morning. Jon and the film crew were using a drone to film us as we rode, flying it above us. It crashed somewhere in a field with high weeds. We pulled over to stop while they looked for it. Near the road stood a barn, and inside the barn I spied a man and a woman working. I was fairly sure we had crashed the drone on their property, so Caroline, Wes, and I pushed our bikes over, explained what we were doing, and asked if they wanted to talk.

The woman stopped her work, lit a cigarette, and shook her head. The man put his hands on his hips and studied us for a moment.

"Anything you want to say to people?" I repeated.

"Nah," he said. "I don't want to be famous. That's why I live out here."

I got the point. He was telling us to get lost. Some people don't want to talk, and that's okay. We nodded, waved, turned our bikes around, and wheeled back to the road.

Meanwhile, Jon had found the drone, a bit beat-up but salvageable.

The rest of the morning passed slowly. We were heading toward Adrian, Texas, and for miles there was nothing except the road and the blazing sun and the constant pain of my butt on my bike seat. The skin lubricant made it possible to ride, but every pedal stroke still hurt. I'd seen Caroline suffer with the same ailment, and now I couldn't help but be impressed with her. She'd never once complained. Undoubtedly she was way tougher than me. I wondered if I could go the distance if my problem didn't improve soon.

We rode all afternoon on Route 66 and stopped at a truck stop close to the Texas border for dinner. I felt famished. Una began a conversation with an older couple sitting in a booth, and soon she led them over to the booth where Vela and I were sitting. They sat with us, and I ate while we talked. I was that ravenous.

Their names were Jim and LaDonna, and they were immediately fun to talk with. Jim was solidly built and sported a white walrus mustache. LaDonna had one of the kindest faces I've ever seen. They held hands as they sat at our booth and mentioned they'd been married for forty-five years. When I asked how they'd met, Jim smiled and told me they'd met at a dumpster.

"Well, we need to clarify that," LaDonna said with a laugh. "Jim was in the Naval Academy in Maryland, and I lived in the same apartment complex as his parents. I was just taking the trash out one night, that's all."

Jim grinned. "I was on leave and sitting inside my folks' place, reading. I saw LaDonna walk outside, and I thought, 'I need to meet her.' So I headed outside and said, 'Are you LaDonna?'"

"And I said, 'Are you Jim?'" she added. "That's how we met."

"She had the most gorgeous 1971 Mercury Cougar," Jim said. "But it had an oil leak. I told her I could fix that. So I did. Then she had a piano that needed tuning. Well, I could tune a piano too. That's how we got to know each other."

I chuckled and asked Jim to tell me a bit about his career. He'd graduated from the Naval Academy in 1972 and served in the navy for twenty-one years. He had commanded a submarine and been all around the world in it, including under ice caps.

"Wow," I said, with genuine amazement. "Thank you for your service. What was the coolest thing you ever saw in your submarine?"

"Actually, it was the teamwork," he said. "About 150 people were in my sub, and when you're gone from home and underwater for 285 days, you get to know each other real well."

"Ever get claustrophobic?" I asked.

"No," Jim said. "If you were claustrophobic, you'd never be able to qualify."

My father had worked for the National Security Agency for years, and I had been raised in Maryland until I was fifteen. We swapped stories of military and government life and various people and places we knew. Jim and LaDonna had two children and five grandchildren, and we all talked about our kids and grandkids for a while. Jim struck me as a brilliant man who'd done some incredible things in his career, and LaDonna seemed compassionate and wise and kind. I asked them if they had any concerns for the world today.

"I tell you what," Jim said. "I think it's great. The world is much better off now than it has been. Sure, there's a lot of sadness, a lot of bad things. But people are healthier than they've ever been. If you study history and look at the condition of the human species, we've never had it so good as today. The average lifespan in ancient Rome was thirty-five.[1] World history has been about constant battle, constant war. Even with all the hard things today, we enjoy far more peace than we've ever had in the history of the world. The environment is improving. It's not perfect, but many things are getting better. I worry about homeless people today, for whatever reason they are homeless. We should be able to do better at improving the human condition and solve that homelessness problem. But overall I believe the world is in good shape."

The conversation shifted and touched on a smattering of subjects: 3D printing, searching for new planets, today's entrepreneurs and some of the remarkable things they've done.

I asked Jim and LaDonna about their faith, and we talked about how most cultures believe in a supreme power. It looked like Jim was ready for a deeper conversation, and he seemed eager to engage in this subject matter. But their food came just when I was going to ask them more pointed questions, so they stood up to return to their table. The good-byes were over before we had a chance to go further. And that was okay. I was still thrilled I'd had such an intense conversation about a variety of subjects with strangers at a café.

After our meal we kept riding on Route 66 and finally, after a total of 106 miles, reached our destination of Adrian, Texas. We stopped for the night at a unique, older roadside motel. My entire body was tense and sore. It wasn't comforting to think that we hadn't even reached the midpoint of our trip.

As the sun was setting I met a younger-looking couple named Vic and

Aida, who lived in a corner room of the motel. We talked for a while in the parking lot. They both spoke with strongly accented English, explaining that they were from Armenia and had lived in Texas for the past five months.

Vic, who looked maybe a decade older than his wife, had arrived in the United States in the mid-1990s, but had traveled back to Armenia several times. In 2016 he'd attended a protest rally for freedom in Armenia. When he spotted Aida at the rally, it was love at first sight. They developed a relationship while he was still in Armenia and corresponded after Vic returned to the United States. Eventually he returned to Armenia again and asked Aida to marry him. They married, did all the immigration paperwork, and were able to come to America together.

"I very much love my wife," Vic said in his halting English.

Aida smiled and said she loved her husband back.

I asked them to tell me more about the freedom rally. Aida explained that freedom meant a lot to them because Armenia had been part of the Soviet Union and had only become independent when the Soviet Union collapsed in 1991. But for years afterward Russia still controlled Armenian lands, and there was a lot of conflict, fighting, and killing. The borders between Armenia and neighboring Turkey and Azerbaijan are severely blockaded to this day, and overall the country is still only considered partially free. They were both worried about family members back in Armenia.

I told them about a good friend of mine in college who had helped me get back on track spiritually. He was Armenian, and he'd had a huge impact on me. I was so thankful that his parents had immigrated and brought him to America. They both nodded and smiled.

I asked what had brought them specifically to Adrian, Texas. Vic explained that a friend of his had stopped in Adrian while driving from Austin to California and had spotted an old Stuckey's restaurant that had been for sale for five years. The building needed a lot of work, so he'd been able to buy it for very little money. He'd invited Vic and Aida to partner with him in the business, and now they were living in the motel and fixing up the restaurant with hopes of being able to open it soon.

I congratulated them on their endeavor, and then we talked about their faith. They'd both grown up in the Armenian Apostolic Church, a national form of Christianity. They read the Bible regularly and attended a Catholic church in Adrian. Aida said she was glad to have freedom of religion in America and talked a bit about the Armenian genocide in the early part of the twentieth century. She explained that Turkey, a Muslim country, had considered Armenia, with its mostly Christian population, to be a threat to Turkish security. So between 1914 and 1923, Turkey had arrested, deported, imprisoned, and eventually slaughtered some one and a half million Armenian men, women, and children.

"Our ancestors lost much," Vic said. "There are many hard memories."

We talked about grief and sadness and their desire to move forward and build new lives in their new country. I asked how they hoped Jesus could help.

"I hope that with Jesus I would live my life correctly," Aida said.

"Yes," Vic added. "And I am always thinking about how I can be true to my family and my new country. I was a soldier back in Armenia, in the army, and fought the Russians. When I came to America, I was asked, 'If something bad happens to America, will you join the American army?' I said yes. I will do whatever is needed." He turned to his wife. "But mostly I hope I can just live my life correctly and we can enjoy our life and have children someday. We will run our restaurant and live a happy life."

Vic had clearly seen some difficult things in years past. Undoubtedly so had Aida. I asked if I could pray for them, for their future and their families and for freedom in the country they had left. They said yes, and both immediately took hold of my hands. I prayed a blessing over them.

After that they very warmly invited us into their home, although it was nothing more than a motel room, and showed us various artifacts from their home country, including some purifying rock salt they used for prayers, incense they burned, and a prayer book that Aida usually kept underneath her pillow. They were both very kind people. Aida gave me a small beaded-leather wall hanging as a gift for Vela. It had been made by her sister.

We said our good-byes for the evening. As I walked away I couldn't help but think how exciting it was to meet new people. Sometimes it feels difficult to initiate a deep conversation because of the potential for that conversation to go wrong or become divisive or awkward. But Vic and Aida were proof that sometimes amazing things happen. Encouraging and meaningful connections can be made.

Back in my motel room I iced down my saddle sores. I was in pain, but at least I was able to sleep.

The next morning Vic and Aida joined us for breakfast. They talked throughout the entire meal, then Aida took Vela back to their motel room so that she, too, could see the things Aida had brought from Armenia. Vela remarked to me later just how earnest Aida had been. It was clear she really wanted to connect with others and to tell her story. All she needed was a listening ear.

After we said our good-byes, I thought more about yesterday's inter-actions. Jim had a remarkably positive view of the world after all he'd seen in his military career. Vic and Aida were looking toward the future with great optimism and strength despite the suffering in their lives. They had all faced challenges involving warfare and had endured conflict and strife, yet they had such a hopeful outlook, and they were so quick to be warm and open with a stranger.

I thought about how a lot of the division in the world can be tied to fears of the future. What role did hope play in overcoming the barriers between us?

Hope moves us forward, toward something new. Hope says that things can get better even if there's no proof yet. Hope prompts us to open up or to be open to listening because we might find common ground. Or inspiration. Or simply find ways to show respect and support.

Maybe, I considered, hope is an important part of openness—the openness we need to take down walls and really hear one another.

— 14 —

BLOOMING FIELDS AND
HOSPITAL BEDS

It was June 7, the twelfth day of the ride. Before we left the motel that morning, I had a short talk with Ramona, the motel's owner. She was a middle-aged woman with long, straight hair, glasses, and a quick smile. Ramona and her husband, Roy, had owned the motel for only three years and were still fixing it up. It had been a lot of work, she said. The balcony needed to be replaced, and the top floor wasn't open yet.

Ramona's dad had owned a gas station, and her mom had owned a café, so she had grown up with an ethic of hard work instilled in her. We talked about the town of Adrian, and she said about 175 people lived in the area. We talked about kids and grandkids, and then the conversation turned to God.

"I talk about God to anybody like y'all who I come across," Ramona said. "Anybody who comes to the motel who wants to talk. One real sweet lady had been going through a rough time. Her son had committed suicide, and she was just up in the air in terms of where he was now, you know. Even her family members weren't very supportive, and her faith just wasn't there to help her out emotionally. We talked for three hours one night, and she said, 'You're the only person who's truly listened to me about this.' We still talk now, even though she lives in another state."

"That's fascinating, Ramona," I said. "You must have some real opportunities to care for people and be a listener."

"I try to share God as much as I can," she said. "To me, God is number one. The main message of Jesus is that he's the Savior of the world. If it wasn't for him, so many people would be lost."

I sensed sincerity in her beliefs. The conversation shifted, and we talked about her ancestry a bit, then about science and a little more about the area's history. I asked if I could pray for her and her husband and she said yes, so I prayed that as they continued to fix up their motel, God would help them continue to be a light and a beacon to anybody who came through their door.

Our support vehicles were packed and ready to go. My saddle sores were still giving me a hard time, but I had no choice except to slather up and push through. As we headed out on the service roads along Route 66, we passed beautiful fields of thistles in bloom. All around us, for as far as the eye could see, spread a flowery carpet of purples and blues, greens and pinks. The colors and vastness of the fields were breathtaking, and I found myself staring, drinking in the spectacle.

Wes and Caroline and I were riding alongside each other behind the van. After about four miles I shouted, "These fields just go on forever!"

"Each field is connected to the next," Caroline shouted back.

"Like people," Wes said with a grunt.

"Agreed," I said. "I think it's so telling how few people we've met on this trip have been unwilling to talk with us. I dunno, maybe a total of only one or two people clammed up. Everybody else wanted to talk."

"People want to know they're connected," Caroline said. "That's why they want to talk. Everybody is connected to somebody else, and we're all connected to the whole human race. That's why people are okay with talking to strangers." She grinned. "Even crazy strangers riding bikes across the country."

We were quiet then, lost in our respective thoughts, and we rode and rode. The spread of blooming fields stretched as far as the eye could see. Occasionally I rode higher in my saddle than normal, trying to take some pressure off my rear end. As amazing as the ride through the fields was, I found myself already looking forward to that evening at the motel, when I could ice my sores again, and to tomorrow, when we'd take our first day off. The prospect of doing nothing but gathering myself, doing laundry, and taking naps was enticing.

I had never undertaken any challenge quite like this, one so physically demanding and so long, and I sensed that if I'd taken the trip alone, I never would have found the strength to power through some of the difficult spots we'd experienced already. That realization was a good reminder that we all need more help than we think we do. I glanced at Wes and Caroline, at the vehicles behind and ahead. I was so thankful for a team to help me push through to the next level.

Near Amarillo the thistle fields ended, and we came upon the strange sight of ten old Cadillacs upended and buried nose first in the dirt. The cars were spray-painted bright colors and all placed in a row in the middle of an otherwise barren field. We stopped to take a closer look.

It had been raining, and large pools of muddy water lay all around the cars. Known simply as Cadillac Ranch, the collection of vehicles was meant to be a funky, eclectic art project, open to all. Visitors were encouraged to bring spray-paint cans and add their own graffiti to the vehicles.

As we wandered around the Cadillacs, I met a young couple named Russel and Nina. They were from St. Louis, Missouri, and headed for the Grand Canyon. He was a thirty-two-year-old truck driver, and she was a nineteen-year-old cake decorator at a bakery. They were both fresh-faced and lots of fun. The age gap didn't bother them, they said, and one of their big goals as a couple was just to get out and see as much of the world as they could.

"I feel like I'm wasting my time if I'm not out and about," Nina said.

"Yeah," Russel said. "It's all about getting out and doing things, just trying to stay young for as long as you can."

I wondered aloud about what interested them most, and Nina talked about animals. She had a dog and a cat at home and loved caring for them. Russel loved traveling, riding skateboards, and seeing new things.

I described how we'd been taking this trip, listening to people talk about life's deeper matters, and I asked if they had anybody in their lives they talked to about spiritual things.

"I have a friend, Sophia, back in St. Louis," Nina said. "She's a real spiritual soul. We talk about emotion in general, faith, and spirituality. I feel it's very important to be connected to everything, to care for others, and to show love to everybody. Otherwise the world would be a terrible place."

Russel adjusted the cap he was wearing. "I've often wondered if there is a God," he said. "Like, maybe there is, and maybe there isn't. Or maybe there's a higher power, but he's nothing like he's usually portrayed. I don't know what God is like, so who am I to say? Although I do believe that when you die, your soul goes somewhere."

"It's not far-fetched to say God is bigger than anything and beyond our understanding," Nina said. "I think there's a little bit of that in everybody. Like that connection I was talking about. Because you can connect with anybody if you just see that other little part in them. Connection is definitely something people want and need to make the world a better place."

"We were just talking about that this morning," I said. "How everybody wants to connect."

"That's definitely what I'm about," Nina said. "We're all in this together."

Russel nodded.

"Let me ask you this," I said. "Sometimes this subject can divide people, but I don't think it always has to. What's the first thing that comes to mind when I say the word *Jesus?*"

"He's mostly a symbol," Nina said. "I don't know much about organized religion, to be honest, and when I was growing up, we didn't go to church regularly, just once in a while. I'd say Jesus is a symbol for everybody to come together. He's definitely something that everybody can feel, and there's no doubt about that. There's something more to life than just the here and now."

"I'm not big on religion either," Russel said. "Never have been. But I also don't mind if people follow a religion. I have nothing against it. I've always looked at religion as a good set of guidelines to follow. To just be a decent human being. And it works, too, because if people didn't have something to believe in, then what's the point of all this?" He motioned around at the landscape. "Now, I'm not saying Jesus is real. God could be something else completely, like I was talking about."

"Here's what comes to my mind when I hear you talk," I said. "You both just seem like such fun people who I'd like to get to know more. And you have a strong sense of something guiding your lives. Like, you want to be good people, you want to love others, and you want others to be good too. I'm curious—what's the compass that guides you? How would you articulate that?"

"I like to see people being happy," Nina said. "If I can help anybody in any way, I try to do that."

"Absolutely," Russel said.

I gave them our card, and we took some photos together. Nina was an artist and made stickers, and she pulled one from her purse to give to me. It showed a fun cartoon character that matched the colors of my bike perfectly. I stuck it on the front of my bike right away, and Nina grinned really wide. She expressed how happy she was that somebody liked her sticker enough to put it on his bike.

Nina and Russel were so friendly. It had been great to talk with them, even though we didn't see the world in the exact same way. I would have loved to have had another conversation with them, but it was time to say our good-byes. I hoped my question about what compass guided them would get them thinking along the right track. I offered to give them a copy of the gospel of Mark, and they accepted. I've always thought that reading the stories of Jesus helps people in big ways.

As we continued to wander around the ranch, we saw that travelers had left cans of spray paint behind for others to use. Vela grabbed a can of blue paint, took off her shoes, and waded out into the mud to paint #CC2C—hashtag Conversations Coast to Coast—on a Cadillac. We all cheered her on. I painted a messy blue cross, then we climbed on our bikes again and kept riding.

I felt good. Despite my saddle sores I was going strong, and overall the day's ride was going without a hitch. But then Wes's phone rang, and he pulled over to take the call. A good family friend of his, Tilde, who had cystic fibrosis, had just been put in the hospital and diagnosed with pneumonia. She was in the intensive care unit, having a hard time breathing, and they didn't know if she would live. Her sister had died from cystic fibrosis. We all saw the gravity of the situation immediately.

Wes doesn't show much emotion as a rule, but he was clearly shaken by the call. We talked a bit, just the two of us, and I asked him what he needed from us most just then. He said he wanted to ride by himself for a while, and I nodded. He rode ahead of the first support vehicle for a good many miles, processing his concern for his friend.

The afternoon sun turned hot as we cycled on. At a roadside lookout we pulled off to view the terrain. All around us was the rugged beauty of the painted mesas—peach-colored rocks and green sagebrush, hazy blue sky and the occasional white puffy cloud. It was as beautiful as the fields of blooming thistles, but so different.

We continued on, and the roads grew flat again. Wes returned to us, and the three of us rode side by side again. I patted his shoulder as we rode along and asked him again if there was anything we could do. He didn't say much, and for some time all we heard was the whizzing of our bike chains and the occasional cry of a bird.

Our destination was coming into view, and by that point I couldn't wait to be done for the day. The sun had been beating down on us, and my muscles felt rigid and unyielding. The past ten hours had been such a roller-coaster ride of ups and downs. All I wanted to envision now was unwinding at the motel, sitting on a shady bench in the cool breeze after supper, eating a frosted Pop-Tart, and singing Glen Campbell songs. Yet the morning's image of blooming thistles kept coming to mind.

All those fields—so much beauty—mile after mile. Then, only a few hours later, Wes had received the call about his friend. I thought about how beauty and pain coexist in our world. One moment we're rejoicing over the beauty of a landscape, over fun and deep conversations. The next moment we're sorrowing with a teammate whose dear friend is struggling for air in an ICU bed.

Those two images bled together, and tears stung my eyes. I had to consciously inhale and exhale until I found my composure. Even then, I started asking myself bigger questions. Were we doing any good on this trip? We were having conversations with people, deliberately trying to talk about deeper matters, strategically setting out to prove a hypothesis that the divisions in America didn't need to hinder conversations. We were having courteous talks with people and finding common ground even when we didn't agree. Yet would those conversations actually accomplish anything? Even after our trip was over, there was still going to be conflict. People were still going to argue, fight, and bicker. Friends with cystic fibrosis were still going to get pneumonia. Dark stuff in the world would persist.

We rode and rode, and the image of the blooming thistles kept merging with the memory of Wes on his phone, taking the call. The images interlaced until they became a swirl in my mind. Beauty and pain. Pain and beauty. One continuous circle of the day's events.

Maybe, I thought, *one key to life is to embrace all of that together.* When I looked at Jesus in the Gospels, I saw a Savior who attended fun wedding parties with his friends. Yet Jesus also wept with Mary and Martha when their brother, Lazarus, died. Jesus embraced the full gamut of human emotions.

The more I kept my mind focused on the totality of what Jesus experienced, the more grateful I felt. God gave us the ability to feel highs and lows, and he experienced those highs and lows in the person of Jesus. Beauty and pain mixed together. Jesus was there in blooming thistle fields and hospital beds all across America.

I hoped that as we went across the country connecting with people, looking at both the beautiful and painful parts of life together, we were helping people see and feel Jesus. As they were living out the highs and lows of their stories, he was reaching out to them in love.

I also thought about how Jesus continued in his ministry even though dark stuff existed in the world. The reality of hardship didn't slow him down or mean he was failing his mission. He just kept bringing his light and love everywhere he went.

I prayed that we'd keep doing the same and knew God would accomplish what he wanted through it.

— 15 —

GOING THE DISTANCE

That night Vela and I slept in an old railway car. The team was staying at a bed-and-breakfast, and the converted car was on the grounds. We were out in the middle of nowhere, and I loved that the place was so remote and our room was so quiet when we lay down. I expected to get a lot of sleep that night.

No such luck.

Our car was refurbished and clean, but it had a small air conditioner that turned itself on and off all night. When the AC was on, we froze. When it was off, we roasted. The temperature couldn't be regulated, and the unit made a loud jarring noise every time it clicked on or off.

To make matters worse, just at sunrise I heard a loud bellowing outside. The noise was so extreme it woke me. I stuck my head outside the door to see what was wrong. A baby calf had somehow wandered off by itself and become stuck on the wrong side of a fence, apart from its mother. It was bawling. I didn't know what to do to help the calf. She wasn't in danger, just hungry. Whoever cared for her would find her soon enough.

I sighed. That concluded one of my worst nights of sleep yet on this trip.

After breakfast we all milled around slowly. A few team members slept in until midmorning. The rest of us wandered around the grounds of the B&B. In the afternoon we did laundry. Some people took naps. Mostly we kept to ourselves.

The package with my new, softer bibs arrived, but that didn't help my mood much. I felt grumpy and sleep deprived all day. So did many others. I'd been so desperate for a day off that I'd created this image in my mind of the team bonding happily while we rested. But it turned out that we all just needed some time to ourselves.

That evening we all perked up and grilled steaks, feasted, then talked, sang, and prayed as a group. A sense of peacefulness descended upon us. We still had a long way to go on our trip, but I think we all were beginning to understand better the work it took to move a group of cyclists across the country.

That night I didn't sleep well again. The calf had found its mother, but the wind had picked up outside, and the air-conditioning unit was up to its old tricks again. I woke up, exhausted, at 4:45 a.m. The wind still howled, and I knew if it kept blowing like that, we were in for a challenging day on our bikes.

Fortunately, two friends from Dallas, Tim and Tony, had arrived the day before. They would be joining the cycling group for a few days. I'd known these guys for years, and I knew they'd breathe new life into our team. They were ready to roll.

But as I feared, once we bundled up in windbreakers, climbed on our bikes, and started to pedal, the wind pushed us sideways. A weather app said the crosswinds were blowing at thirty-three miles per hour. We needed to lean sideways into the wind to just stay upright on our bikes. Dust and sand swirled around us. The grit filtered through the seams of our clothing and mixed with our sweat. My legs, arms, wrists, and neck chafed. My eyes stung.

Gusts came and went. Whenever the gusts died, we nearly toppled over. We'd adjust, and then another gust would punch hard. My shoulders were up near my neck and tense, and I had to work to get into any sort of flow on the bike and stay focused. Everything felt unsafe. After only five miles I wondered if we needed to call it a day and quit.

Our destination for the day was Foss, Oklahoma, 103 miles away, and we'd just had a day off, so we wanted to stay on schedule. When we could we all hunkered down in a pace line next to the van. Wes kept his mic on and was in constant communication with the lead driver, Glenn. As the wind continued to slam us from the side, Tim and Tony moved to ride at our flank, between us and the main gusts, to give us a bit of a break.

Soon enough the weather went from bad to worse. It started to rain. The temperatures dipped, and the rain turned to sleet. We were quickly drenched and cold, but we kept riding. I knew nobody on the team was a quitter, and today would require us to pull out any reserves of endurance we had left. I often rode in the back of the pack, my eyes glued on the other riders, feeling responsible for everybody's safety. The tension ate away at me. At times it felt hard to breathe. As mile 20 rolled by, and then mile 30, I again felt tempted to quit.

All across the country, apparently, the weather was crazy that day. We heard that a storm had broken over Dallas. Sudden cloudbursts and high winds had been reported all over the city. Our daughter Sheree was planning on joining the ride soon, but she currently was still back in Dallas. She'd stopped by our house to pick up something and called Vela, frantic, because a tree branch had fallen on our roof. The power was out throughout our neighborhood, and Sheree couldn't get into the garage to check on the damage inside.

Vela spent most of the rest of the morning on the phone with our insurance company. A seminary student from Brazil was house-sitting for us. Fortunately she'd been out of the house when the branch hit, and Vela was able to coach her through the madness. Vela called a roofing contractor to assess the damage and learned we'd need a new roof. Several hours later she learned that the power was still off. Vela called the seminary student to ask if she could empty our fridge if things didn't improve soon.

Meanwhile, we kept pedaling. About 11:00 a.m. we were passing through Mobeetie, Texas, population 101, the oldest town in the Texas panhandle, and one of our riders needed a restroom quick. We found a tiny café, virtually empty, and piled inside to use the facilities, then bought snacks at the café so we wouldn't be freeloaders. Besides, on this trip I was always starving.

As I wolfed down a bowl of bread pudding, an older man ambled into the café and eased into a booth like he was a regular. We struck up a conversation. He introduced himself as Herman Boone and said he was a direct descendant of Daniel Boone, the famed American pioneer, explorer, and frontiersman. I told him I was happy to meet a person with such a unique lineage.

Herman was maybe in his early eighties, weather-lined and soft-spoken. He described how he'd grown up along three miles of the Brazos River and never knew what a fishhook was because he'd been taught to fish with his hands. When he was a boy, horses and wagons had still been used for transportation on the family farm, and they hadn't gotten electricity at his house until he was twelve years old. After he completed college he taught high school agriculture classes, raised cattle, and served as a county official. We talked about the Korean War. One of his relatives had fought in it and considered it a miracle to come out on the other side alive.

"You've seen a lifetime of change, Herman," I said. "Tell me how faith in God factors into all this for you."

He gave a little nod. "Well, without divine guidance I wouldn't be where I am today. I figure God is much the same as Mother Nature. If you can't live with Mother Nature, you can't live with God. I watched a documentary on TV not long ago that said man is so much smarter today than he was yesterday. But there's not a lick of truth in that. We're not smarter today, not a one of us. Every generation does the same thing."

He was off and running, and I let him talk for quite a while without interruption. He believed there were far too many religious groups today for anyone to sort out truth from error. He believed the Bible was mostly reinterpreted from the original documents, not translated straight across. He went on a rabbit trail and talked about how a true horseman could glance at a pile of horse manure and immediately tell by the size of the pile what size collar that horse would need. He told me most of his philosophy of life, that we all just need to be good people to be right with God, and that he believed the Old Testament and New Testament contradicted each other.

Instead of pointing out the places I disagreed with him, I said simply at his last point, "And that's why people need to go back to the Bible to see what it says."

He paused as if in the middle of a thought, and said, "Well, you're right about that."

As Herman continued to talk, I struggled with finding the right mix of wisdom and patience and God's guidance to know when to speak and when to listen. I had encountered thinking like Herman's several times already on this trip, where folklore and orthodox theology had been stirred together, and the outcome was a blend of truth, opinion, and outright error, all spun with genuine charm.

As I sat across the table from Herman, I wondered if I should press in more with him. I wanted to question some of his beliefs and see how open he'd be to hearing mine. I desperately longed to present another picture of what Jesus was like. But I didn't do that. Instead, we talked some more about the town, and he showed me a photograph on the wall he'd taken of three bulls. I liked it so much that I asked him if it was for sale. He said, "Well, I'll sell it to you for what I got in it. Fifty bucks."

Right on the spot I bought the photograph to take home as a souvenir. I thought we might be able to talk some more then, but several of Herman's buddies drifted into the restaurant. He explained that church had just let out and everybody wanted to get a good seat for lunch. Suddenly the once-empty café was full of folks. Herman left me to talk with his friends, and everybody was laughing and chatting at once. I was meeting people right and left, and it felt like a regular party.

Before long Herman sidled back to me long enough to say, "Just remember one thing: never try to help someone who doesn't want your help." Then he was off and talking again, lost in the group.

Maybe that was my answer. Herman didn't want to hear me speak. Not yet. Not today. He only wanted me to hear him speak. And sometimes I needed to be content to leave a conversation like that. I could only pray that God was doing a work in his heart—one I might never see, but one that was real and deep and true anyway.

The crowd that had gathered was a regular hoot, and they were full of tales from the history of Mobeetie. Apparently back in the 1800s, when it was founded, it was a "wild and wicked town," as one older man put it with a gleam in his eye. I listened to story after story about gunslingers, gamblers, prostitutes, cutthroats, and drunks. An especially dramatic story involving a shootout sounded like a movie script—a saloon girl jumping in front of a bullet to save a man's life while ending her own.

I was told that the townspeople had originally wanted to name the town "Sweetwater." When they discovered the name had already been taken, they chose Mobeetie. A Cheyenne scout had said the word meant "sweetwater" in his language, but he'd been a trickster. It actually means "buffalo dung."[1]

The talk was really fun, but I had a hard time going below the surface in the midst of it. I tried a few times but the crowd kept bouncing back to history, and I didn't want to discount the value of that. Sometimes it's more difficult to get below the surface, and maybe that's okay.

I glanced at my watch. We had stayed at the café for nearly two hours, far longer than we'd normally take for a mere bathroom break. Surely some sorts of divine appointments were happening, even if I couldn't see them.

I said my good-byes to Herman and his friends, and we headed back out into the wind and rain. We rode for another hour and stopped for lunch, then we rode all afternoon in the stormy weather. At mile 90 we stopped for supper at a pizza joint, where we got news that things were settling down back in Dallas.

We still had a few hours of light left, and I really wanted to get in the full 103 miles for the day, so after dinner I said, "I'm going to keep riding for a while." It wasn't an order for anyone else to follow. Not even a directive. But to my delight all the riders jumped on their bikes and kept going right along with me. We knocked out the last 13 miles and reached our campground at last.

It felt really good to say we had gone the distance on a day that required such a high measure of endurance. All day long we'd fought strong, blustery crosswinds, and I'd felt a lot of tension on the bike. It would have been so easy to quit at mile five, when I'd first questioned the day. Or at mile 40, when we stopped for the bathroom break at the café. Or at mile 50, when we had lunch. Or at mile 90, when we had dinner.

We could have jumped into the safety and comfort of our support vehicles at any time and ridden the rest of the way with no problems.

But we hadn't. And I felt good about that.

As I crawled into bed next to Vela, I thought about how when any kind of road grows difficult, a million excuses crop up not to finish. The temptation always exists to jump into safety and comfort and *not* go the distance, no matter what the situation.

We had reached Foss, Oklahoma, 1,300 miles from our starting place, with slightly more than 1,700 miles to go. Rethinking my conversations with Herman Boone and with other folks of his ilk, I didn't have all the answers figured out. I still lived in the tension of being on this trip to listen while aching to present the truth.

But I was determined to keep listening.

And I would go the distance.

— 16 —

COME TO THE PARTY

The day dawned early and bright, with yesterday's harsh winds mostly abated, although some lighter winds still blew. Two more riding buddies from Dallas, Richard and Wyche, arrived to join the team for a few days, as did Sheree. I was happy to have them all there, especially Sheree. At age thirty-one, she was a smart and strong rider. She regularly biked 200 to 300 miles per week, and she knew how to ride at a consistent power, which helped when taking the lead with a pack.

I was glad to have Wyche and Richard riding with us too. Wyche always carries a backpack when he rides filled with sandwiches, medical supplies, anything needed for a long trip. Though I'd been known to mock him about the backpack, I was typically the guy asking for stuff from it.

Richard is a doctor, a kidney specialist, who genuinely loves people. He and I have had many conversations over the years about how to care for people holistically—body, mind, spirit, and soul. It was fun to ride with a group that included these guys, and the mood among the cyclists was energetic and full of spirit. With Tim and Tony also riding with us, we now had five more cyclists helping us draft than we did a couple of days ago. Hopefully Caroline, Wes, and I could pick up our pace.

Our plan was to ride 118 miles today from Foss to Edmond, Oklahoma. We needed to get there because something exciting awaited us at day's end. In preparation I donned a blue-and-orange T-shirt that read "Great Cycle Challenge" on the front.

The Great Cycle Challenge is a program sponsored by the Children's Cancer Research Fund. Back when I was doing the legal paperwork in preparation for the ride, I had met with a banker named Eddie and learned that his seven-year-old son, Jaden, was battling cancer. Eddie and I had developed a friendship in the time leading up to the ride, and today I wore the T-shirt in honor of Jaden. Even better, Jaden and his dad and mom were scheduled to meet us in Edmond. A few folks from our church were driving out, too, and we were going to have a party with gifts and a dinner in honor of Jaden, just to encourage him and his family.

We headed out on smooth, flat roads through the Oklahoma heartland. The countryside was green and lush, and we passed cornfields and wheat fields and rich tilled soil. Sheree led the train, and we all rode at a good clip.

After pedaling 15 miles, we pulled over at a McDonald's for breakfast. There I met a thirteen-year-old named Jack who was with his grandparents, Howard and Loretta. The grandparents' niece attended our church back in Dallas, and through her they'd heard we'd be riding near their town. The grandparents had driven Jack out specially to meet us because, as he explained to us, he "wanted to meet somebody famous."

I told Jack that today we were riding for Jaden, a boy with cancer, and we talked about what it might mean to be young and go through medical procedures. Jack recorded a video message for Jaden, saying simply, "Hi, Jaden, we're cheering you on." Then, with his grandparents' permission, he rode in the van with Glenn, Judy, and Vela, for about ten miles so he could watch us cycle. He really got a kick out of that and said it rivaled going to Disneyland. That made my day.

Outside of that same McDonald's, before we started riding, I met two middle-aged men. One immediately declared himself to be a minister, and the other jumped right in to say they were both conservatives and had no apologies. That surprised me because I hadn't brought up politics or religion or anything of depth. I suspected that maybe they'd taken some flack somewhere along the line and were feeling defensive.

I asked what was most important to them. Without knowing what I did for a living, or even whether I was a Christian, one man launched in by saying, "Well, we're both believers in God and in our Lord Jesus Christ. That's the most important thing to us."

"That's cool," I said, and looked at the other man to speak.

"I've been absolutely amazed at the direction our country is going," he said. "So many things that were almost unheard of when I was young are commonplace now, even celebrated. I just feel like we're headed in the wrong direction. Abortion is a problem in our country. Homosexuality is a problem. I don't hate homosexuals, but the Bible says that's not an acceptable lifestyle. Those are two big issues that I believe are affecting our nation in a negative way."

"Interesting." I wanted to see where this would go. "Tell me, how do you as Christians follow the call to love everybody, and especially to love people who have a different view than you? How do you love a person while also speaking God's truth to them?"

The second man spoke. "Our place isn't to judge. That is God's place. But we have to speak truth. God changes a person—that's his job. We can only speak the truth."

It was a short conversation. After we talked a bit more, I thanked them for their time and shook their hands. I wondered if I should have dug deeper with them, but I was fairly sure I'd heard enough. It wasn't my place to judge these two Christians, but I needed to evaluate their approach as I considered my own approach to people.

I was having trouble with the way they'd led the conversation. They hadn't known who I was. They hadn't known my belief system. What if I had been a non-Christian and maybe somebody close to me had had an abortion? What if I had been a homosexual, and these men had introduced themselves as Christians and immediately let it be known that they disapproved of my lifestyle?

Their views could be classified as traditional, and since I hold to a literal interpretation of Scripture, I could see how they'd arrived at them. But I also could see how their demeanor could come across as rigid, even uncaring. They had led the conversation by stating their allegiance to Christ and then immediately talked about what they were *against*, not about what they were *for*. They hadn't told me about a Savior who cared for the world, who invited all people to come to him.

I considered the kinds of people Jesus had befriended. Lepers, the outcasts of the day. Prostitutes. Tax collectors, who were frequently reviled. Jesus invited people like that to eat with him. He spoke to them gently, warmly. He let them know he was for them, not against them. When speaking with nonreligious people, Jesus never went for the jugular. But these guys had basically jumped in and done just that.

I reminded myself that my job wasn't to point this out to them. My job was to be kind, courteous, and respectful of all people. My job was to listen, to seek to understand. Maybe they felt like their views were under attack, so they believed they had no choice but to declare them boldly and stand firm.

I had to admit, however, that I didn't feel much like talking to these men for long. There is a place for truth. And there is a place for love. And that place is always together.

We rode until lunchtime and stopped at a hamburger joint, where I met a middle-aged motorcyclist named Steve. He had an easygoing smile and described how he'd always been passionate about sports, mostly snow-ski racing and bicycle racing. Then he'd bought a motorcycle and never looked back. We talked about riding and about his new granddaughter, who he was quite enthusiastic about. This conversation wasn't long, either, although when I asked him what he thought about God, he smiled and said Jesus was "critically important" in his life. I hadn't mentioned what I did for a living or let him know I was a Christian.

Steve wished us well on the road as we traveled and encouraged us to stay safe. We shook hands. He smiled again and rode off.

In my mind Steve stood in clear contrast with the two Christian men I'd met at McDonald's. Both conversations had been short, but Steve had led with his smile and exuded encouragement. It felt like he genuinely cared about us.

I thought about how so many Christians can quote John 3:16, perhaps the most famous verse in the Bible: "For God so loved the world that he gave his one and only Son, that whoever believes in him shall not perish but have eternal life." But only a handful of Christians can quote John 3:17, the following verse: "For God did not send his Son into the world to condemn the world, but to save the world through him."

The first verse relates to a Christian's message. The second verse relates to a Christian's demeanor. I was pretty sure Steve knew John 3:17.

Inside the diner we met a guy named John who lived in the area, a friend of Glenn and Judy. He was a triathlete, a strong competitor, and a deacon at a local Baptist church. They'd arranged for him to ride with us for the remainder of the day. This proved to be a godsend. The area had experienced huge rains and flooding the day before, and John was able to lead us on an alternate route to avoid the water. We were really flying. John knew the roads well and was riding fast—almost too fast, like he was trying to get in his workout rather than leading a group of riders, three of whom had recently ridden more than 1,300 miles, on a day that was steadily growing hotter.

We rounded a corner near a convenience store and rode into a neighborhood full of old, rough-looking homes. I noticed an older man with a cane sitting on a chair in his yard, smoking a cigarette. A woman stood talking to the man, and a little girl was playing nearby. Their front lawn sported a sign that read Puppies for Sale. This was too good to pass up.

"Hey, let's stop here," I called to John, who was still in the lead. Fortunately he heard me and put on his brakes, as did the rest of the pack.

The puppies were irresistible. There were nine little pit bulls, cute as all get-out. We played with the puppies for a while and talked with the folks. The woman was the daughter of the older man, and the little girl was his granddaughter. We talked about the puppies and about the neighborhood, then I asked them what they thought about God. The woman said she hadn't been much of a churchgoer until about two months earlier, when a neighbor had invited her. She'd started going and loved it. She didn't know much about God yet, she admitted, but she was eager to learn, and she said good things were happening overall in her life because she was getting in touch with her faith.

This felt refreshing. We'd heard many stories on this trip about the abuse of church power. But this woman's story was evidence that church can work. Now she was feeling encouraged and refreshed, or at least heading that direction, all because a neighbor had cared enough to have a deeper conversation with her.

I wanted to do something for this family. It didn't seem like they had much money, and the grandfather with his cane looked like he'd fallen on some hard times healthwise. I picked up a puppy, scrutinized it, and asked how much. Fifty bucks. Everybody on the team looked at me like I was nuts.

Vela walked over, scratched the puppy behind the ears, and asked, "What exactly do you plan on doing with that, Neil?"

"Well, I thought I could buy this puppy," I said with a chuckle. "Then she could ride the rest of the way cross-country in the van—on your lap."

Vela chuckled back. "Oh, that'll be the day."

I grinned. Vela and I have been together long enough for her to know when I'm joking, although I was serious about buying the dog. "We have a name for her already."

"What's that?"

"You know the answer."

Vela gave me a knowing look and laughed. When Vela and I had been starting our family, there was one name I'd always wanted to call a baby girl. The name had sounded beautiful to me and seemed like the perfect union of our names, Neil and Vela. But I'd never been able to make it stick.

"Her name is Neila," I said.

Vela only laughed harder.

I turned to the little girl and said, "Hey, I'd like to buy this puppy from you. But would you take care of her for me, because I can't take her along on the trip? You can still have the money now."

The little girl looked at the grown-ups, then nodded at me, her eyes bright.

"Here's what I want you to do," I said. "Find one of your friends. Make sure it's okay with her parents. Then give this puppy to your friend for free. Can you do that?"

The little girl looked at her mother and grandfather again. They both nodded. "I can do that," the girl said. "Thanks."

We said our good-byes to the family. They thanked us for the fifty bucks. I petted Neila one last time and gave her a kiss on her puppy nose, then handed her back to the little girl and climbed on my bike. As we rode through the neighborhood, John the church deacon fell back through the pack to ride beside me. For some time we rode side by side without saying anything.

"You know," he said at last. "I've passed through this neighborhood any number of times and seen that grandfather sitting outside on his lawn, smoking a cigarette. This is kind of a rough neighborhood. If you want, I could stop by there sometime just to check in on the family for you."

"I'd like that," I said. "Maybe you could pick up a six-pack of Dr Pepper and some snacks for them—just something fun as a gift. And tell them Neil says hi."

He grinned. "I'll do that for sure."

We continued the ride, and somehow the air felt cooler. The pace didn't feel as rushed. John was getting it. We all were. We rode all the way into Edmond—118 miles total—to where the party for Jaden was scheduled at a place called Deckle Smokehouse BBQ.

Overall it had been a good day. A couple of carloads of folks had driven up from Dallas for the party, and we all shook hands and hugged and said hello. But there was one important person missing.

Vela filled me in. News had come in earlier when we were on the road, but I'd missed it while on my bike. Jaden's health had taken a turn for the worse. He was feeling too sick this day to make the trip.

My face fell. I looked around at the group. The love was here. The food was here. The people were here. But we were missing the guest of honor.

I turned to Vela. "Maybe we should have the party anyway," I said. "We'll have it in Jaden's honor. Take pictures. Write notes. Send Jaden and his family a word of cheer."

"I'm never one to miss a party," Vela said.

Day 1. Setting out from Santa Monica on a 3,000-mile ride of a lifetime. I couldn't believe it was actually happening.

The first conversation of the trip. John and Melissa were heading off on a bike ride of their own. Yes, people really do want to talk.

Finding conversations in the middle of nowhere. It's fun for me to meet new people in unexpected places. Wes (right) shares a laugh with our new friend, Hanson, a mechanic.

At the end of our conversation with Sergeant Major and Joe, we got a chance to pray. Left to right: Sergeant Major, Joe, and Neil.

Cleaning my bike while downing a recovery drink after an 88-mile day.

Riding across the Mohave Desert. Left to right: Neil, Wes.

Traffic stopped for construction on the road. Waiting in line became an opportunity for quick conversations and connections.

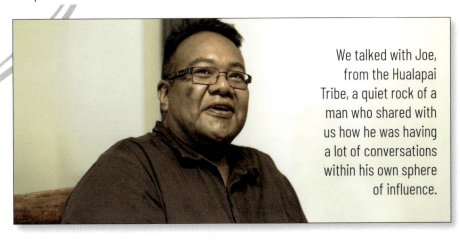

We talked with Joe, from the Hualapai Tribe, a quiet rock of a man who shared with us how he was having a lot of conversations within his own sphere of influence.

Una joined us in Arizona and brought a spark of energy to the team. She became a cheerleader and shoulder massager for everybody.

Having lunch with Mike. Listening to a painful story of being abandoned as a child.

Jeffrey and Marcella gave us this gift of expensive handmade pottery.

(Left to right) Vela, Una, Caroline, Jeff, Wes, Marcella, Jeffrey, Judy, me, and Glenn, snacking on freshly baked tortillas.

My Sikh buddy, Kiki, and his son in front of their motor home.

Talking shop with two cowboys in a Texas diner.

Herman Boone, direct descendant of Daniel Boone, in Mobeetie, Texas.

Wes, Caroline, and I were joined by a team of riders on a 104-mile day from Tulsa, Oklahoma, to Joplin, Missouri. Left to right: Wes, Neil, and Caroline.

Caroline and I spoke with this beautiful and gentle soul in Hartville, Missouri. She simply wanted a listening ear.

Diana, our new Muslim friend, with me in Carbondale, Southern Illinois.

The hills rolled on forever between Eminence and Farmington, Missouri.

(Below)
I was able to speak with Art and Lori in front of their motor home. She kindly bandaged my arm.

Johnette and Kelly and their daughters on moving day. We helped carry their couch into their new place.

Riding through Virginia, I spotted Tamika and her puppy out on their front porch. After some initial reluctance to talk, Tamika ended up speaking with me for quite a while.

Worn out but triumphant at the finish line.
Annapolis Pier, Maryland.
Left to right: Wes, Neil, and Caroline.

Photographs by Jonathon Link

The tantalizing aroma of barbecue drifted through the air. After riding 118 miles, the smell was almost too much for me to handle. I said a few words and let everybody know what we were doing. We toasted Jaden, then I loaded up a plate of food and got busy with my teeth. So did everybody else. People laughed and told jokes and chatted and had fun—all in Jaden's honor.

Soon enough I started talking with the restaurant's owner, Andrew. We talked for a while, and he indicated he followed Jesus. He pointed out a plaque on the wall that I hadn't seen yet, a kind of motto for his restaurant: "Welcome to your happy place."

When I saw that sign, I teared up a little. I thought about the events of this day. We'd ridden in honor of Jaden, who'd seen his share of hospital rooms. We'd bought a puppy from a family who looked as if they could use another fifty bucks. We'd met several people who'd described themselves as Christians. And now we were eating at a happy place in honor of a family who needed encouragement.

Back when Jesus was with his disciples on earth, meals were a super important thing. When you invited somebody over to your house for a meal, you were making a statement. You were saying, "I want to invite you into my life" and "I want to be your friend."

That's what I was learning out here on this ride. By listening to people, by being genuinely interested in their stories, I was essentially inviting people to a meal—sometimes with physical food, but always with spiritual and emotional communion.

Isaiah 55:1–2 came to my mind. In those verses thirsty people are invited to a party. Hungry people are invited to a feast. "Come . . . eat what is good," God said through the prophet Isaiah, "and you will delight in the richest of fare."

I filled my plate with food again and returned to the party.

— 17 —

LIVING WITH IMPERFECTION

The night felt short, and I was tired when I awoke. We'd just been through two huge days—118 miles the day before and 103 miles the day before that in strong crosswinds. On the schedule today was a 107-mile ride from Edmond to Tulsa, Oklahoma. I felt a strange combination of excitement and exhaustion. To complicate matters, at breakfast my eyes started to itch.

I have bad allergies. I'm allergic to all grasses, mold, dust mites, and most trees. We'd known for years that I was allergic to cats, so we'd always opted for a dog, then it turned out I was allergic to dogs too. To combat the allergies, I regularly use an inhaler and take two different pills each night. This morning I definitely needed my meds, so after breakfast, I headed back to my room to grab them. Then it dawned on me: Vela had a rental car for the day so she could do some errands, and she had left the motel early. She had taken the suitcase we shared, and all my allergy stuff was in it. I didn't want to call her on the road and ask her to return. I decided to tough it out.

My eyes were still itching when we checked out of the motel. A young woman named Rachel was working the front desk. I described to her what we were doing on the trip, and she wanted to talk with me.

Newly married, with dark shoulder-length hair, Rachel smiled easily and constantly. She mentioned her strong passion for her parents' new business, a day-care center for dogs. Her dad had been an advertising executive for years, and her mom had been a physical therapist. But her dad had grown disillusioned with the business, and her mom felt the need for a change. So the parents had asked themselves what their true passions were. They loved dogs. They switched careers and opened the doggy day care.

Rachel knew tons about dogs. She talked about the intricate ventilation systems in the day care and described with great detail the eight types of baby wipes that can be used on dogs' feet. It was cool to see her talk so excitedly about her parents' living out their passion.

I asked Rachel about her faith, and she referred again to her parents. They went to church regularly, and her mom did a daily Bible study.

"I've always been more logical and questioned things more," Rachel said. "My mom lives more on the blind side of faith. Like, she believes everything happens for a reason, and everything's going to work out. But questioning things helps me to process."

She added, "I do try to do thirty minutes of self-care every day. I take a time of quietness just to think and reset myself for the day. Usually I'm thinking about how to help others or how to improve myself somehow. I'm taking baby steps to expand my faith, and my mom gave me a scripture-a-day calendar. I read a verse from it each day and think about it."

Rachel said that chronic migraines ran in her family. "For several years I lived with a 24-7 migraine. The pain was so bad. I tried everything. I even cut off all my hair once, just to see if that would help. Lots of learning happened for me during that time, such as how to cope and breathe. Now I get only a couple migraines a week. I learned during that time that if you choose, you can live sad and frowning. But it's much easier to smile and be thankful for the things you do have."

Again, she spoke with a smile. I thanked her for being so friendly and hospitable. Her demeanor was a real blessing, and I found it noteworthy that when it came to her passions and her faith, so much of her sense of self was still tied to her parents. That's not uncommon with young people, and I've seen similar things play out with teens and young adults in our church. A person's faith emerges over time, and part of the process of the teenage and young adulthood years is developing a faith of one's own. Rachel and I said our good-byes, and I started riding.

My allergies became worse. Something hung thick in the air, maybe pollen from trees or grass. At eight miles in I could hardly see. My eyes itched and burned. A crosswind blew against us, and I squinted as I pedaled, my eyes barely open. This was getting dangerous. I pulled back behind the other cyclists, kept pedaling, and wondered what I should do.

Just then I spotted Caroline make a sudden swerve and hit a terrible pothole in the road. The impact caused a pinched flat in both tires. Everybody pulled over so Caroline could change out both inner tubes. Wes helped. I spent my time sitting on the ground with my head down and my eyes closed. My eyes were on fire. I was sneezing and forcing myself not to rub them. I finally called Vela and asked her to find us on the road and bring my eye drops. Fortunately she wasn't too far away, and she arrived before Caroline's bike was fixed. But it was too late for me. My allergies had seized control of my body by then, and the eye drops didn't do a thing.

I paced up and down the shoulder of the road, wondering how I was going to continue the ride. Then it hit me. If I forced one eye open, maybe I could let the other eye rest while I continued to ride.

I took some gauze and tape and completely bandaged one eye. Everybody looked at me like I was nuts. Vela gave me that quiet "Oh, dear" look. But I shrugged off their concern, hopped on my bike, and started pedaling. I could just make out the landscape with my one open eye.

Wes rode up to me before long. "I was wondering about where we stayed last night," Wes said. "If the motel had a freshwater pool or a saltwater pool."

"Freshwater," I said. "Why?"

"Well, shiver me timbers, if it had been a saltwater pool, maybe a sharrrrrk got you." He spoke in a stereotypical pirate voice, mocking my eye patch. "Maybe there's something you need to tell us. Like, arrrre you hurt?"

I croaked out a chuckle.

After two hours the bandaged eye indeed felt better. So I pulled over again and switched the gauze and tape to the other eye, but I only needed it for a little while because the allergy meds finally kicked in. Both eyes felt better, and I was able to take off the tape for good.

When we reached a roadside produce stand near Chandler, Oklahoma, we pulled off the highway to check things out. I could hear a tractor running somewhere nearby. The building was made of metal and stocked almost like a convenience store. Inside were snacks, drinks, fresh produce, toys, tools, and older movies on DVD, like the proprietors were trying anything and everything to make a buck. I introduced myself to the owner, Jim, an older man with a long white beard who wore a straw hat, overalls, and a plaid short-sleeved shirt. Right away he launched into his story.

"The bank's about to take my farm from me," he said. "We been settled on this spot since 1965. There were six of us kids and my mom and dad, and we all worked the fields together for years. I became an ironworker later on and moved to California, built high-rises, then came back here to help my dad. When he died in 2003, I took over the place. Weather's been killing us last three, four years. Too much rain. Climate's changing. We have longer falls, and our springs are too wet to get crops started. The wild hogs and the deer, they're everywhere and eat every-thing. They kill us too."

"I'm so sorry to hear that," I said. "When farming was going better, did you love it?"

"Yeah," he said. "It's hard work, but I've done it since I was a little bitty boy. I'm sixty-five now, and we've always grown seventy-five to a hundred acres of produce each year. We used to have a peach orchard with fifteen thousand trees, but they're gone now. I been broke the last three, four years. We're trying to get the family raised and the grandkids growed up before I kick the bucket."

Just then Jim's son, Jimbo, and his granddaughter, Aubrey, showed up. Jimbo was a sturdy-looking farm boy of a man who wore jeans, a trucker hat, and a white V-necked T-shirt. He had long sideburns and a scraggly goatee. Aubrey sported a mass of blonde hair. She said she was five years old and stayed glued to Jimbo's side with a shy smile.

I asked Jimbo to tell a bit of his story. He talked about working with his father since he'd been younger than Aubrey and how he loved working the land. He'd been born with a liver disease and gotten a transplant at age twenty-three. Since then his health had improved. He yanked up his T-shirt and showed me a scar that ran underneath the length of his rib cage.

"My mama left me when I was two years old," Jimbo said. "So my dad's raised me my whole life."

I looked at Jim, and I looked at Jimbo. "Seems like you really respect your dad," I said. "Is there anything you'd like to say to him while we're all talking?"

"He's always been on my side," Jimbo said. "I love working with him. He's supported me in everything I ever tried to do. I got three kids today, and how my dad raised me is helping me raise my kids right. They're heavy into sports. The boys wrestle and play football and baseball. Aubrey's into gymnastics and played T-ball this year. I can't thank my dad enough for being so good to me."

Jimbo said all this in his father's hearing, and it felt good to know that one of my roadside conversations had facilitated some encouragement between a father and son, particularly when times were so tough for them. I hoped this good conversation would spur another good conversation between the two of them later. We talked some more about parenting and the economics of farming. Then I asked about faith.

"Well, if it wasn't for God, we wouldn't have been able to do what we done," said Jim. "We try to take care of stuff, treat people right, and do our best. That's all we can do. I grew up in church, although we're not part of a church right now. But I say Jesus was the sacrifice of everything for everybody." His son Jimbo nodded at this.

I asked if I could pray for them, and they both nodded again. "Yeah," Jim said. "Pray that we keep this place. We're doing everything we can, but I don't know if we're gonna make it."

I prayed for them, and we bought some pickles and a couple of cantaloupes from their store. Jim brought out a knife, and we sliced into the cantaloupes right then and there. Without exaggeration I can say it was the best cantaloupe I'd eaten in my whole life. We shook hands all around, and I thanked them for talking. I wished I could have stayed longer. They were heartland folks, the backbone of America. I hoped everything turned out okay for them.

My eyes were feeling much better now, but the day's difficulties weren't over. We weren't back on the bikes long before Wes hit the back of Caroline's bike and went down hard. He'd been drafting behind her, and his front wheel caught her rear wheel. It's particularly difficult to draft when a group is made up of both fresh and tired riders. Caroline was behind our newer riders. Those who had joined recently were able to surge with more power than us. Consequently their pace was less steady.

We all stopped, and Wes checked out his injuries. The road had torn through his bibs and flesh, and he had a baseball-sized raspberry on his hip.

"Aw, no problem," Wes said, already joking about it. "This is just an ant bite."

"And I thought I was the one having problems seeing," I said with a grin.

Wes laughed. "Man, that's what I get for making fun of you."

We doctored up Wes and were soon back on the road. We rode through the small town of Sapulpa and met a sheriff's deputy with the last name of Clark. I thanked him for his service and asked him what he'd like to say about his profession.

"Being in law enforcement is a calling," Deputy Clark said. "We have a lot of great people on the force who care about the citizens in this area. Sometimes people forget that, and as we all know there can be bad apples in any industry. But for the most part there are really good people in this line of work."

We talked about some of the tougher things he'd seen. A few years back, a patrolman who was a close friend of Deputy Clark's took his father on a ride-along. They'd been involved in a crash, both the patrolman and his father had been killed, and Deputy Clark had ended up working at the crash site of his good friend. He said it had been really hard.

Deputy Clark was on the job when I was talking with him, so he wasn't able to describe his faith with much detail. Yet he said that faith had definitely factored in to helping him get through the difficult time of grieving for his friend. I thanked him, and we went on our way.

We rode into Tulsa a few hours later. Sheree and I were riding next to each other as we neared the Arkansas River and a short, steep incline came into view. Sheree told me it had a name: Cry Baby Hill. She had ridden in the annual bicycling road race called Tulsa Tough, so she knew all about it. The race loops around in a big circle, and the hardest part is Cry Baby Hill.

I didn't have much gas left in my tank, but both Sheree and I are competitors, and this was too good of an opportunity to pass up.

I glanced at my daughter.

She glanced at me.

The race was on.

Sheree took an early lead, but I caught up with her. I surged forward, then she surged ahead.

Wes was in front of me, and I tried to get past him, but he blocked me. "Get out of the way!" I shouted. Wes shrugged and moved over.

I pedaled with all my might. Every muscle ached. I dripped with sweat. I passed Sheree and never looked back until I was at the top of Cry Baby Hill.

I'm sure she let me win.

If it had been a real race, she would have beaten me. But that day Dad still triumphed. At least that's what I was bragging about by the time we reached the motel.

We got settled and had dinner. Afterward I sat outside on a bench and thought about the past twelve hours. It had been a day of ups and downs, for sure. Talking with smiling Rachel at the start of the day was positive. My allergies were negative, as were Caroline's two flat tires and Wes's hitting the pavement. It was clear that there was a lot of love between Jim and Jimbo, the struggling farmers, and that was positive. But meeting them felt sad, too, because of the economic hardship they were going through. Talking with the sheriff's deputy was positive, but it was clear he'd seen his share of difficulties as well.

The people I had talked with that day had been quick to share their painful experiences. Sometimes we're reticent about asking people to talk about the hard times they've seen, but I was learning that talking about the hard times can provide the biggest openings for connection. That made sense to me because Jesus came for people with needs. Plus, it seemed that within every difficult experience, some kind of gold could be found.

The more the trip progressed, the more I kept being confronted with the imperfectness of life. There are days when I simply need to tell myself that things are what they are. I don't need to second-guess myself, and I certainly can't solve everybody's problems. I just need to ride both the ups and the downs. To live through each experience and to keep praying with gratitude for each breath I take.

— 18 —

WHEN WALLS COME DOWN

The next morning I spoke at a prayer breakfast in Tulsa. About fifteen Christian men met weekly in the spare room of a country club for breakfast, study, and prayer. A friend of mine led the group, and he'd invited me to join them.

At the meeting we got into an intense conversation about the effects of listening to people's stories and welcoming people into deep conversations about Jesus. Not everybody agreed with me. They were used to more traditional styles of talking to people about Jesus, styles that involved less listening and more preaching.

Yet as I kept communicating what I was learning on this trip, the tone in the room seemed to change. Many of the men had started out with their arms folded, taking an almost skeptical stance. But the more I told about who I'd listened to on this trip and how their stories had unfolded to me, the more the men leaned forward in their chairs and became engaged, asking questions of me—and the more we truly grappled with how to have conversations with people about stuff that matters.

I brought up 1 Peter 3:15, where the apostle told believers: "In your hearts honor Christ the Lord as holy, always being prepared to make a defense to anyone who asks you for a reason for the hope that is in you; yet do it with gentleness and respect" (ESV). I told the guys that we will honor whoever we put in our hearts. If we make Jesus number one, then conversations about faith will flow naturally out of that. The conversations will emerge not with arguments and division but with kindness, courtesy, and respect.

"God has convicted me more than ever on this trip," I said, "that I really need to be gentle with people and their stories."

Overall the talk seemed to go well.

Because of the prayer breakfast, the riders and I didn't get on our bikes that day until 10:00 a.m. We planned to ride 100 miles eastward from Tulsa and end up in Joplin, Missouri. Complicating matters, we were fighting another crosswind, although it wasn't as bad as the one a few days earlier.

As we passed through a small town, I saw a man come out of a store carrying a fishing pole. He was with a young boy, who also had a fishing pole, and I pulled over to talk. The dad was named Joseph and the son Nathan. Joseph had tattoos on his arms, three-quarter-inch gauges in his ears, a spike through his lower chin, and two tiny gold rings in his bottom lip. It was the kind of look that sometimes keeps people away. But as we talked, any walls his edgy appearance might have built up quickly came down.

We talked about fishing and fatherhood and the best places to raise kids. A half mile down the road was a creek, and the father and son were headed there to fish from the historical bridge that spanned it.

Joseph brought up the subject of faith before I did. "Faith means salvation and forgiveness to me," he said. "That's through Jesus, and that's important because in the last four years I got into some trouble through substance abuse. I got invited to a church here in town and went through a program called Celebrate Recovery. They take you through a process where you get sober and faith helps you. Jesus has worked some real miracles in my life. I've become a leader in the group, and in three weeks I'm going to graduate from drug court. From there, well, I'm just going to keep going forward, living one day at a time." He shook his head, and his eyes teared up. He looked proud and joyful and encouraged all at once.

"Wow, that's awesome!" I said. "Thanks for being so honest. We're here to celebrate with you today."

"Every day I wake up and thank God I'm sober," Joseph said.

We talked some more about the changes in his life, and he invited us to go to the fishing spot with them. We gave them a lift in our van, and the riders met them down at the bridge. It was off the highway, down a dirt road in a wooded area. An old iron bridge spanned a babbling thirty-foot creek overshadowed by trees.

Nathan, who looked to be nine or ten years old, hadn't said much yet. At the river he baited his line, cast through the crossbeams of the bridge, and set his hook right into the river. It was a beautiful cast, particularly for a kid. He opened up and explained to us how to cast.

It was a good moment. Joseph and Nathan had obviously experienced some pain, but here they were now, a father and son, fishing together— and all seemed right with the world. Jesus had done a good work in their lives, and the dad had gone from lost to found, from a person controlled by addiction to someone who lived each day with sobriety and gratitude.

I felt encouraged not only by the conversations I'd had with these folks but also by the conversations Joseph had had with others long before I'd arrived. We hung around for a while, talking and watching them fish. Then it was time to hit the road.

We were biking on a long, straight stretch of highway in Oklahoma when a huge eighteen-wheeler cattle hauler came up behind and then roared past us. The trucker gave a long, loud blast of his horn, and I didn't know if it was a safety measure or just a good ole boy trying to scare a bunch of bicyclists. (I suspected the latter.) The truck disappeared in the distance, but as he'd passed I thought I'd seen a distinct flash of red, white, and blue paint on his cab—something I could recognize if I saw it again.

Twenty minutes later we reached the tiny town of Vinita and pulled up at a café that looked a little rundown. Outside the café was a herd of pickup trucks and a cattle hauler with a streak of red, white, and blue on the side. I wouldn't bet my life that it was the same truck, but it looked very similar.

Judy had read a Yelp review of the café that said, "Don't let the outside appearance discourage you," so we ambled inside. And the moment we walked in, a table of guys eyed us. Folks can get territorial about their favorite diners. I get that. They don't like outsiders on the best of days. And if these guys were the same ones who had honked at us, I knew they could give us trouble.

I've never been one to back down from a challenge, but I was hungry and tired and didn't feel like a confrontation. I walked over to an empty table, sat down, and placed my order. An older man wandered by, and I couldn't help but strike up a conversation while I waited for my food.

His name was Larry, age seventy-one, and he sat down with us like he owned the joint. Larry wore an old trucker hat, jeans, cowboy boots, and a plaid shirt. I started to ask him a question, but his cell phone rang. He shushed me and took the call. He yakked for a while, then hung up, and I started to ask another question, but his phone rang again and he answered. He shut up the caller before long and gave me his full attention. His manner was no-nonsense as he talked about his town, his family, and his work.

"This part of the United States is probably more religious than either the West or East Coasts," Larry said. "Everything bad starts on the coasts and heads inland, although by the time it gets to us, we can usually sort it out." I wanted to laugh when he said that, but I stopped myself. He added, "I grew up in a Holiness church—it's from the Nazarenes—and

I still go there, although not as much as I did. I'm a believer. Folks are prone to wander away from church if there's too many outside influences. Like recreation. People have everything and anything to do on Sundays now. They go to ballgames. They're always out doing something different. But I tell ya, the worst thing in our country is abortion. That bothers me more than anything. It's just wrong. I was always taught it was wrong. It's wrong now. And I don't waver on that like fellas do when they're running for president."

The waitress plunked down my plate of food, a sizzling pile of steak, cut up and fried with onions and beans. I inhaled, and the aroma was heavenly. I didn't quite know where to go with all Larry had just talked about, so I said simply, "Looks good, doesn't it?"

"It does indeed," Larry said. "I guess that meal can be custom ordered. I have to laugh because them boys over by the wall are cattlemen, and I saw the same plate on their table." He raised his eyebrows. "But those same boys who pride themselves on cattle . . . they was eating *chicken*."

I laughed right along with Larry. Before I could ask him more questions, he said his good-byes and took off. I chowed down quickly, then glanced over my shoulder. The good ole boys were still there, so I took a deep breath, wandered over to their table, and introduced myself. They nodded at me to sit.

Three men lounged around the table, all wearing cowboy hats. Two were younger, one was older. All three were thickset and muscled, like they were no strangers to hard work. Or to cracking the skulls of city slicker outsiders.

"You're doing what?" the first man said, his voice incredulous. It felt like he wanted to test me. They all did. Sometimes it takes a while before trust is earned. People can test you lots of different ways.

"Riding bicycles across the country," I said again. "We want to be kind, courteous, and respectful, and we're hoping to have conversations with people about stuff that matters."

"Stuff that matters?" asked one of the younger guys. He snickered. "Like hemorrhoids?"

I chuckled along with them, which seemed to set them at ease. The older man explained that the other two were ranchers, while he was a cattleman, owned a construction company, sold real estate, and did a bit of everything.

I looked around at the cowboys. "So what's most important to y'all?"

"Air." The older guy cocked his head. "You know . . . oxygen. We gotta have it to live." He laughed, and we all laughed with him.

One of the younger men adjusted his cowboy hat so it sat lower on his eyes. He was built like a bale of hay. No neck. All biceps. "I'd say family and religion."

"Yeah, and being happy," the second younger man said. "Life's too short to go through it unhappy."

"You guys all seem like you're pretty happy," I said.

"I'd say we are," the bit-of-everything guy said. "I set out to be a billionaire when I was young. I was pretty high-strung back then. But I settled for working jobs, keeping my bills paid. Riding my horse wherever I want to. I wouldn't be happy living in a city. Too many people."

"We have that in common," I said. "I hate being cooped up in an office. That's one reason I'm riding my bike across this country—to get outside."

He nodded and explained how he'd set out to be an engineer. But he'd spent one summer in a cubicle with no windows and changed his mind. It was like torture, he said. They all chimed in, saying they loved being outside, although they had hard days too. Today all three had been up at 5:00 a.m., out in a field in the rain, loading up six hundred head of cattle.

The older man said he believed that family came first and he'd do anything to help his family. His demeanor had relaxed, and he wasn't cracking jokes with every sentence anymore. He talked about how cattlemen could be misunderstood, particularly by "politically correct folks" who didn't eat beef.

Finally our talk turned to faith, and I asked them what they thought about Jesus.

"He's the Son of God," said the man with the biceps. He sounded sincere. The others nodded. "He's the one who sacrificed everything for us to have a spot in heaven as long as we believe in him and follow him and try to live the best way we can. Everybody has a life, and everybody has a past, but God forgives, and for me God is most important."

We talked some more, and the guys all got to laughing again. It was clear that they led every conversation with good-natured ribbing. Larry, the man with his phone always ringing, showed up again and asked if I could come outside and see his pickup truck. I said "why not" and followed him out. He showed me a semicustom Chevy truck, wildly painted and lowered. He was clearly proud of his work.

Biceps followed me out too. He got to talking with Caroline and asked if he could ride her bike. He was maybe two hundred fifty pounds of solid farm boy, but Caroline let him. She was pretty certain the bike would hold him.

He hopped on as the other two cowboys moseyed out and whooped and hollered, cheering him on. He looked funny riding a bicycle in his blue jeans, plaid shirt, and cowboy hat. I laughed along with Caroline and the cowboys and hollered that if he could ride a horse, he could surely ride a bike. He let out a *yeehaw*, took his hands off the handlebars, and nearly toppled over.

It was all good, clean fun in their eyes—and ours too. At first glance they'd been nothing but redneck cowboy-truckers to us, and we'd undoubtedly been nothing more than city-slicker tree huggers to them. But when Biceps at last stopped and climbed off the bike, we all shook hands like friends. All because we wanted to start a meaningful conversation.

The other riders and I hopped on our bikes again and rode all afternoon until we reached the small town of Miami, Oklahoma. I stopped and introduced myself to three guys in a park playing Pokémon Go. Their names were Dakota, Daniel, and Dalton. They were all twenty-five and had been friends since elementary school. One was married, with kids.

They talked about their jobs and how economical it was to live in a small town. They were thoughtful young men—smart, educated, and polite—and the conversation felt unrushed. It quickly went beyond the weather. They talked about the bonds of long-term friendship and how they appreciated generational roots that ran deep.

I asked them about faith. Daniel's father was a preacher, and he'd been raised in church but abandoned his faith as a young adult. "I personally don't believe anymore," he said. "We had to keep going to church until we turned eighteen, then my dad gave us a choice."

"Do you have any idea why you don't believe anymore?" I asked.

"There's no proof of God," he said. "There's more scientific proof of evolution."

I asked Dakota what he believed. "Same thing," he said. "As a kid I was forced to go to church whenever I spent the night at Daniel's home. I don't see any actual proof of there being a God. There could be someone out there. But I haven't seen any proof."

"That's interesting," I said. "Just for fun, let me ask y'all this: What would God need to do to prove himself to you?"

"I'd want him to take a corporeal form and appear to us," Daniel said. "He could tell us right there of his existence."

"Yeah," Dakota said. "I'd want to see a visual representation of him. I wouldn't ask for anything, though. I feel my life's already complete."

Dalton piped up. "If we figured out he was real, you wouldn't really want to ask for anything. You'd want to change your ways."

I turned to Daniel. "You used the word *corporeal*. That means earthly or bodily. But it's not a word you hear every day. Where'd you get it from?"

"Video games," Daniel said.

We all laughed.

"When you used that word it surprised me," I said. "Because if you read the works of theologians, you find they use that word. The whole deal about Jesus is that God did show up in corporeal form. Part of Jesus' message was that he was God in human form and that by seeing him people could see God. I wonder, if we could go back in time, if that would be the proof you'd need."

Dalton said, "Yeah. If someone asked me what superpower I could have, I'd choose time travel. I'd want to go back and see dinosaurs or Caesar and even Jesus, just to see and observe everything."

"Here's something to chew on," I said. "Consider this an invitation to think of God in a fresh way, beyond the church you grew up in and what your parents told you. We believe in Caesar today because some guys in the past wrote about him and the manuscripts we have about Caesar are deemed reliable. You can get to know Caesar today when you read about him. It's similar with Jesus. The manuscripts that make up the Bible are reliable. You can get to know Jesus today when you read about him in the Bible. And the Bible does actually say that Jesus was God in a corporeal form."

We talked some more about topics ranging from cycling to teamwork to aging. I affirmed their ability to converse about meaningful stuff. Then I challenged them to dig into Scripture—for the first time, if they hadn't done so before, or anew, if they'd only interacted with it during their childhood. Of all the people I'd encountered on the trip so far, these three young men in small-town America had impressed me most with their intellect, sincerity, and depth.

It had already been a long, full day, but we still had miles to go, and rain was threatening. So we got back on our bikes and continued riding.

The rain came before long, but it was gentle and even soothing. When we finally pulled into our motel at 8:00 p.m., we were feeling good. We'd bicycled 104 miles and had lots of conversations and lots of fun.

The amazing thing to me was how many walls we'd faced. When I looked at people without knowing them, it was easy to find reasons to keep my distance. It didn't matter if I was talking to traditional businessmen at a breakfast, edgy young dads with lip rings, joke-filled cowboys in a café, or smart young men playing Pokémon Go, everybody led with their walls. But when I stepped forward with just a bit of courage and took the time to ask people to tell me their stories, it was amazing how quickly their walls crumbled. They wanted to tell their stories.

With the barriers down, we were just guys hanging out over breakfast.

We were fathers talking about fishing.

We were fun-loving guys sharing laughs at a café.

We were thoughtful people talking about time travel in a park.

— 19 —

BREATHING LESSONS

My chest felt clogged. My gut was doing flip-flops because we had eaten dinner too late last night. My limbs didn't want to move. My head felt fuzzy.

It was June 13, the eighteenth day of the ride.

We had started the day in Joplin, Missouri, and I'd felt flustered this morning from moment one. Apparently my team members felt the same way. None of us had slept well. The accumulating pressure of riding day after day, sleeping every night in a new location, and eating food on the road was wearing on us all. Our conversations were going well, but I was learning just how much energy it takes to truly listen, concentrate, look people in the eyes, and stay engaged.

Glenn and Judy had made a Walmart run the evening before to get supplies for the trip and had eaten at a fish place with some friends they'd met on the road. Glenn is allergic to shellfish, so he'd ordered salmon, which he can eat without a problem. But something had gone haywire because he'd been up all night, violently ill. Judy had cared for him, so neither of them had gotten much sleep. They suspected that shellfish had somehow contaminated Glenn's food. He'd given us a wry look in the morning and said simply that he would soldier on. Judy said that at least she'd be able to doze in the van. The commitment level of the team continually astounded me.

Despite my stomach flip-flops, I found I could still eat breakfast. In fact, everybody except Glenn brought an appetite as we shuffled into a local diner and wolfed down pancakes, eggs, hash browns, and bacon. Afterward I met a group of older guys at a nearby table who said they breakfasted there every week. I was tired and almost didn't feel up for a conversation, but one of the guys mentioned he'd been up all night serving at a homeless shelter. I figured if he could keep going, so could I.

The guys were all gray-haired, kind, funny, and content. Salt-of-the-earth types. All were retirees, and their number included a former doctor, a former professor, a former CPA, a former bank examiner, and a former state senator. I caught their names at the beginning—Bud and Ken and Pete and Howard and Gary and Bill and Dave and Richard— but several of them called each other by nicknames, so I quickly lost track of who was who. One guy motioned around the table and said their motto was, "This is the highlight of our week; isn't that sad?" That made us all guffaw.

They got semiserious and explained that their breakfast club was much more goal-oriented than they let on. The camaraderie, the interaction with each other, the stimulating conversation helped keep them sharp and fulfilled a purpose. That purpose became clear as our discussion continued. I asked if they disagreed over substantive issues, and they all said yes. For instance, when it came to politics, most of the guys were conservatives, but they had a token liberal in the group, who they spoke of proudly.

"We might disagree with each other," Bill said (at least I think it was Bill). "But it really doesn't matter. You gotta keep the peace."

"Yeah," Bud said. "I vote Republican, but I'm married to a Democrat.

We keep two TVs in our house—one blue, the other red. *That's* how you keep the peace." Everybody laughed.

We talked about books and music and sports. Every other sentence was punctuated by a joke. I asked what was most important to them, and Gary said, "God and country." Bill said, "Family." Pete said, "Friends." Howard said, "The fact that we're all still here today. That's really important." They all laughed again. Then I asked what concerned them the most, and the mood turned serious.

"The decline in civility of public discourse," Bill said. "Part of the problem stems from education. Somehow we have failed to teach the young people in this country that America was never designed as a place to win the argument. It was designed as a place for the argument to go on perpetually—and hopefully in a civil way, by developing consensus but not unanimity. The minute somebody wins that argument, you've established a tyranny. These days, unfortunately, everybody's lined up on opposite sides. They're only committed to victory for their ideology, to defeating the other side. But that's the antithesis of what we need in America today."

"Sad but true," I said. "We've come to value victory over relationship."

"America is the place to hold a debate," Bill added. "It's not the place to win it." As I watched and listened, I saw that these guys had learned how to stop and breathe in the middle of their debates.

Gary set down his fork and looked at me pointedly. "If your aim on your trip is what you say it is—to be kind, courteous, and considerate while talking to people who don't normally agree, then you're gonna need some prayer. Can we pray for you?"

This was a shift, but I nodded, and the men bowed their heads like they'd done this often. "Be with these guys as they travel across the United States," Gary prayed. "Bless them as they meet fellow Americans in an effort to build consensus and love and respect. Through Christ's name, amen."

Our conversation was drawing to a close. The more these retirees talked and joked with each other, the more I found myself admiring them. I began to hope that someday I would have what they had: a group of friends who met regularly, supported each other, and could talk about anything.

We shook hands all around. I went to the cashier and paid our bill, then headed outside. I was beside my bike when I noticed that two of the retirees had followed me out to the parking lot.

"Hey, you forgot to wait for the offering," one said. "We passed the plate." He handed me a fistful of bills.

"Oh, man, thanks so much," I said. "But we're not asking anybody for money."

His voice was firm. His smile was sincere. "You're doing a good work, and we want you to have this. We insist."

Moved and appreciative, I accepted the gift. They both shook my hand. After they returned inside, I counted their "offering." It was more than two hundred dollars. The gift encouraged us hugely.

With our late start to the ride and everyone feeling tuckered out, we struggled to keep a good pace once we were back on the road. An hour dragged by, then another. The fresher riders had returned home, so only Caroline, Wes, and I were riding.

No crosswinds blew at us. The landscape was not at fault. It was pleasantly dotted with gently rolling hills and leafy trees, bright in the early summer sunshine. But still we struggled.

We saw a turtle moseying along in the middle of the road, and we stopped to place it safely by the side of the road. We passed four turkey farms. We slowed even more. I mentioned aloud that I could use another three hours' sleep. Caroline murmured her assent. Wes's face was drawn and tight, and he didn't say anything. Something was definitely off with him.

I tried to pick up the pace, but nothing seemed to work. I didn't know what to do. On one hand, I felt like spurring the team onward. On the other hand, I knew that everybody was dead tired, me included. I felt the tension of trying to balance our goal of riding 100 miles each day with our other goal of stopping to talk with people. On top of all that, my bike was giving me problems. It needed adjustment, and maybe that was a sign.

The further we rode, the more the day dragged. I checked in again with Caroline. She looked exhausted but grunted that she was okay. I turned the other direction and asked, "You doing okay, Wes?"

He was quiet for a good ten or twenty pedal strokes. I wondered if he had heard me. I glanced at him again.

"Physically I'm fine," he said at last.

"How are you emotionally?"

"Not so well."

"Wanna talk about it? You don't have to if you don't want to."

He mumbled something that I didn't hear, so I glanced back at him again. His mouth was tight, and he was shaking his head. He was choking back tears.

"I got another call this morning," he said. "You remember that my friend Tilde is in the hospital? Well, she's not going to make it. The doctor said they're making a decision about what to do. Her family is hurting so bad. I can only imagine how much pain they're in. I'm just a friend, and it's killing me. It's hard to think that we have all these advances in medical technology and equipment, but we still can't do anything for her."

We rode for a time in silence while the news of Wes's burden spread heavily over us. There wasn't much to say except to convey we were there for him. Wes was sorting through his emotional pain in addition to the physical strain we were all under, and I knew one could easily compound the other.

About an hour away from lunchtime, we made a pit stop for snacks and water and spoke with an older woman who'd stopped her motorcycle in a parking lot. Her name was Karen. She worked as a school bus driver during the school season, and she was riding from Lombard, Illinois, to San Diego by herself to see her son. Her motorcycle had three wheels, and Karen explained that she'd recovered from a stroke but now had the beginnings of Parkinson's. Folks had told her to give up motorcycling, but she loved the freedom of the open road. So she'd bought a kit and converted her bike to three wheels so she could continue riding as long as possible.

I tried talking about spiritual matters once or twice, but nothing much was connecting. Her responses weren't negative. Her demeanor simply told me that she wasn't ready to go there. That was okay. Karen was friendly and relaxed and seemed to be in good health at the moment. We talked about motorcycles and maps, different routes across the country, and what it was like to ride alone in contrast to riding with a group.

Our conversation didn't get terribly deep, but what impressed me most of all was that she was living her dream in spite of hardships. She hadn't let her difficulties derail her. She'd simply made adjustments and kept going. I wondered what kind of courage it took to be in your late sixties with medical issues and heading cross-country by yourself on a motorbike. She was still doing what she loved to do, still doing what she could with what she had. Talking to her, I felt pure admiration.

We started pedaling again and rode into the afternoon. It became hot and dusty. My bike was becoming harder and harder to shift and was making nasty noises. We passed cornfields. Wheat fields. Acres and acres of newly planted crops. We were starving, but there was nothing for miles around that offered sustenance. No convenience stores. No restaurants. No gas stations. We stopped at a roadside pullout and ate from the back of the van, picnic style. I adjusted my derailleur cable in hopes of helping my bike.

One of the female support team members needed to use the restroom, but no facilities were showing up on the map for miles. Just then an older farmer in a red pickup pulled over. We talked for a few minutes about nothing and everything, and our team member's predicament was made known. He offered to drive her up the road to his farmhouse to let her use his facilities.

It felt weird to say yes. Dangerous even. But our team member was in agony. So a few of the women and one of the guys jumped into the truck, and away they went. They were back before long. The farmer wasn't an ax murderer, just a friendly gent helping out his fellow Americans in need of a bathroom.

We continued riding, but by now all our bikes were getting a bit cranky, just like me. After another ten miles my bike would hardly shift, and in another five it stopped shifting altogether. We all pulled over by a roadside store to get a cold drink.

When I came out after having a short conversation, Wes announced to the team—without talking to me first—that everybody was tired and that we needed to jump into the van and get to a bike shop while we still had time.

My limbs felt jittery. It was late afternoon, nearing dinnertime. The day was so hot. Our pace all day had been so slow. I looked at Caroline and Wes, then looked at our mileage meter.

Fifty-two miles.

We were so short of our goal.

For a moment or two I protested and paced in the dusty parking lot. Glenn and Judy looked exhausted. The other two riders looked as beat as

I felt. The rest of the crew hung their heads. This day had brought with it a lot of moving parts, and we were all off our game.

Wes was right.

I knew that a big part of the integrity of this trip was that we rode hard each day. We couldn't cut corners, and if it had just been me riding, I might have pushed on, misery and all. But I also knew that people mattered more than miles.

"Let's get in the van," I said. I was angry. Frustrated. My statement was a command.

In spite of my terse tone, an audible sigh of relief escaped from the group. We packed up, climbed aboard, and started driving toward Springfield, Missouri. The whole way I battled myself and my expectations, wondering if I'd made the right decision.

After reaching the city, we found a repair shop. The technician asked me to explain the problem. He was young and fit, with a shaved head and a clean, direct style. He put his hands on my bike, and I held onto it, too, my hands clenched tightly around the handlebars. I guess I must have been talking too fast, communicating from a place of frustration, because he stopped me at one point and said, "Breathe. Okay, bud? Just breathe."

I stopped short and stood looking at my bike with its seized-up gears, still wrestling with all the self-imposed tension I felt. This trip had been fantastic so far, but there was so much inside me that needed processing.

"Breathe," he repeated.

I unclenched my hands. Stepped away from my bike. Breathed in through my nose, out through my mouth. Let my bike problems rest in his hands.

"I'm learning," I said.

— 20 —

DAY BY DAY

I don't think I stirred at all in my sleep that night. Depth came quickly to my slumber and cradled me until morning. When I awoke I felt refreshed, grateful, and enthusiastic about the new day, our nineteenth of the journey.

On today's plate was a ride through the Ozark Mountains—some 6,000 combined feet of climbing. Rain was forecasted at about 2:00 p.m., and I knew the ride itself would be grueling. Yet my prayer first thing in the morning was not so much for stamina to ride, and not even for conversations I hoped we'd have, but simply that today's ride would be fun again. I prayed for joy. Overall I hoped it would be a good day for our team.

I believe God respects a prayer like that.

This ride had already offered up its difficulties. There had been heat, cold, and wind to contend with. Lousy sleep schedules. Upset stomachs. The inevitable tensions that come when traveling with a group of very-much-humans. Yet God promises joy as a benefit of living life with him. The Bible refers to joy as a "fruit"[1] and describes it as being "filled with all the fullness of God,"[2] something that can happen even within adverse circumstances.

And I was practicing the discipline of letting go. If I didn't talk to a single person today, I would flow with that. If we only went 20 miles, I wouldn't push the team any harder. I walked out of the door of the motel and put on my windbreaker against the imminent rain, then thought to check my phone. A friend had sent a prayer in the form of a text, part of a poem written by retired minister Ted Loder that encouraged me to seek quietness with God, soothe my tiredness, and release the end of my compulsiveness.[3]

I wanted all of that. The quietness. The release. The end of my compulsiveness. I headed toward the van, and the team was gathered and ready to go. I could only grin.

We left the motel in Springfield just after 7:00 a.m. The fact that we were actually out the door and on the road and pedaling by the time we'd agreed on felt like a new record for us. Not once did we take a wrong turn—another first. The route led us down some wide highways. The overcast sky soon cleared and emerged blue and bright. After its time in the shop, my bike was shifting smoothly.

We paralleled Interstate 44 for a while, riding on a service road. Then the traffic cleared out, and we pedaled up and down beautiful green and winding hills. Farmhouses dotted the landscape. Several properties had grazing horses out front, looking posed for iconic country portraits. We passed wheat fields again, and the breeze on our faces was gentle and kind. So far the day was turning out well.

At lunchtime we stopped at a diner in the town of Hartville, Missouri, population 608, where I met Krystal and Kenny. They were seated at a table with a little girl about four years old who told me her name was Addison. Krystal smiled readily, and Kenny seemed affable. He spoke with a thick Southern accent. Addison licked an ice cream cone while we talked.

I soon learned that Kenny and Krystal were cousins and that Addison was Krystal's daughter. Kenny had lost his wife nine months earlier. He had two children of his own, ages seventeen and fifteen. He teared up as he told me about his wife's passing, then stopped talking, overcome by emotion. I laid my hand on his shoulder while he struggled with his tears, and Krystal finished the story for him, saying simply that he was grieving quite intensely and needed a lot of prayer. The wound was still so raw. Krystal described how she was staying close to her cousin through this difficult time, providing part of the family support he needed.

"You're a good cousin, Krystal," I said.

"I really care about him," she said, with a determined smile in his direction. "He's family."

I turned to Kenny and offered some words of encouragement. He nodded and said he was okay, and Krystal went on to describe how she'd also lost her brother and mother within the past three years, and now her father was close to death too.

"Wow, that just sounds so hard," I said.

"It is," she said. "But God has given us grace to deal with it."

I nodded. "It's a broken world."

"It's a real world with real pain," she said. "You just have to live day by day."

Krystal said she was currently working nights, doing billing audits at the local Holiday Inn, but she hoped to be a veterinarian someday. Kenny had been a truck driver and traveled all over the United States and Canada, but now he worked as a handyman. A week ago a tornado had dropped down in the area and mowed a narrow swath through town. Krystal and Kenny described how they'd scrambled to run from the storm and hidden in the courthouse, which was deemed the safest building in town. A few houses had been flattened, doors had been ripped off, and power lines had gone down, but fortunately nobody had died. The whole community had been shaken up, and the storm had caused a huge mess and disruption throughout the area. We'd seen a bit of the destruction as we rode through.

In spite of its depth, our conversation wasn't long. We talked about faith a bit more, and both Krystal and Kenny said they were Christians with a strong love for God and Jesus. What impressed me about these folks was how committed they were to helping each other and their community. Krystal was smart and educated and had dreams for the future, yet she stayed in this small town because she loved the people in it, working the night shift so she could help care for her family. Kenny loved driving a truck, but he knew it made sense to be near family while he grieved, and he'd taken the job as a handyman so he could stay put. They stood up to leave, and we said our good-byes.

Still in the restaurant, I spoke with a seventy-seven-year-old woman named Annie. Caroline was already talking with her when I walked up. Annie was soft-spoken and frail looking, wearing a hat that paid homage to veterans who'd served in the Vietnam War. She spoke with a constant careful chuckle, a sound that indicated affability more than comedy. Her husband had served in Vietnam, she explained, and had passed away three years earlier. Wearing the hat made her feel closer to him, she said. Again came the little chuckle.

I asked her more about her family, and she described how she'd lost three family members—her first husband to a heart attack, then her son and her second husband, the Vietnam vet, to different kinds of cancer.

"You've had a tough road, Annie," I said.

"Yeah," she said. "But I just look up and keep on trucking."

I nodded my head in sympathy. "Do you ever want to say, 'Why, God?'"

"Oh, I've asked him about that, and I don't know all the answers," Annie said. "But he's up there. Jesus hears and cares, very much, even in the midst of all that difficulty. Actually, I would say *through* all that difficulty he cares. Knowing there's another day—not just for me, but for people in general. The sun rises each day and sets each day."

"That reminds me of a promise in the Bible," I said. "The Lord's 'compassions . . . are new every morning.'[4] You know that one?"

"I do," she said. "I know that one very well. Sometimes I just pray, 'Okay, God, you gonna give us another day? Okay, go ahead.' That's how I live. Day by day."

There was that phrase again: "day by day." I'd heard it from Krystal a few moments earlier.

I asked Annie another question, and she got into a longer story, closing her eyes at times, perhaps in reverie. Her voice was so low that it was hard to catch exactly all she was saying. When I did hear her, some of her discourse didn't sound quite coherent. I asked Annie if she would speak up slightly, and her voice rose for a word or two, then fell back to barely audible.

The story went on for quite a while, and I decided to simply let her talk. Caroline was still standing nearby, and I glanced at her and caught her eye. It was clear that Caroline wasn't catching all of Annie's story either.

Annie talked and talked, all the while smiling and giving her soft, careful chuckle. At last, she finished her story. I thanked her for talking and asked if I could give her a hug. She smiled and said sure, and Caroline hugged her too.

We left the diner, hopped back on our bikes, and kept riding, musing on that gentle soul. We were starting to climb now, the road growing steeper and more winding.

"Did you catch all of that last story?" Caroline asked before long.

"No," I said. "Did you?"

"Just bits and pieces. She didn't seem bothered though."

"Yeah. She seemed pretty happy just to have someone to talk with."

"Yep," Caroline added. "I was glad you were listening. It felt like that's where the value came from—being there with her while she talked. It would have been nice to hear her better. But I guess sometimes that can't happen."

殂

I was still thinking about what Caroline had said, grasping the implications of being a listening presence, as we rode into an area we knew to be Amish country. Soon we came upon an Amish family traveling along the road in their buggy, so we stopped and said hello. They stopped, too, but didn't smile at all.

The father climbed out and stood at a distance at first while he asked some questions of us. We told them what we were doing and asked if we could talk a bit more. He said okay, and the rest of the family climbed out too.

We talked for some time about farming, furniture making, and their family. The more we talked, the more I could see smiles starting to form. He said that he and his wife had fifteen children, although not all their kids were with them in the buggy. A few were grown, married, and raising families of their own.

When I asked if we could take some photos, he said we could take photos of the land and their buggy, but not of them. He explained that it was a theological issue for them. They followed the Old Testament command not to make graven images, and they considered photographs of people to be graven images. He added that sometimes people would agree but then would take photos of them anyway.

We respected their wishes, snapped only the permitted photos, and said our good-byes.

The skies were clear for another hour of riding. The road grew steeper, and we sweated and grunted against the climb in elevation. Then clouds began to lower and rain threatened, but we still felt buoyed by the strength of this day's conversations.

A roadside park beckoned us. The clouds lifted again as we pulled off the road and parked our bikes. The area was so beautiful, we simply had to check it out. A newly constructed wooden bridge connected two banks over a creek, its water tumbling by in shades of white and blue. The sun peeked through the trees, revealing hues of green and gold in subtle variations. All around us was a feeling of tranquility.

Mike and Lynn, a couple in their early forties, were standing beside the bank, gazing at the water. They wore T-shirts, shorts, and running shoes, and I strolled over to make conversation. When I asked what was new in their lives, Lynn said they'd both been through major life changes in the past ten years. She had once weighed 415 pounds, and Mike had weighed more than 400. Two lap-band surgeries had failed for Lynn, so they had decided to get serious about making life changes. They'd started eating healthy, planning their meals, and going to a gym, and gradually the weight had come off. Lynn had lost 235 pounds, and Mike had lost 200.

"Praise God," Lynn said. "He was with us throughout the whole journey. Being overweight had really been an issue we both had to deal with. And now . . ." she hesitated. "Well, we get to live life now. We get to be healthy. We get to do things like this"—she motioned with her hand to the creek—"Just walking around outside, enjoying this scenery. We couldn't do that before, when we had all that weight on us."

Lynn and Mike's story fascinated me, and I asked a few more questions. They talked about how the physical strain on their bodies wasn't what it used to be. It was difficult to maintain their new weights, but they were committed to the process, and it was worth it.

"When you stop eating a bunch of junk and get into a whole-food diet, it clears your brain," Lynn said. "I can think more positively about the world. I do better at my job now. We've progressed in so many areas of our lives, and I attribute that to a change in mindset. Do more. Live better. Have fun. Live healthy. You're worth it."

She had mentioned God, so I asked how faith factored into their weight loss.

"I believe God appointed us for a reason," Lynn said. "Mike and I went through our most difficult times and came out the other side, and it happened so we can share our story today and help others. Our message is that nobody needs to settle. If you're overweight, that doesn't need to be how your story ends. There's a whole other life on the other side of being overweight. The devil's way is always the easy way. Whenever you overeat or eat poorly, you're harming your body. It's easy to do that. But there is a better way of living, a way that helps you."

"That's right," Mike said. "God is a loving God, and he has a purpose for each person. He cares where you've been, and he cares where you're going. I start each day with a devotional that I read with a friend, and I find it very helpful overall. It's true: losing weight is hard, but it's so worth it in the long run. We feel so much better now, and we're able to do things we were never able to do before. We used to buy three airplane tickets for two people. Now we only buy two. We're able to do Segway tours. At amusement parks we can fit in the rides now. We've even gone horseback riding. I tell ya, when you're four hundred pounds, you're not getting on a horse. But now we've found horseback riding is really fun. There's a ton of diets out there, and everybody's body works differently. You just have to find the healthy lifestyle that fits you, and then keep at it. Day by day."

There was that phrase again—and I loved hearing it in the context of Lynn and Mike's story. They were so encouraging. We talked for a while longer before giving each other good-bye hugs. Then the other riders and I hopped on our bikes and pedaled the rest of the way into Eminence, Missouri, arriving ahead of schedule. We would be staying on a ranch outside of town.

The entire ride that day had felt fun. The weather had held. We had been shored up by a better sleep last night. Even the hills hadn't seemed too difficult. We'd had surprising conversations with people we would have never met outside of this ride across the country. And there'd been this sense that God was leading us each roll of the journey.

Moment by moment.

Day by day.

— 21 —

THE VALUE OF EVERY
INTERACTION

A rainstorm blew in during the night, a major deluge, so when June 15 dawned, we decided to wait until the rain let up before we started out. This meant getting on our bikes late, but there was nothing we could do to change the weather. I looked out the window of my room and tapped my foot, watching the sky dump buckets on the cedar trees around us, then I took a deep breath and a cue from the words of King David in the Bible:

> I do not occupy myself with things
>> too great and too marvelous for me.
> But I have calmed and quieted my soul,
>> like a weaned child with its mother.[1]

The sky continued to pour, and we continued to wait, and I knew my day would go better if I trusted God like David and didn't try to force anything. I couldn't force the rain to let up, and I couldn't force conversations, and I couldn't force how quickly we rode from point A to point B. That theme seemed to emerge day after day on this trip, and day after day I seemed to wrestle with it.

I decided to see if I could find somebody to talk with while it rained.

Kathy managed and co-owned the hundred-acre Coldwater Ranch, where we were staying, and I found her in the dining room after breakfast. A middle-aged woman with glasses propped on her head, Kathy said she was the eighth generation of her family to live and work on the ranchland, although it hadn't been occupied that whole time. I marveled at that. Before she managed the ranch, Kathy had lived in Columbia, Missouri, where she'd worked as an insurance agent. Life in the city had stressed her out, so she'd decided to travel back to Eminence, where her mother still lived, and see if she could build a life on her family's land.

"Whether you're religious or not, I had an experience that gives me chills," she said. "Can I tell you about it?"

"Please do," I answered. I had yet to tell her I was a pastor.

"When I first came to the ranch, I gave myself six months to decide whether to stay or return to the city," Kathy said. "Before I left the city, I said, 'Okay, Lord, I need a sign, and you're gonna need to make it really clear.' Now, when I was driving to the ranch, about ten miles out of town, a semi drove straight toward me. I had to put my pickup in the ditch. The rear axle caught and bent, and I flipped end over end.

"As I lay there in my truck, hanging upside down, an old man came along—really ancient. He stopped, addressed me by name, and said, 'I'm going to stay here with you and wait until help arrives. I know your dad would want me to do that.' He named my father, too, and said he used to work with him. Now, my father had been dead for many, many years. And nobody had lived on our land for forty years. I wasn't known in these parts.

"The man stayed with me until my mother drove up. She helped me get untangled from the truck, and I was all right. The old man left without saying another word. My mother asked who he was. She didn't know him. I told her I didn't know him either, but he'd said he knew my dad and he'd known me. My mother said, 'That's impossible. Your father's been gone for far too long.' To this day, we have no idea who he was."

"Wow," I said. "You think he was an angel?"

"I honestly do," she said. "It wasn't my time to die, and whoever that old man was, that experience was my sign."

We went on to talk about horses—Coldwater Ranch specializes in horse camping and riding trails—the beautiful scenery surrounding us, and the dynamics of running the ranch over an eight-month tourist season. I asked her what it looked like for her to connect with God here.

"Before I came here I nearly checked myself into a stress unit," she said. "There's something about this ranch that just heals you. A few years back my son moved home. His dad had died not long before, and my son was grieving and in a bad way. I told him, 'If you let it, this place will get in your soul, and it will calm you.' See, we live in the woods here, surrounded by all the sounds of nature. It quiets you. And it did that for us both. There's something here. You feel good. You feel home. That's how I get close to God."

"I'm curious," I said. "Who is God to you? How do you define him?"

"God's in my soul," she said. "He calms me. Things come up from time to time that are gut-wrenching. I'll go out on the property, all alone, and I feel I can actually speak to God. I like to be alone when I talk to God because there's not that stigma of somebody saying, 'Hey, there's some nut out in the woods talking to herself.' So I go out alone and pray like that a lot, and it helps. Something traumatic happened not long ago, and I prayed a lot. I felt like God was right there with me. I wasn't asking for anything except peace. God calmed me. I knew God was with me, and I felt blessed."

Kathy told me several more stories after I stopped asking questions, and I just let her talk for a while. When people talk free-form, they tend to remember things as they talk, even processing and clarifying things within the conversation. She mentioned several times that she'd gone out alone in the wilderness to pray, so at last I asked her where she had learned how to pray.

"When I was young my dad was Baptist, and we grew up in a house of prayer," she said. "He was ill a lot and died when he was only forty-four. There were lots of times before he passed when he just prayed. He asked God for more time with his family. He prayed that we could make ends meet. I watched that model and took it in. After I grew up and moved to the city, I was away from my faith for some time. It felt like I just didn't belong in the city, like it wasn't really me. Now I pray a lot, and I pray directly to God. I know in the Bible it says, nobody gets to the Father except through Jesus.[2] So I include Jesus in my conversations, but I always address God directly. Maybe that's odd."

"I don't know that it's odd," I said. "I think it's your story, and your story is beautiful. Thanks for telling it to me."

She nodded and chuckled in reply.

In the Lord's Prayer, Jesus taught that we *can* pray directly to God as our Father. (This was a fairly new concept to Jesus' disciples, who first heard that teaching.) It's striking in the Gospels how many times Jesus refers to God as Father.

If I had been thinking more quickly, I would have said this out loud, but instead I stayed quiet and chewed on Kathy's words. She had naturally brought up Jesus as she told me her story, and as she talked, I sensed that I was tiptoeing with her into the wilderness, this place of soul-searching and peace. She connected with God, and God was going to sort things out with her, and I hoped that I could have a second conversation with her someday.

At the end of our time together, I gave Kathy a copy of the gospel of Mark. As she accepted it, she said she'd read it. I believed that if she revisited Jesus' story with that same openness she brought to the wilderness,

God himself would begin to sharpen her theology. I hoped for so much more for her. But I'd said enough for now. I trusted that God would bring another person into her life to continue the conversations.

The morning hours crawled on. It was still pouring, and I heard thunder in the distance, but we decided to start the ride anyway. We hopped on our bikes and headed out over hilly terrain in the rain. Fortunately, within ten minutes of riding, it let up, and we soon found our groove on the bikes.

We rode up a steep hill, then flew down the other side. Wes was arcing back and forth like a water skier behind a boat, just having fun. Then another hill came upon us, and we all buckled down and pushed hard to the top. From the crown I caught a glimpse of the next few miles. Just hill after hill after hill.

By lunchtime we were winded, so we stopped in a small town and went into a convenience store. They had candy cigarettes at the front counter, which I hadn't seen since I was a kid. Candy cigarettes are a horrible thing to sell to children, totally inappropriate, but when my brother and I were young, of course we loved them. Somebody in the store—it may have been me—remarked that they're harmless enough until you stick one in your mouth and light it on fire. Everybody laughed.

I introduced myself to the woman behind the counter, Debbie, explained that we were riding across country in an effort to have deeper conversations with people, and asked if she wanted to talk. She said she didn't. But she handed me a pack of candy cigarettes, chuckled, and said they were a Father's Day gift for me—on the house. I laughed, accepted the gift, and walked out of the store. A few team members lingered over purchases, and when they joined me outside, Caroline said, "She wanted to say good-bye to you."

"Huh?"

"Debbie. You left before she had a chance to say good-bye. She told me that after you left."

I looked at Caroline, hoping she could elaborate. She shrugged. I walked back inside and bantered with Debbie for another five minutes. Nothing deep, just a casual chat. Again I asked if she wanted to be interviewed, and again she cheerfully declined. She'd only wanted to say "so long" to me, she said. That was all.

Debbie and I said our good-byes. I thanked her again for the gift and left, scratching my head. The riders and I climbed on our bikes, and we were five miles down the road before it hit me.

You can connect with a person over many things. Over sports. Over shared activities. Over the fence as backyard neighbors. Over fun. Debbie hadn't wanted to talk formally with me. Yet by going back inside the store to say good-bye, I had, at the very least, affirmed the truth that she was valued. She was seen.

Once again I reminded myself to slow down with people, even when a conversation didn't seem deep. Any conversation could be more significant than it first appeared.

As we were riding by a field full of cows, I spotted a young guy pouring diesel into a tractor. He had a bemused smile on his face, so I pulled over and asked what I needed to do to get some free steaks. He laughed, stopped what he was doing, and moseyed over. I explained what our ride was about, and he introduced himself as Ryan and said he'd talk.

An old Cadillac pulled up just then, and a young woman got out and immediately spit a wad of tobacco juice on the ground. Her back was toward me. She turned around, looked me in the eye, and laughed. Her actions were so nonchalant, they made me laugh too. I could see baling wire and seed in the backseat of the Caddy.

Ryan introduced me to his wife, Bethany. He was twenty-five. She was twenty-three. He explained that they cut hay on a different farm and trucked it over to this farm for feed. They had sixteen cows, a bull, and thirteen calves. They'd both grown up in the area and loved farming. They talked about the strong work ethic needed for farming and how everybody in the area was friendly. They valued family and being closely connected to the land. I asked them about faith, and they both said they believed in God. Bethany had been the more spiritual one when they got married, but she'd brought Ryan along. Now they were going to church together.

"Jesus has changed my outlook," Ryan said. "I tend to treat people better. I notice that some people mess up and lie. But you just gotta forgive them, although that can be hard. I pray about it a bunch."

"Interesting," I said. "What's hard to forgive?"

"People can take advantage of you." Ryan was getting real. "Folks have done me wrong. It's hard for me to let go."

Bethany's brow wrinkled. "Ryan was lost as a person when I first met him. His attitude was terrible, and he was mad all the time. He didn't understand what there was to live for, and so I prayed for God to show him that God has bigger plans for his life. I think the Lord has given him a more positive outlook on life now."

We talked about marriage—specifically about spouses disagreeing and making up again. We talked more about prayer and patience in praying. Ryan also worked for the Missouri Department of Conservation, and we talked about the strategic planting and harvesting of trees. We talked about living in cities, and Ryan said he'd never want to live in one, but Bethany said she might for a while. Mostly, she added, they were content living where they were, doing what they were doing.

I smiled at that. They both struck me as grounded people, content with their lives and where they were heading. If they had suddenly been transplanted in a city, people might have called them hicks. But there was something so straightforward and charming about this couple and the lifestyle they'd chosen. Despite their young age, they seemed like they had much of life figured out. A sense of peace and solidity hung about them. They were connected to their heritage and their occupations, clear about who they were. I found it refreshing.

Soon the team and I were riding again. The rest of the day the road followed the constant rise and fall of rolling hills. After 90 miles we pulled into Farmington, Missouri, our destination for the evening, and headed to a restaurant for supper. Altogether we had climbed more than 7,000 feet of elevation. We were famished.

In the lobby we waited to be seated, and I sat on a bench, waiting for team members to exit the restroom. A young man came out of the restroom first. He looked like he might have been college aged, but I wasn't sure. He sat across from me, stared my direction, and didn't turn away. I stared back. He was shorter than me, with thick glasses and a cheerful round face. Something seemed a little off about him, but I couldn't discern what it was.

It's easy to turn away when you encounter folks who look a bit different. But I made the conscious decision not to flinch. He kept looking directly at me, and I wondered where this was going. I decided to be quiet and let him take the lead.

"Hi," he said, after about a minute of staring. "My name's TJ, and I'm a brain-cancer survivor."

"Wow," I said. "That's cool. My name's Neil. Nice to meet you."

He stood, came over to me, and shook my hand. He parked himself right next to me on the bench, and we started talking. He explained how he'd had twenty-six brain surgeries over the years. The first, when he was nine months old, had been performed by the famed Dr. Ben Carson.

I asked him a number of questions about the surgeries, and he talked quite a bit. I told him some about our trip, and he asked a lot of good questions.

After a while an older man came out of the restroom, sat against the far wall, and watched us. I was pretty sure he was TJ's father, but he didn't talk to us at first. He just sat and watched.

Our table was ready. I said good-bye to TJ, then walked over to the older man and introduced myself. Sure enough, he was TJ's father. He was happy that I'd taken time to show interest in his son. I told the man a bit about our ride and asked if I could give TJ one of our T-shirts. He said sure, so I went out to the van to get one, brought it back, and handed it to TJ, who rewarded me with a smile. He joined us for a team picture, then they headed to their table.

The restaurant was serving all-you-can-eat catfish. Our hungry team definitely got our money's worth. The food was delicious, and we ordered coffees and Cokes with dinner and pie for dessert. When we finished, we walked to the front to pay the bill, but the hostess just shook her head.

"It's taken care of," she said. "That older man you were talking to when you first came in—he paid it all."

Wes spotted him outside and ran to say thanks. "I didn't do it for the thanks," the man said. "Just enjoy the gift."

I was still thinking about TJ the next morning when I received a message on Instagram from a young woman named Larah, who explained that she was TJ's sister. "What you didn't know was that it was TJ's birthday yesterday," she wrote. "Thank you. You really made his day."

When I read Larah's message, I couldn't help but tear up. The whole day coalesced in my mind. We had started the day by talking with a woman who found God in the quietness of her land. We'd talked with a young couple who presented themselves as the next generation of pioneers. I'd barely talked with a woman at a convenience store, but some sort of connection had been made with her, at least some recognition that she found valuable. And I had tried to truly listen to a young man at a restaurant who'd been through some tough times. It had made his day.

Every interaction is important—I knew it then without a doubt. Wherever we are. Wherever God has placed us. Although many times I wondered how God was going to follow up a conversation, the key for me was simply to start one.

— 22 —

EXPECT THE UNEXPECTED

On the twenty-first day of the ride, I awoke to find it was raining hard, and as I looked out the water-drenched window I wasn't sure if we'd be able to do much that day. We were scheduled to cross the Mississippi River. But word had already come that a section of roadway near the river was flooded, so we needed to take a different route than planned. We'd have to start the day by riding in the vehicles for about half an hour until we crossed a busy bridge and then found rideable roads. Reports said that much of this area of Missouri was flooded, and it was the same on the other side of the bridge in Illinois. So that meant anything could happen.

I wanted to expect God to do the unexpected, but all I could see was this pile of problems. I had to consciously activate my faith to tackle this day.

As I loaded up my bike in the van, I thought about how easy it is to be faithless. We were three weeks into our trip, and we'd seen incredible things happen so far, yet there was something in me that expected the blessings to run out. I don't know why exactly. Maybe I was looking at God through a scarcity mentality. I know he is good and that he loves us, and I knew it that morning. But I wasn't sure if he would enable me to talk with anybody that day. Would we be on roads where we wouldn't be able to see anybody? Would we even be able to ride?

To top it off, Wes had received news that his friend Tilde had passed away. He made several calls, and we surrounded him with prayer and love. We also talked with him about pragmatic issues, including the possibility of his returning home. He decided it would make more sense for him to finish the trip. Still, he was hurting.

We finished loading the vans and it stopped raining, but the skies stayed gray. As we headed off in the vehicles, we saw lots of water on the ground in places it didn't belong and spotted very few people. The river was swollen and fast-flowing when we crossed it. Traffic was thick on the Illinois side, and we drove for several miles before deciding to ride.

At last we climbed on our bikes. Immediately it started raining again. The farmlands were flooded on both sides of the road, and as we pedaled, all we could see to our left and right was water. Occasionally we passed houses and businesses—all flooded as well.

When you hear news reports of flooding, it's hard to appreciate the magnitude of destruction that water can cause. Then you see it up close for yourself, and devastation takes on a new meaning. We rode and rode through the flooded landscape and didn't see anybody to talk to. One stretch of highway was reduced to one lane because of the flooding.

A couple of hours into the ride, Caroline needed to use a bathroom. There was no place to stop. Finally we spotted an open fruit stand, but as we pulled up I noticed a sign that read No Public Restrooms. We went inside anyway, pleaded our case, and asked if they'd make an exception. The woman shook her head and said their toilet wasn't working. As we left a team member wondered aloud, just out of earshot of the proprietor, if that was true. We kept riding, but there were no gas stations. No restaurants. No convenience stores. Nothing.

Finally we saw a house out in the middle of nowhere that didn't seem directly affected by the floods. I glanced at Caroline, and she nodded. All the windows of the house were dark and covered. The house looked scary. A Mack Truck was parked in the yard.

A man and two women, maybe in their early thirties, and a young boy were outside the house milling around. They didn't look happy, and it didn't look like they wanted any company. We pulled over and, sure enough, they didn't want to talk. I stayed courteous and explained our predicament, particularly about the need for Caroline to use their bathroom. At last they relented.

Caroline went inside. I kept hoping and praying the people would soften, but I found no conversational chinks in their armor. When Caroline reemerged, she looked spooked at whatever she saw inside. We conveyed our thanks, wished them well, and kept riding.

The rain let up. In another forty-five minutes we came to an old fruit stand near Jonesboro, Illinois, and stopped. There I met a woman who'd worked at the stand for the past thirty-five years. Her countenance looked troubled and grumpy and perhaps a little saddened. This much rain could do that to anybody. We talked a bit about the area and the flooding, and I tried to ask her a few deeper questions, but all her answers consisted of one or two words. I decided to give up and said thanks. We kept riding.

At lunchtime we stopped by the side of the road and ate from provisions we carried in the back of the van. No people were around. Doubts crept into my head. This might become our first day with no real conversations. We finished lunch, hopped back on the bikes, and kept pedaling.

The wind picked up. Another bad weather front was heading our way. We hit mile 50, then 60. The rain started pelting us. At mile 75 the skies opened up and unleashed everything they held. Temperatures dipped. Lightning cracked across the sky. Thunder boomed in the distance. We took cover under a rickety carport by the roadside and debated whether we should quit for the day. Always the hardhead, I insisted that the foul weather wouldn't bother us much. We bundled up and kept riding. The roadway was tight, and traffic whizzed by us. We were drenched in minutes.

At mile 77 hail started to fall. At first the pellets were small, merely inconvenient. We rode another mile. The hailstones grew bigger, now big enough to hurt. Just after mile 78, the team called a halt for safety's sake. I wanted to wait it out and get back on our bikes soon, but I was voted down. We stowed our bikes and hightailed it into the vehicles. Our biking time that day was finished. Dismayed and soggy, we drove the remaining way into Carbondale, our planned stop for the night.

The team unloaded the van at the motel, gathered luggage, and went inside ahead of me. For a few moments I stood in the rain and watched them. What a day this had been. We were all cold and wet and tired. Wes was grieving. Nothing had happened by way of conversation. I had pushed the team too hard. Again. And we still hadn't ridden the full distance today. All I wanted now was some dry clothes, food, and a bed. For twenty days we had experienced abundant and meaningful conversations, but this entire day was shaping up to be a bust.

A silent prayer passed through my mind. *God, would you please provide a way for us to do what you've called us to do?* As I did, I was pushing away my doubts and activating my faith, removing the limitations on what I believed God could do. So what if all I could see didn't look promising?

Glenn was handling the reservations. By the time I got inside, he already had keys for everybody. I was just about to head to my room when the young woman behind the front desk said, "Did I hear right that you are on a trip across the country looking for people to talk with?"

"That's right," I said.

"My mother might be interested. She's got a story. Hold on."

The young woman, who managed the motel, went into the back, and a middle-aged woman with a pleasant face emerged. She'd been getting some boxes from the motel, just hanging out with her daughter. The mom wore jeans and a T-shirt with the word *Inspire* across the front. She introduced herself as Diana, and we made ourselves at home in the lobby. She motioned to a Naugahyde chair, and I apologized for my damp conditions. She smiled and said not to worry about it. I sat.

Diana sat across from me. Bits and pieces of her story came out in a rush. She'd been adopted as a young girl and grown up in Illinois. Her adoptive parents had taken her to church as a child. After college she had married a Middle Eastern man. They'd had a baby together and moved to Amman, Jordan. After the terrorist attacks of September 11, 2001, she'd returned to the United States. Somewhere along the line there had been a divorce, although I didn't catch the exact sequence.

"There's no child support in the Middle East," she said. "No way to enforce anything like that. I was on my own, but still I headed back to Jordan to get my son. By some grace of God, I got him out. I brought him home and raised him here."

A multitude of questions sprang into my mind, but she shifted gears and said in an escalated voice: "In today's political environment, if you're not wealthy, people think it's because you did something wrong. If you're not rich enough to buy a home and a newer car, then you must not work as hard as others. But that's not true. I work just as hard, if not harder, and it doesn't mean I'm less deserving than other people. As a single mom, I've rented for years. Things happen. You don't have the best credit. You get a job and a credit card. You lose your job. You can't afford to pay your bills. You can't get by. These days I have a job, but I can't afford health care. What happens when I get sick?"

It sounded to me like nobody had listened to Diana for a while. She wanted to be heard and respected. "Can I say something?" I asked.

"Sure."

"I have a daughter who's a single mom," I said. "She's a social worker, and the work is highly important, but she doesn't make much money. She works hard, and she rents." I looked at her closely. "Diana, I want to say to you: I don't think of you as 'less than.' I believe you work very hard, and I just want to affirm you in that."

There was a moment's pause, then she said, "Thank you." Her tone softened. "I try. If people aren't helping each other and only helping themselves, it's just not good. It'll only get harder in this country if that's the way it continues."

We talked about politics some more, with me assuring her I would be kind and respectful no matter her opinions. Then I asked her about faith.

She chuckled while rolling her eyes. "So . . . shockingly, I don't look like the average Muslim, but I am Muslim. I've had people say negative things to me about Islam, things they've heard in the news or whatever, simply because they don't think a White person could be Muslim. And I get it. There are extremists in every religion. Extremists make the news. Jim Jones was Christian. We all must be like Jim Jones if we're Christian, right?

"The basic teachings of Islam are to be kind and charitable. I recently unfriended someone on Facebook because she said that Islam was a horrible religion and all Muslims were evil. I've been a part of the Muslim community for years, and I can say it's the complete opposite of that. Islam is not a horrible religion, and Muslims are not evil. The people who actually practice true Islam know that there's punishment involved if you do something wrong, so kindness is the best route for you to take. It's good for others, and it's good for you."

Now it was my turn to chuckle. "You know, Diana," I said. "I have a job outside of riding my bike. I'm a pastor of a Christian church, and I feel honored to talk with you."

"Thank you," she said, obviously a little surprised.

I went on, "I'm curious—when did you become a Muslim?"

"I got married in 1990 and became a Muslim in 1995. It wasn't an issue for my husband initially, but when I became pregnant with our son, my husband wanted us to be on the same page. I agreed. I'd met a kind young woman from the apartment building next to us, where we lived in Chicago. She was Muslim, and she impressed me by her actions, by her way of carrying herself and how well she got along with her husband. She was the person Allah put in my life. Through her I saw that I didn't actually need to convert to Islam. I already was a Muslim just by my actions.

"I don't feel I lessen Jesus in any way or Muhammad in any way. We are taught that they were both men and sent by God. There's only one God, and we're all children of God. That's how I've always felt, ever since I was a little girl sitting in Sunday school. I didn't know anything about the prophet Muhammad back then. But my belief now is that God made us, and the examples we get from men such as Jesus and Muhammad are what guide us where we need to go."

"Thank you for trusting me with that," I said. "May I press in just a bit?"

She nodded.

"You mentioned the people who adopted you took you to church as a child," I said. "How did they handle you becoming a Muslim?"

"I have a very religious but not overbearing grandmother," Diana said. "I went to her because if there was going to be a problem, I thought it might come from her. So I explained that I was a Muslim and what it meant, and that I was going to do the whole Islamic thing. I asked if she was upset. She said, 'Diana, anything you need to be to make you a good human being and cause you to believe in God is fine with me. It's all just what gets it done for you.' Most people, if they read the Bible and read the Koran, find there's not a lot of difference."

Everything within me wanted to challenge this head-on, yet I took a different approach, a listening approach. "Wow, interesting," I said. "You mentioned the rhetoric of the day, how there's a lack of respect between people with different viewpoints. So let me ask you this: How, in your estimation, can people disagree and still have respect for one another? Like, if I lived in this town, could we be friends and have coffee together? I'd like that. Over time we would trust each other to go to deeper levels. How might we disagree and have respect for each other and still get into things?"

Diana smiled. "At the end of the day, you have to have your own convictions. I have to have mine. We can respect each other's ideas and beliefs and still learn from each other. When people ask me about Islam, I start the conversation by saying, 'I'm not here to convert you. I'm here to help you understand what I believe. If you have any questions, hopefully I can help you answer them.' That way people are more comfortable with talking. People always want to be right, but in the end it's God's decision who goes where. I've had Muslims tell me my father went to hell because he's Christian. And I've had Christians tell me I'll go to hell because I'm a Muslim. Someone wise once told me, if you've lived a good life and done well by your neighbors, and if you've not harmed anybody, then it's up to Allah what will happen in the end. All kinds of people can go to heaven."

We talked about how God is the only judge of what's truly inside people's hearts. I agreed with her on that. We talked about some of the harder verses in the Bible, such as where Jesus said he was the way, the truth, and the life and that no one could go to the Father except through him.[1] We didn't see eye to eye on that, but our conversation didn't get heated. I talked about a community center associated with my church back in Dallas that provides language skills and job training for refugees, a number of them Muslim. She thought that was a good idea. And I let her have the last word.

"I think if people just relax a little," Diana said. "So many more things can be done when people work together."

We shook hands. Her demeanor had changed by the end. Her smile was broader.

This conversation was exactly what this trip was about.

No, we didn't agree about much. But we weren't fighting. We were courteous and kind to each other. We had talked about deeper matters. And the door was open to further conversations—either with me or with whomever God put in Diana's path. Or in my path, for that matter.

She wished me well and hoped less rain would fall on our trip. She told me she appreciated me listening to her. And she gave me a hug.

It was a day when I'd chosen, despite misgivings, to expect the unexpected. And that's exactly what I'd found.

Why had I ever doubted?

— 23 —

MEETING PEOPLE
WHERE THEY ARE

Before I left for the trip, I'd had a lengthy conversation with a friend about the places and positions we were born into. We're not completely products of fate, or whatever a person might want to call it these days. Yet we're all initially assigned a place in life that we have no control over. We talked about how any one of us could have been born in a different place or time or generation or to different parents. We might still be the same person, but our life would have turned out vastly different.

I was reminded of this conversation as the morning of June 17 dawned, overcast but bright. More rain was forecasted, but so far it was holding off. It was day twenty-two, the official two-thirds point of the trip, and we had a lighter day scheduled, only 84 miles, although lots of climbing was on the agenda. The plan was to head from Carbondale to Cave-in-Rock State Park, just across the Ohio River from Kentucky.

As I gathered my supplies for the day, I flashed back to that pre-trip conversation and recognized the advantages that I held as a White, educated, middle-class male—advantages that Diana hadn't had. She'd mentioned the many challenges she'd encountered as a divorced woman, a single mom, and a Muslim. And she'd felt she had to prove her worth because she worked a blue-collar job rather than as a banker or a doctor. I had tried to affirm her, and our conversation was a good reminder to me to see others with eyes of compassion. I only truly know about my own experiences, but I can try to understand more about others' lives by listening to them with openness and empathy.

The thoughts were coming fast and furious. I let them settle into my gut as we climbed on our bikes and rode through rolling farmland over long, smooth roads. The countryside was blanketed with green. Lilacs sprouted alongside picket fences. Homes displayed colorful flower baskets hanging from porches. Everything seemed manicured and freshly mowed, and the air smelled rain washed and fresh.

By the side of the road we spotted two hikers, a guy in his late twenties with a long, bushy red beard and a teenager about fifteen. We stopped to talk. Both had wiry builds and were carrying loaded rucksacks. The man, Zack, told me he worked as a youth center facilitator, basketball coach, and online poker player. He explained they were midway through a 157-mile, six-day trek. They both loved the freedom of hiking as well as overcoming challenges such as finding water and sleeping outdoors in the rain. One of the best parts of hiking was the sensation of slowing down time, Zack said. That statement intrigued me, and eventually the conversation wound around to matters of faith.

"It's all a big blank," Zack said. "We don't have enough information to know if God truly exists.[1] I do lots of reading in philosophy and science. The past and the future could be an illusion. The present is the only thing we know for certain. My folks were religious, and I grew up with religion, but when I was about thirteen I gave it all up. There just wasn't enough information for me to believe. My brain doesn't have a choice of what I believe. I'm either convinced or I'm not. If I can't be convinced, then it's better to keep those things separate from the things I am convinced about."

"Interesting," I said. "So you're the type of person who, if you get convinced about something, you go all in. Would that be a correct assumption about you?"

"Absolutely," he said. "If I am convinced of something, it's because I know it's true. If I'm not convinced, then I don't want to live my life in that area."

I turned to the teen. "How about you? What are you convinced of?"

The teen scratched his shoulder. "There could be a God, I guess. It's hard to know."

"It makes sense to think the way you do," I said, addressing them both. "It's hard sometimes for people to approach God through religion. Or people like to put God in a box, as if they understand everything, but that only backfires. This universe is so big. I've hiked and biked in so many different places on this planet, but I've only scratched the surface. One time I met a guy who drew a circle on the ground with his finger and said, 'This represents all the knowledge we have. Don't you think there are things that are real that are outside this circle?' I had to think about that for quite a while." They both nodded.

I asked them a few more questions, and we talked more about philosophy and epistemology, the study of how we know what's true. I asked what they would need to be convinced that God is real. Zack said he'd have to believe in the reliability of the Bible. We had a good conversation around that for a while, then the conversation shifted away from deeper matters, and we talked some more about hiking.

After that Zack made it clear we were done talking. It was as far as he wanted to go in the conversation. That was okay with me. Some conversations only go as far as they go, and it's an issue of respect to let a person disengage with you and leave. They both struck me as fun guys to hang out with, and I appreciated Zack's frankness. He had to be fully convinced before he believed in something. That showed integrity.

After we said our good-byes, the other riders and I climbed back on our bikes and kept going. Near lunchtime there wasn't a town in sight, but we came across a small grocery store that had a covered seating area. The store was painted a jaunty red, like you'd see on a barn, with white trim around the windows. A couple of outdoor tables had chess pieces set up. We sat at the tables, munched on meat-and-cheese sandwiches, and joked about how a game of chess would take too long.

When lunch was over I sat down on a bench outside the front door and ate an ice cream sandwich. I'm not usually a big ice cream eater, but anything and everything on this ride looked and tasted good. I was eating huge amounts and a wide variety of foods.

A muscular guy sat down next to me on the bench and dug into a bag of chips. I soon learned that his name was Mark and he was a former special-ops navy officer who'd worked in explosive-ordinance disposal. He was riding his bicycle cross-country, too, but he'd started in Washington, DC, and was riding west.

I thanked Mark for his service, then asked him a few deeper questions, but he declined to go that direction, saying he wasn't interested. I said no problem, and we kept eating our snacks while chatting about bike riding. He'd been on the road for a month already. He asked why I wanted to talk about deeper stuff, and I said the state of the country had bothered me. People were divided over too much, so I wanted to see if I could go out and have conversations with people from all walks of life and viewpoints. I wanted to see if I could talk about deeper matters and still be kind, courteous, and respectful, no matter what people's backgrounds, creeds, or politics were.

He nodded to that, and the more we chatted, the more Mark warmed up. He planned to travel on his bike for six months, not simply going one direction across the country but north and south as well. He told me he'd been in the navy for twelve years and had recently retired due to traumatic brain injury from working with explosives. "My bell got rung so many times that every once in a while my brain wouldn't shut off," he said. He scratched behind his ear and described how he'd done two deployments to Afghanistan and two more deployments to Iraq. "I knew that before I moved on to the next chapter of my life, I wanted to close up that chapter first. This trip is my reprieve."

I told him about my friend who's a Navy SEAL and who had described to me some of the difficulties he'd encountered overseas. I asked Mark how it had gone for him.

"I'm happy to get away from it," Mark said with a slight smile. "I had a rough go, and I kept finding myself in situations where I never knew if I was just being stubborn or if the universe was trying to tell me something. I kept pushing through and overcoming every obstacle I encountered, and finally life handed me an obstacle I couldn't overcome. I look back now and wonder if I ever belonged in the military in the first place."

We talked about how sometimes when difficulties come into our lives, some people pull closer to their faith while others go the other direction. They don't want anything to do with God anymore. I told Mark I was a pastor and asked him where he fell along the faith spectrum.

"I don't share your beliefs, but I respect them," he said. "I've had plenty enough close calls, and that causes me to believe in something spiritual out there, although I don't know what it is. There were times on a mission where I knew something was up, something wasn't right. Then somebody would get hurt, somebody would get killed. So I got better and better at trusting those instincts that had warned me." Here he looked directly at me. "I know there's definitely something greater than us. But I don't believe in the Christian faith. I met a kind chaplain overseas, and he and I would actually do Bible studies together. But it just never resonated with me."

"Never resonated. That's interesting." I didn't say anything after that for a good long while. I was looking straight ahead as we sat on the bench together, and I could feel him still looking at me. Finally I added, "You know, when I hear from people who've had similar experiences, I often wonder what it would take for things to resonate. What would it personally take for Mark to say, 'Okay, I think I believe'?"

He relaxed and threw an elbow up on the bench behind him. "I don't think it's as simple as one answer. I'm not sure if I could truly say. But, you know, I think what you're doing right now is a great thing—this getting out and talking to people and listening. While on this ride I've been hosted by some churches. They often serve as a good resting point. If someone's there at the building, they invite me in. But I've also been in situations where you get the feeling that a person doesn't really want to hear your opinion. I truly do believe that the best thing you can do for another person, regardless of their faith or opinion or origin, is to listen."

"Hm, I love that," I said, finishing the last of my ice cream.

We talked some more about empathy. About his time in the service. About biking. Mark observed that it was so easy out on the road to see other people as anonymous, as defined by the car they drove or the bicycle they rode. Yet if we see people as anonymous, he added, then it's easy to be angry or divisive instead of understanding people or where they're coming from. That was a good observation, I agreed.

Our snacks were done. Our conversation was wrapping up. Mark indicated it was time for him to go, and just like with Zack, I respected his wishes to move on. Sometimes we feel this pressure to dig as deep as we can or go as far as we can in a conversation, but that might not be what people are ready for.

Mark and I exchanged social media contacts and shook hands. For a guy who hadn't wanted to talk to me at first, he had really opened up. The more I was willing to listen, the more he was willing to talk.

Wes and Caroline got back on the bikes and kept going. We rode all afternoon up long, straight inclines until we came to the state park. We'd climbed more than 4,000 feet that day. The rain had held off, and the day had turned out to be gorgeous. Now, my stomach insisted, it was nearly dinnertime.

The park where we were staying was fully green and leafy, and our cabin was perched high on the hills above the Ohio River. Vela and I looked out over the water and saw boats and barges heading up and down the waterway. I couldn't help but give her a kiss.

We headed to the restaurant up the road. Dinner was roast chicken and baked potatoes with blackberry pie for dessert. I gorged myself, then headed back to the cabin. As I settled on an Adirondack chair on the deck, I thought about my profession.

I relished being a pastor. I considered it a privilege and a call. Yet I wondered how often I said things that people didn't really want or need to hear. Each week I prepared to give people a sermon from the pulpit. My sermons were generally well received, and I believed they had their place as a point of value in the overall spiritual conversation. But I also wondered if I was sometimes guilty of tossing out sermons, viewpoints, opinions, and topics that buzzed across my congregation as unwelcomed as houseflies buzzing through the air. Was I answering questions that people weren't actually asking? I knew I was regularly telling people plenty of good things, but was any of what I was saying being received?

What I had seen on this trip so far was that the more I was willing to listen, the more people would talk about what was truly important to them, and the better I would get to know them and understand their points of need. I had been assigned a place in life, and other people had been assigned theirs. So if I truly wanted to connect with people—whether through a sermon or through a conversation—how much more strategic might it be to ask people first what was on their minds?

I wondered if often as pastors or as Christians we were so eager to lead people on toward where they needed to be—finding all that God desired for them, experiencing Jesus as Savior and Lord—that we missed the opportunity to connect with them where they were. I needed to understand where people were coming from. What they'd grown up with. What experiences had shaped them. Then we'd truly be talking. And then we might find an authentic connection point between us and see what our exchange of perspectives might inspire in each other.

As I started to imagine how I might incorporate more listening in my work at home, I thought about how Jesus meets people where they are. How he meets me where I am. Loving people the way Jesus loves them would mean trying to do that too. Giving people more time and attention, more empathy and respect. And coming to know people's hearts and stories the way he does.

— 24 —

DARKNESS AND LIGHT

The cabin was amazingly quiet when I awoke the next morning, June 18, the twenty-third day of the ride. Rain had fallen overnight. I got up early and watched the flowing river for a while from the deck, then I hiked along the beach in the stillness of dawn until I came to the cave that Cave-in-Rock State Park is named for. I made my way inside and found that the cave grew dark and narrow after twenty or thirty paces.

I turned around and paused for a moment, standing in darkness but looking outside to the light, wrapping my mind around the desire to be present with Jesus wherever I was. Inside a cave. On my bike. Having conversations with people. In everything I did, I always wanted to remind myself to see the light. I said a silent prayer of thanks for the day, then headed outside to join the rest of the team.

For today we'd scheduled a longer ride of 105 miles to Hardinsburg, Kentucky, with a climb of more than 5,200 feet ahead of us. Before getting on our bikes, however, we hopped into the support vehicles to drive into town for an early breakfast and then a ferry ride across the river.

As we exited the park, the road circled around, and we grew confused. We found ourselves driving the wrong direction on a one-way lane with a car coming toward us. We stopped the van and rolled down the window to ask directions so we could straighten things out. The driver let us know in no uncertain terms that we were absolute knuckleheads. We gave her no argument. She was right that we were going the wrong way. Yet her demeanor was less than helpful.

Fortunately we got ourselves straightened out, made our way into town, and found a restaurant. Surprise: the same woman who'd been so nasty to us turned out to be our server. She must have been late getting to work. She tried to smile at us, and we tried to smile at her, but the whole situation felt awkward. I didn't know how to make things right or if I should even try. Sometimes you have to let a situation reflect its truth without trying to fix it.

The service took more than an hour. The food was subpar, and our server never warmed up to us. Yet things took a brighter turn afterward. Glenn went to pay at the register and noticed an older man moving about behind him. Glenn said, "Go ahead. Don't wait for me." The man said, "Nah, I don't have to pay. I own the ferry in town."

Now, that was somebody I had to meet!

He wore jeans, a plaid shirt, and a red baseball cap. I soon learned that his name was Lonnie and he was seventy-eight years old and spoke with a Midwestern twang. We started visiting, and he invited me over to his office four blocks down the street.

Essentially the town of Cave-in-Rock, population 286, still exists because of this man. Twenty-six years earlier the ferry across the Ohio River had been set to be shut down. And if the ferry had died, then the town would have died with it. It was a smaller ferry, holding only fifteen cars. Lonnie and his wife, Shirley, had saved a little money, so they'd just up and bought it.

The ferry continued to keep the town going. The ride across the water was free, and it transported some five hundred cars a day.

I could see by the sparkle in his eyes how much Lonnie loved his community. The river was the biggest employer, he said, and he described how his town was the place where everybody from the surrounding countryside came together to meet—mostly at the churches. That was my opening. I asked Lonnie what he believed in.

"Jesus," he said simply. "What else is there? God holds this town together."

He took me back in time and described how he'd met Shirley when they were in high school. She'd been a brilliant girl who graduated from high school when she was only sixteen. They'd dated and married a few years later. He'd become a contractor and worked to build highways near Chicago. She'd raised their children, taught Sunday school, and helped run the family business. In time they'd come back to southern Illinois and invested in farming. They'd enjoyed fifty-seven loving years of marriage. But then Shirley had contracted cancer. She'd fought it with everything she had, but it had finally gotten the best of her. Shirley had died two years earlier, and when Lonnie showed me her picture in his office, he teared up.

"That was a real hard good-bye." He cleared his throat, and the stories stopped while Lonnie blew his nose into his handkerchief. I looked at him, and he looked at me, and it felt like a moment of connection between us. We both knew the joys of a long marriage.

Then he launched into more stories. Lonnie had a deep river of stories.

He told me about some of the larger rock formations in town and how the town boasted the largest fluoride deposit in the United States. We talked about fishing and politics and more about ferries and tugboats.

I mentioned how as a teen I had installed radios in tugboats on the

Mississippi when I was working for my dad. Then Lonnie listened while I told a story of my own.

One time I was working on a tugboat with my younger brother, Chuck, and I told him to put up an antenna while I worked in another section of the boat. While he worked I kept hearing the horn blow—loudly.

After an hour Chuck came to me, totally disheveled, and said, "Oh, really funny, Neil, blowing that horn in my ear the whole time."

I gave him a puzzled look. "Not me," I said.

I followed Chuck back to where he'd been working on top of the captain's bridge. A wire went from inside the bridge to the top of the bridge. The captain would normally pull the wire to set off the horn. Chuck had been stepping on and off the wire the whole time. He didn't know he was blowing his own horn.

Lonnie laughed. Here was a guy who loved tugboats, and I'd had my own tugboat story to tell. It wasn't just me listening to him anymore. He was glad to hear a story from me about something he was interested in. We'd gone to that place of mutual storytelling.

He showed me all around his office. Our conversation returned to faith, and Lonnie said this area of the state was quite religious, with a lot of God-fearing folks in the region. I asked him what he might say to someone who didn't believe.

"What do you have to lose?" Lonnie said. "Jesus gives you hope. All we got is hope."

Lonnie told me how he'd been hurt in an industrial accident in 1983, and his organs had started shutting down afterward. The doctor had told him to go home to die, that there was nothing more they could do. So Lonnie had gone home. Shirley had prayed. Their church had prayed. Slowly, surely, Lonnie had gotten better.

"I don't understand these things," Lonnie said, "why one person lives and another person dies. They're beyond me."

"I think they're beyond all of us," I said.

Through the huge picture windows of his office, we could look out across the river and see the ferry. After a few moments I wondered aloud about the ferry's schedule—and if the team and I would miss it.

"Don't worry," Lonnie said. "I'll hold it for you."

And he did.

He walked me outside and over to the ferry just as the rest of the team arrived at the terminal. Lonnie clasped my hand with both of his hands, squinted, and nodded as if in approval. We climbed aboard, the ferry blew its horn, and the boat broke away from the shore. The cool wind of the Ohio River caught us all.

I watched Lonnie grow smaller on the bank and gave him one final wave. He took off his hat and tipped it our direction.

This man had never been onstage or made the national news, at least not that I knew. But he had loved his wife and his family, and he'd saved his town. He seemed like a man who had experienced a lot of genuine success. I was in awe.

Once off the ferry we started riding again, but my lengthy conversation with Lonnie had slowed us down. By lunchtime we had only pedaled 30 miles. We ate quickly and agreed to pick up the pace. We cycled for another 20 miles, then stopped at a gas station, where I met a grizzled man outside the store. Tall and bespectacled, he was a jittery sort who spoke very quickly. I asked a few questions, and he took off on an intense monologue. He talked about the history of crime in the area and the Ku Klux Klan. He wasn't making much sense, and out of the corner of my eye I saw team members edging away from him.

When I finally got a word in, I asked what had brought him to the area. He talked about coming from California, then launched into a diatribe against Hispanics and the Hmong people, insisting it was getting too hard to trust your neighbors in that state. I let him talk for a while, just listening, then I asked a carefully worded question about faith. His response set me on edge.

"It really takes religion to make man do evil things," he said.

I asked him to explain, and he told me about being kidnapped, beaten, and raped by a priest when he was only eleven years old. As an adult he'd figured out how to sue the church. Then he had turned to Scientology for a while and gone through their training.

His speech became more forceful, aggression just barely under the surface. He spiraled back to the subject of being hurt by the church and said with a snort, "If it wasn't for Jesus, I would have killed them all."

I wasn't sure if this guy was off his nut or genuinely traumatized, and I had to fight the temptation to write him off. He talked for another fifteen minutes or so. And the more he talked, the more convinced I was that he'd genuinely experienced a lot of heartache. Although there was no way to fully sort out his story in this short time, I wanted to offer him compassion—at the very least, a listening ear. As he talked and I listened, he did seem to dial down his intensity a little. At last we shook hands and said our good-byes.

As the team members and I continued riding, I thought about how I'd given him an inch of listening and he'd given me a mile of talking. Listening can be like that sometimes. People can be bursting with angst, ready to blow like a volcano. When people have been wounded, it's easy for them to lash out at the nearest person, even if the nearest person never did them any harm. When you encounter people like this, it's not always easy to give them a listening ear. Yet it is a needful ministry.

We continued along the route and found ourselves in Amish country again. Cows grazed in open fields, and we passed another horse and buggy on the road. The serenity of the land filled me with peace—such a contrast from the intensity of my last conversation. We spotted a tiny store in front of a farmhouse and stopped for a quick look. It was filled with items for the

Amish community: linen, German Bibles, baby blankets, simple clothing, and grammar books. We spoke to the proprietors for a while, then kept riding. We pedaled past a lumber mill and entered a deep forest. The air around us grew dark, but soon we burst out into the sunshine again. We were making better time than we had in the morning and hit the 105-mile mark by early evening.

We ate at a diner in Hardinsburg. That took a long time. Then it took us some time to find the place we'd reserved for the next two nights, a large waterfront house on Rough River Lake. Everybody was exhausted when we reached it at last. We were at that point when we all needed our own space, although we were getting along okay. But there weren't enough bedrooms at the lake house for us all to have privacy. Wes didn't want to share a room, so he jumped in the van and spent the night in a nearby hotel. I understood completely.

The next day we took a welcomed day off and did as little as possible, although Wes, Jeff, and I did drive to a shop in Hardinsburg to get the bikes worked on. Wes and I both had bottom brackets that needed replacing, but the shop didn't have the parts. The technician shot a ton of grease into our brackets, and we hoped for the best.

After that the guys dropped me off at a lunch place, where I met with a mentor of mine from college days. Jim had been in our wedding, but I hadn't seen him for years. He had driven an hour from his home in Owensboro to see me.

I was so glad to see my old friend. A faithful, understated guy with a great family and a deep relationship with the Lord, he'd helped teach me to listen to people by listening to me. He'd been one of the first people I ever fully trusted to talk to about my life. But now it was my time to lend a listening ear because Jim was going through a deeply painful season in his own life. His college-aged son had recently been in a car accident, lingered in a coma for thirty days, and then died.

Jim and I spent three hours together that afternoon, looking at both the darkness of suffering and the light of God's beauty, and pouring into each other's souls. We shed tears and talked about the longing we both felt for heaven. It wasn't an easy talk, but connecting deeply as longtime friends bolstered us both.

That evening the team and I grilled steaks and played Ping-Pong at the lake house. Afterward we talked about where we were as a team. We had a lot of love and respect for one another. Yet we also had to acknowledge the sheer challenge and arduous logistics of working together so closely for more than a month. For the riders, this meant the physical work of bicycling as well as the mental work of learning to ride together and draft off each other. The support staff, meanwhile, had to keep everything running smoothly. Plus, they were riding in slow-moving vehicles day after day, traveling more slowly than you'd drive through a school zone. That took its toll.

We also talked about the conversations I was having with people. I told them more about meeting Lonnie, a man who was clearly stable and accomplished in spite of the pain he'd gone through. I related a little more from my talk with the troubled man at the gas station who seemed to be struggling toward peace. Then I shared a bit about my relationship with my mentor Jim and about some of the pain he was experiencing lately. The contrast of those three stories struck us all.

We had nine days of the trip left, and I encouraged each person to make the most of the time remaining. I didn't want us to coast to the finish. I wanted us to finish strong. Surely there would be more contrasts ahead, more highs and lows, more respect and tension.

More darkness and more light.

— 25 —

SIMPLE, CLEAR PRIORITIES

I emerged from our day off feeling refreshed. The other team members looked more alive too. It was a rainy, misty morning when we left the lake house on June 20. We had 100 miles to go that day, from Hardinsburg to Harrodsburg, Kentucky, and we pedaled out eagerly over tree-lined roads still wet from the morning's downpour.

At noon we pulled over in the small town of Sonora because I had a phone interview scheduled for a radio program. I found a sheltered area near some train tracks and phoned the studio to do the interview, but there was no response. Nobody on our team had realized we'd crossed over into the eastern time zone. It was actually 11:00 a.m. at the radio station, not noon, so I'd called in an hour early without realizing it.

Vela and Jeff had left in one of the vehicles to pick up a new team member, Sarah, from the airport. Sarah was flying in to assist for a few days. So the new plan, now that we knew the correct time, was to stay put and wait until they returned. I was a bit bummed at changing plans and having to wait but decided to make the best of it. We all ambled over to a nearby diner and sat down. I ordered meatloaf and mashed potatoes with strawberry shortcake for dessert. I chowed down.

Delores, an older woman with a kind face, owned the café with her family. When I asked if she could talk, she said she was really busy but hesitantly agreed to give me two minutes. The restaurant was a gathering place for the community, she said, when I asked about her diner. Each Thanksgiving she stayed open for anybody who wasn't connected, who might not have a family to eat with. She had her regulars each year, and if any of them didn't show up, she'd check on them to make sure they were okay. We talked about the kindness often evidenced in smaller communities, and she asked me to sign her guest book.

The conversation appeared to be over. But as I was signing the book, a picture on a nearby display case caught her eye, and she asked if she could tell me a story. Something had arisen in her; she desired to talk more. It felt like a magical moment. This opportunity to go deeper in our conversation was serendipitous—nothing I had conjured up. I nodded, and she continued talking.

"Mom died in 1999," Delores said. "We were really grieving. I was coming home one day and planned to swing by the cemetery where Mom was buried. I wasn't much of a strong believer, but I'd been asking for a sense of Mom's presence. The sun was really bright that day, shining through the clouds. When I looked up, I swear I saw an angel.

"I rushed home to get my camera. I only live three minutes from the cemetery. When I came back, the angel wasn't there. I took a few pictures anyway, and when the pictures came back from developing, you could see the profile of Mom in the sky. You could see her glasses, nose, the way her hair curled up in the back, even her earring. Mama always wore earrings.

"I didn't say anything to anybody about the image in the photo because I figured they'd think I was crazy. But when my son came home from work, I showed him the picture. He looked at it and said, 'That's Grandma.'"

Delores showed me the picture up close, and I had to admit that it looked like a person's image in the sky. "What do you think, Delores?" I asked. "You think that was a gift God gave you?"

"I do," she said. "He was letting me know Mom was okay, because I was definitely asking him. The experience reinforced my belief in God."

I knew Delores had work to do. So I thanked her for her time, watched as she disappeared into the kitchen, and marveled at the story she'd just told me. Twenty years ago, if somebody had told me that story, I might have responded out loud with skepticism. I might have argued that God doesn't work that way, at least not according to what I knew about God.

But over the years my theological biases have been stretched and even broken in places. I've learned that things don't always neatly fit inside our boxes. And I've had plenty of seminary professors who'd agree. Who's to say God wasn't giving Delores a specific bit of encouragement? At the very least, it wouldn't have done any good if I'd been argumentative with her. Delores and I had established a connection, and if I'd seen her the next day, we could have talked more.

I was still thinking about this when a young woman named Megan sat down at a nearby table with her young son and her teenage brother. We started talking. Megan and her brother both worked at their family trucking company, which hauled grain and fertilizer. Megan had been to university and was the bookkeeper for the company.

When I asked her what she most enjoyed about living in the area, Megan talked about her family and how everybody in the community pretty much got along. Then with a grin, without being prompted, she described a community event they all enjoyed called the Bucksnort Festival, which I thought was a terrific name.[1] They had live bands and parades, food trucks, games for the kids, and lots of down-home celebrating.

The festival had given everybody in the area something to look forward to each year, Megan told me, but it wasn't being held anymore. I didn't ask why. What interested me most was the tiny note of sadness in her voice. It seemed as if perhaps a brief window in her heart had opened. I saw an image of longing, an expression of her wanting something more. I asked her about her dreams for the future.

"I don't really have any big dreams," she said. "I want my kids to be happy, and I'd like to retire someday. I believe in Jesus, and I'd like my kids to believe, but I'm not going to force them. I'm going to teach them principles along the way in hopes they'll learn what they need to."

It was a short conversation, packed with value. At least it felt that way to me. The time for my radio interview was coming up, so we said good-bye, and I headed back to the sheltered area we had found, where I could have a fairly undisturbed phone conversation. On the walk I thought about how there's sometimes a bias against the South in other parts of the country. People think Southern folks aren't as sophisticated as the rest of the nation.

But Megan was educated and articulate and had expressed herself thoughtfully and carefully. She didn't appear to overly strategize her life, as people often do in the big city of Dallas where I live. Yet there was something grounded and winsome about her way of living. She missed the Bucksnort Festival, and that bit of longing revealed far more about her than was communicated by first appearances. I sensed she missed a whole way of life that seems to be disappearing from our country. I also sensed she had a lot to offer the world.

When I reached the shelter, I paced up and down until the correct time, then called the studio again. The interview went well. A train whistle blew in the middle of it, and a loud truck rumbled down the road at nearly the same time, but I kept my cool and asked the host to wait a moment until it grew quieter again. I talked about the big goal of our trip, how we wanted to engage people and hear their stories all across America.

"I'm not trying to force anybody to believe anything," I said. "I'm genuinely interested in hearing what people have to say. We're in a culture right now that feels really confrontational, but it doesn't need to be that way. We can connect on deeper matters, even if we disagree, and still be respectful of each other."

The radio host agreed. We talked for a good half hour, and the show ended. Then Caroline, Wes, and I hopped on our bikes again and began the afternoon's ride.

We pedaled up and down gently rolling hills. The overcast skies lifted, and the sun broke through. A breeze blew, and corn stalks swayed gently in the fresh air.

We'd learned about a family from our church that was traveling through the area. Around 3:00 p.m. we rolled into a small town to find our friends standing on a street corner, cheering and waving, holding posters and signs. That gave us a boost of encouragement. We visited with them for a while, then continued on.

At Harrodsburg we hit the 100-mile mark just as evening fell. As usual I was starving. The aroma of grilled meat wafting from a Mexican restaurant was so inviting that we simply had to stop. Everybody wolfed down their respective tacos, chicken enchiladas, carne asada, and steak fajitas. The food was delicious.

I talked with the managers of the restaurant, a husband-and-wife team, Leigh and Jorge. With them was their little daughter, Charley. Leigh's father, Wayne, stood nearby, eagerly weighing in on the conversation.

We talked about the ins and outs of running a restaurant and about the history of the area. They told me Harrodsburg was the oldest permanent English settlement west of the Allegheny Mountains.

I asked the three adults what was most important to them, and Leigh talked about her family and children. "I just want to raise kids that contribute something good to society," she said, and I agreed we needed more of that today.

Jorge's parents lived in Mexico, and he lamented that he didn't get to see them much. He missed them a lot.

Wayne talked about how neighbors matter and how each person has obligations to others. "We have to care about people," he said simply.

The conversation turned to spiritual matters. Leigh and Jorge both talked about the importance of believing in God but admitted that running the restaurant left them little time for church. Wayne was a strong believer in Jesus Christ, and in Wayne's presence Leigh admitted that her dad wanted her and her husband to go to church more.

"I feel like even though you're not going to church, it doesn't take away from your love of Jesus," Leigh said. "We listen to Christian radio in the car all the time. Our children go to a Wednesday night program at the church. We're constantly praying for our kids, family, and friends. Church is amazing, but you can still have a great relationship with Jesus even though you don't go to church."

I wondered if she said this more to her father than to me, but I didn't express that thought. We all just grinned.

That night the team and I bedded down at the Shaker Village of Pleasant Hill. It was dark by the time we arrived, and the grounds were pitch black. The accommodations were simple—all the guys in one cabin, all the girls in another. It was late when we hit the sheets, and I was exhausted. It had been a day of conversations with people in small towns, a day of seeing the simplicity of hopes, dreams, interests, and passions outside of big cities.

I thought back to Delores, who opened her diner year after year on Thanksgiving and checked up on the regulars if they weren't there.

I thought of the young couple I'd just met at the Mexican restaurant, how Leigh just wanted to raise her children to be productive citizens, how her dad said we have responsibilities to help others, and how Jorge missed his parents. Their desire to take care of people and to keep close to one another was so apparent, their priorities in life so clear.

And I thought about my conversation with Megan, the young woman who missed the Bucksnort Festival but said she didn't really have big dreams. That conversation replayed in my mind the strongest. My head was on the pillow, and I was inches away from sleep, but I was still mulling over how we often think that life is so difficult to figure out. And sometimes it is. But other times we make it overly complicated.

I know I do. I'm a planner. A doer. A strategist with a chess-playing mind who's always thinking five moves ahead. But sometimes, in the midst of all my plans and actions and strategies, I can forget to really live.

After all, what is life, really? We grow up, get educated, find a job where we do something purposeful, hopefully fall in love and get married, have kids and teach them to be purposeful. Serve God. Help our neighbors. Grow old.

And that's life.

I didn't want to live distracted, forgetting what I know matters most. I wanted to give myself entirely to loving the people around me. Connecting and building bonds. Doing my best with each day. Simple, clear priorities.

Megan wasn't caught up in what she was going to make happen in the future. Her way of living communicated something about the ministry of Christ to me. Jesus said, "Do not worry about tomorrow, for tomorrow will worry about itself. Each day has enough trouble of its own."[2] That's what Megan appeared to be doing. Living in the moment.

As I drifted off to sleep, I concluded I would need to do much more of that myself.

— 26 —

HONESTIES

Those Shaker beds are completely comfortable, and I'd experienced the best night's sleep of the whole trip. Day twenty-six dawned, and I awoke early feeling great. We planned to travel another 100 or so miles today and climb another 6,000 feet. Already the weather was beautiful, with clear blue skies.

After breakfast Wes, Caroline, and I started riding and pedaled through more Amish country, large areas of farmland dotted with old wooden barns. Then we came to more populated areas with houses and average-sized yards. Lawn mowers buzzed. Everybody we passed initiated a wave and a smile. I mean *everybody*! Judy kept count. By late morning her tally was up to more than a hundred.

Next we rode through a more rural area again. Out in the middle of nowhere, people had set up a rest stop for cyclists, complete with a covered area and snacks, water, and supplies, all free. They'd done it just to be neighborly. We stopped and chowed down.

In the city of Richmond, we rode through the campus of Eastern Kentucky University with its stately buildings, manicured grounds, and red-bricked sidewalks. A young man was walking along a sidewalk, so I slowed down, introduced myself, and asked if he wanted to talk. He was bearded, midtwenties, muscular, and wearing a cool black T-shirt and shorts.

Brandon liked the area and the university classes, he said, but wanted to get out of the Bible Belt soon because of its "closed-mindedness." I asked for an example of what he'd seen, and he explained that he'd grown up quite conservative and had even worked as a youth pastor for a while. But he'd been burned by the church and had walked away from his faith. He'd been married at the time, but when all the trouble in the church occurred, his wife had divorced him. Since then he'd tossed it all aside. He didn't even believe in God anymore.

"Obviously it wasn't everybody in the church who hurt me," Brandon conceded. "But I encountered a lot of intolerant people there. Just general closed-mindedness. Homophobia. Things like that. People very resistant to change or growth. People afraid of anybody whose culture was different than theirs."

We talked for a while longer, and it felt like I needed to ask my questions very carefully. At times Brandon would begin to explain more of his story, but then he would stop abruptly, almost as if he'd said too much. I'd ask a few more careful questions, and he'd talk a bit more, but then he'd stop again, as if he was scared he would be berated if he told me everything. I sensed that there was much brokenness in his story, although he made it clear that he didn't want to be pitied.

At one point Brandon said, "I don't want to be treated like I'm damaged goods." When he said that, I felt it. He was almost rebuking me. His words had a sting to them.

The blue sky still radiated the sun's brightness as we said our good-byes. A few puffy white clouds lazed in the sky. Wes, Caroline, and I kept pedaling, heading out of the city. We moved slowly within the traffic, and occasionally we cut through residential areas. Before we reached the other side of the city, we spotted a woman carrying a box out of a restaurant to her car. We stopped and offered to help. She said, "Don't worry about it," and loaded the box. Then we started talking.

Bonnie was middle-aged, friendly, African American. She explained she was always busy, but never too busy to talk. This was her restaurant, which her kids helped her run. I asked how many children she had. She said three, all grown. She stopped when she said this, nodded with a wan smile, then continued with a choke in her voice. About fifteen years ago she'd lost a daughter, who was only nine. One of the older siblings had been driving the little girl to school, and a truck had hit them head-on. Time and again on this trip we'd heard such stories of grief.

"So, we just do what we can," Bonnie said. "It's rough, but by the grace of God we make it."

We had only just met, and already she was telling me some of the harder details of her life. I felt stunned—and honored. "How did you ever get through that hard time?" I asked.

"If it hadn't been for God, I wouldn't have made it," she said. "Folks sometimes wonder, *How am I going to make it today?* but they don't know who I know. God is my life. Everything I do is about God, even my restaurant. It's hard to explain, but when God tells me to do something, I do it. The restaurant's how I make a living, but if I see a need, I try to fill that need. We do meals for kids during the summer in conjunction with the school. Or if a homeless person is around and says they're hungry, we feed them. No questions asked. I live day by day, and I know God's got me."

"Wow," I said. "Really cool."

Bonnie smiled, and this smile was full of life. "To be honest, I was just on my way to buy a pair of shoes for a homeless guy. He came into the restaurant today and didn't have shoes. So we talked, and I asked him if he'd like a pair of shoes. That's where I'm going right now."

"Wow," I said again. I had run out of words.

"I never worry." Bonnie was on a roll, and I just listened. "I know God's going to provide. My husband died four years ago, and times are hard. He was only forty-nine. But God's grace gets us through every day.

"I helped my older daughter through university. She's got her master's degree today. And I'm helping my son through university now. A lot of times he'll say, 'Mama, how are we going to make it?' And I'll say, 'The Lord will make a way.' He's beginning to see that, and he'll even say the same thing to me now. He'll ask, 'How are we going to make it?' Then he'll stop and say, 'Oh, wait, I know. *The Lord will make a way.*' That's what it is, right there. Jesus is my all in all. We have nothing to fear."

I was shaking my head at this woman's faith. I asked her if we could pay for the shoes she was going to buy for the homeless man. She laughed and said no. But I asked again. She laughed out loud, nodded, and gave me a hug.

"Jesus brought you along this road today," she said as we gave her the money and exchanged warm good-byes.

Caroline, Wes, and I pedaled out of the city and into the countryside again. The route grew hilly. One hill rolled right into the next. The trees on either side of the road stretched leafy branches overhead, and our way was shady but steep. Coming down the other sides of those hills, we really flew.

We continued to see houses by the sides of the road, and at one point a loose dog gave us chase. He ran full tilt for a good two hundred yards, zipping along beside us, barking his fool head off, just a white and black streak of speed. Finally he petered out and started slinking back to his yard. He seemed like a good dog, and we didn't mind being chased.

People continued to offer waves from their front porches, and Judy kept counting. All in all, she counted 245 waves before the day's end.

The afternoon grew late, and as we neared the 100-mile mark, we stopped for supper. We dined on beef brisket, barbecue ribs, baked beans, potato salad, and coleslaw.

In the parking lot afterward, I met a group of six motorcyclists, part of the American Legion Riders. They were all big guys on Harley-Davidsons, and all had shaggy beards or goatees. They were heading into the restaurant to get some beers. They'd come from New York and Michigan and joked about the routes they took and who got to pick where they went. They rode for charity, mostly, and camaraderie, raising money wherever they went for children's hospitals, schools, scholarships, veterans' homes, and severely wounded military personnel.

"Legion Riders are good people," said one of the men, who introduced himself as Howard. "Work and family are what's most important to us. That and God and country."

I asked the group if they all agreed with Howard, and they nodded and grunted affirmations. Then I picked up on the theme of God and country and asked them to explain more about their faith. Did they ever talk about that among themselves?

"Nah, not really," said one of the guys. "We all have our own beliefs."

One of the guys said he'd married a preacher's daughter. "I'm all good," he added with a grin. "I was baptized Catholic, confirmed a Lutheran, worked at an Assemblies of God camp, and now I attend a United Methodist church. I got all my bases covered."

All the guys laughed, and I laughed right along with them. I asked what they thought about Jesus. Who was Jesus to them?

"A friend," said one.

"The Savior," said the guy who'd married the preacher's daughter.

The guy on the far end shrugged and said he wasn't sure if Jesus was real.

Another guy shrugged and said he wasn't sure either.

We talked a bit more, just about this and that. The conversation started to wrap up, and I said, "Well, thanks, guys. I really enjoyed this." I sincerely meant it. They had all been fun to talk with. The guy on the far end who'd said he wasn't sure if Jesus was real grinned and responded, "Thanks, we enjoyed it too."

That felt good. Here we were again facilitating conversations among friends. The team and I continued on to nearby Natural Bridge State Resort Park and found our accommodations. Although I had a deep ache beginning in my legs from the steepness of the day's route, I felt like God had been in charge of every aspect of the day. We'd had a series of honest conversations, one right after the other.

Our talk with Brandon had revealed that he'd been hurt and had walked away from his faith, but that he didn't want to be seen as damaged. That was honest.

Bonnie had gone through some hard challenges, but she approached her life now with faith and altruism. That was also honest.

And the group of bikers, riding for fun and camaraderie and to raise money for charity, how did I see them? A few of the guys sounded like they had some faith, while others didn't. But all of them felt accepted enough to give honest responses.

This was America. We'd had encouraging conversations about deeper matters today, and we'd received a variety of responses in return. More and more I was observing that the unity in this country was not found in any standardized belief system. It was found in people's wrestling with real life. Whenever we went deeper like that, we were taking steps toward greater understanding of each other, toward more meaning. From what I had observed today, many people were doing that.

The unity was found in the honesty.

— 27 —

COMEDY, TRAGEDY, ASSENT

I t was the twenty-seventh day of the ride, June 22, and I woke up foggy and in pain. My legs ached after yesterday's hills, and I winced at the thought that today's ride called for more. I've always tended to resist pain and tell myself I shouldn't hurt. But this ache thumped me with reality, and I couldn't ignore it. My body was breaking down after all this riding. I wanted to make it to the end and to finish strong, but for the first time I was wondering if I could do it.

We were late getting on the road this morning, which created more tension. The planned time of departure had seemingly been ignored. Again. We'd been late starting almost every day of this trip.

No one person was to blame. Each morning another new reason cropped up. But I was pretty sure I had communicated my wishes to the team clearly, more than once. For twenty-seven days I hadn't gotten what I'd wanted.

What should I do? I wondered. I didn't want to be a nag. I didn't want to be testy.

Just live life, a voice in my head seemed to say as we began to pedal through the Kentucky back roads. That became my new goal for the day: just live life.

The morning roads mostly wound through low-income rural communities. We saw old barns, old fences, old vehicles. I counted eighty-six mobile homes before I stopped counting.

The countryside itself was beautiful and leafy, and the breeze against my skin felt good. I should have been happy, but I wasn't. I pedaled hard, trying to warm up, trying to find a flow, but my legs were screaming at me. My stomach was irritable too. Six days from the end of the trip, I realized I was hitting a wall.

It made sense. I remembered that Hawaii's famed Ironman competition consists of a 26-mile run, a 112-mile bike ride, and a 2.4-mile swim. Each leg is considered a difficult distance for an endurance athlete to tackle. For instance, the running portion of the Ironman is a full marathon. When people run just a marathon alone, that's a huge accomplishment—and they do it maybe once a year—or once a *lifetime*. But on this trip our goal was to ride an average of 100 miles each day. That equates roughly to doing the bike-riding portion of the Ironman thirty-three days in a row. No wonder exhaustion was catching up to me, punching me in the face.

The sky clouded over. It wasn't yet 10:00 a.m., and already I was hungry. We'd eaten a big breakfast, but it never seemed to matter how much I ate; I was always famished. On this trip, if you put it in front of me, I'd eat it. Chicken. Cheeseburgers. Ice cream. Meatloaf. Mashed potatoes. Energy bars. Ice cream. Coconut water. Trail mix. Granola bars. Bananas. Did I mention ice cream?

I'd never been a huge dessert person at home, but on this trip every taste sensation seemed heightened by the vigorous exercise. Every taste bud seemed to sit up and howl with constant demands. That's why it made sense to stop for a midmorning snack at a store we found where each item cost only a buck.

I spotted some electric-blue marshmallow sugar-sprinkled treat thingies, and they looked scrumptious. *Are you insane?* my gut said. I bought a pack, walked outside, and stared the first cake in the face. The shelf life must have been five thousand years. I shoved a baseball-sized spongy gob into my mouth and chewed. But as soon as the convenience store treat slid down my gullet, I knew it was a mistake.

Caroline, Wes, and I hopped on our bikes and kept riding. Sure enough, twenty minutes later, my stomach started doing flip-flops. I hit the brakes, skidded to a stop, and barfed in the weeds. Rain began to fall. I hopped back on my bike, rode some more, stopped and threw up again. It was still raining. I found some beet juice in the van and drank it, thinking vegetables might counterbalance the sugar. Again I hopped on my bike, rode, stopped, and barfed a third time.

It was now almost lunchtime. I was wet, cold, miserable—and I had yet to have a single conversation on this day. I rode for a while longer, then pulled off at a gas station to rinse my mouth and look for somebody to talk with.

Two women were working inside the store. I asked if they'd like to talk, but they were too busy. "Talk with Elwood," said one and nodded toward the back of the store. "He's got plenty of stories."

I found Elwood, a guy in his midsixties with glasses and a mustache. We needed to get away from the noisy front counter, so we moved over to stand in the only empty spot in the store, which was near the freezer case. The AC was blowing. I was wet, freezing cold, and nauseated. Elwood was chewing gum and drinking coffee. He spoke with a strong twangy drawl.

"I'm gonna tell you something that really happened to me one time," Elwood said. "I'm a coon hunter, okay? I was about sixteen years old and treed a coon. But I didn't have no ax to chop down the tree. So I went back to my house and got my dynamite and put it in the tree. I set the dynamite off.

"Somebody said, 'Did you get the coon?'"

"I said, 'No, and I never did see the tree no more.'"

He laughed. "That dynamite blowed everything up."

I laughed along with him. He obviously enjoyed taking me along on this episode from his past, a story he'd likely told over and over. The humor seemed to open a door to somewhere a little deeper. I asked, "Elwood, what's important to you? Like, if somebody is getting to know you and asks you that kind of question, what would you say?"

He scratched his head. "Well, you have to make friends to have friends. That's what my father taught. You can't run around by yourself with your nose stuck up in the air. You gotta get out and mix with people. That's as true today as it was yesterday."

"I like that," I said. "Let me ask this: I understand that this part of the country is fairly religious. Faith, God—is any of that important to you?"

"Very," he said. "Without faith you got nothing. Faith in Jesus. I don't go to church like I should. It's too far from my house. But I go every once in a while. Jesus truly makes a difference. Without him there's no future to look forward to. Life here on earth's just a testing ground—that's what I think. We've all done stupid stuff when we were young. Everybody's got some skeletons in their past. But we got to treat our neighbor like we want to be treated. Everybody's got to get along."

I couldn't help but smile. Elwood was a character, sure and certain, a good ole boy who liked to blow stuff up. But he had his deeper side too. We talked awhile longer, then said good-bye.

It was still raining as I walked out of the store. It had been a fun conversation, and my stomach felt a little better. But I was also struggling with how many times on this trip I'd heard from people who had given up on church. As a pastor I believed that Jesus loved the church, the gathering of people at a local assembly. I wasn't judging anybody who didn't go to church, but I wished that somehow the stories could be different. I wished that people would experience more of Jesus in the local church.

Under an awning on the sidewalk, I met a young couple named Josh and Kaylee. I guessed them to be college aged, although I wasn't sure. Josh was relaxed, with a thin beard and glasses, and looked a little older than Kaylee. She was pretty, smiled easily, and had cool purple-streaked hair. They told me they'd been dating fifteen months. He had his arm around her and looked very comfortable.

We talked about bicycles for a while. Josh and Kaylee said they liked living in a rural area where everything was quiet. We talked about relationships, and I asked them each to describe something they liked about the other person.

"Oh, I love her to death," Josh said. "I love her laugh. Her eyes. Pretty much everything."

"He's just so different." Kaylee smiled warmly but her voice trailed off.

"Than what?" I wondered out loud.

"My whole past," she said, still with a smile. "I've had a really tough life, been through some grueling stuff. Meeting him was a blast of fresh air for me. I was scared in the beginning, scared in the middle. But now it's like, 'Wow, I actually have this thoughtful, kind, gentle person who really cares about me. And he cares about my children 110 percent.'"

That surprised me. "How many children do you have?"

"Three boys," she said. "A four-year-old, a three-year-old, and a twenty-month-old."

"Wow, how great," I said. "Children are a blessing. You know, talking about a tough past conveys honesty and depth, and I'm honored that you told me. It looks like your life is changing now. What's made the difference?"

She thought a moment, still smiling. "It's hard. I was adopted when I was young, and I battle a lot with depression, PTSD, insomnia, and night terrors. But you can't look at each day and say, 'Life sucks.' You have to look at each day and say, 'I can do this. God put me here for a reason.' I used to be by myself a lot. I used to have no one." She turned to Josh. "But I have him now." She smiled again and turned back to me. "He's become a huge rock in my life."

Josh gave her shoulder a squeeze. "Her night terrors aren't as bad as they used to be. Maybe once a month is all now."

Kaylee leaned into Josh. "I was homeless for a while. I was—" here she paused, searching for the right word "—*hurt* as a kid. You don't understand this as a kid. Why nobody listens to you. Why you're mistreated or told you're useless. I didn't have a lot of family support growing up. It was hard."

"But now you're here, still smiling," I said.

"Yeah. You have to. People are going to tear you down and hurt you. They'll tell you that you can't make it in life. But you can't believe that lie." All the while she talked, she rubbed her arm almost compulsively. She looked down at her arm and said, "Sorry. That's a coping skill." She pointed to a small scab on her chin. "This too. I get nervous, so I pick at it."

"That's okay," I said. "You've been through so much, and you're so positive now. I'm curious—what would you say to people who are having a hard time?"

She looked thoughtful. "There's always something positive to think about, even when life's really hard. Maybe you just wake up and say, 'My hair looks good today.' You gotta keep going, keep pushing. Don't let people tear you down. Keep trying to make life better for yourself. When you smile, you're making somebody else's life better. Maybe that person is having a bad day too."

I turned to Josh. "What about your past? Was it better?"

He shook his head. "My past was rough too. My family was on drugs real bad. I witnessed my mom getting beat up by men. As a kid I was beat on by my stepdad. I seen my mom and my sister overdose. My mom was found dead last year in her bed from drugs. All kinds of stuff."

"That's so hard," I said. "How do you avoid bringing all that into this relationship? It looks like you guys are doing well. What gives you the ability to live differently now?"

"I've seen what drugs do to people," Josh said. "I don't want to be like that."

"Me neither," Kaylee said. They had both clearly taken warning from the severe things they'd seen in the past.

I asked if God or spiritual things made a difference for them, and they said they thought about spiritual matters from time to time and believed in God and the devil, but they didn't consider themselves religious.

"I grew up LDS," Kaylee said, referring to the Church of Jesus Christ of Latter-day Saints. "I was abused all those years. That makes it hard to believe now."

"We believe in God," Josh said. "But we definitely have questions. Like, why would God put a kid in those situations?"

Kaylee nodded her head in agreement. "Why would God allow a child to be abused, to be raped, to be made to feel worthless?"

"I'm so, so sorry," I said. "I can't imagine how hard it must be to believe in God, to believe he's good and worth pursuing, when you have been through all those hard things." I thought a long moment before I continued. "I don't want to give you any easy answers about God. But can I say one little thing? You can say no."

They both nodded.

"When I read stories about Jesus," I said. "I think Jesus gets it and cares."

"No problem with that," Josh said, and the admission seemed to lead him to another thought: "There's people all over the world who've been through lots worse stuff than we have."

Kaylee agreed. "God loves each and every person. God allows us to go through trials. Even after what I've been through, I don't think God hates me."

I could see they were both open to matters of faith, both chewing on these ideas, and I shared a bit more about how Jesus connects us to God. But I didn't want to push them. If I'd been younger, more aggressive, I probably could have driven them to pray what's known as "the Sinner's Prayer" to make sure of their salvation. But I didn't want to do that. I felt a restraint within myself. I did not want to exercise any power over these people, particularly Kaylee, who'd had older people exercise power over her so many times in her life.

Instead, I simply asked if they had a Bible. They did. I encouraged them to go home and read the stories of Jesus as found in the four gospels— Matthew, Mark, Luke, and John—and to pray something along the lines of "Jesus, show me you really care for me." They said they would.

That was it. We talked awhile longer, then said our good-byes.

My stomach continued to recover as we rode the rest of the day. The journey to our destination went as smoothly as I could've hoped for, considering the hilly terrain, my aching legs, and my overall exhaustion.

Throughout the day I frequently thought back to my conversation with Josh and Kaylee. I had so enjoyed those positive, thoughtful survivors. Yet I also sorrowed over them. It broke my heart that they were living with wounds because they had lacked a loving home and a strong support system. I believe Jesus sees it as a tragedy whenever a child is hurt or abused.

But they were making lots of progress in their lives. By opening up to me in such depth, they had given me a real gift. I could see we'd had a real connection.

Whether it was Elwood's humor or Josh and Kaylee's pain, you never knew what might become a door to a larger opportunity for conversation.

— 28 —

CURIOUS ABOUT THE FAMILIAR

On Sunday, June 23, my son-in-law Matt flew out to ride with us for a couple of days. Matt's an avid cyclist who regularly rides by himself all around Austin, Texas. It was going to be good to have another strong rider to block the wind for us, particularly because this was going to be one of our hardest riding days: 92 miles with a 6,000-foot climb. We'd be leaving Kentucky and ending up in the tiny town of St. Paul, Virginia.

Our planned route called for us to be fairly far from civilization, more so than on other days. I was curious to see what kind of conversations would take place—if any. My strategy was to let God be God in all areas of the trip.

But I didn't start out with a great attitude at breakfast. Part of this stemmed from exhaustion, but my own stubbornness was a factor too. I felt tempted to do the job of changing my attitude on my own, but nothing much was happening.

So often we pray, then keep running full steam ahead. We ask God to change something for us but keep trying, in our own power, to facilitate the change. I realized I was doing just that. So I switched my prayer to

Lord, change my attitude, then I throttled down my own determination and pledged to watch and see what would happen. I held on to my resolve to lean into the direction of a better attitude. But I wanted to let the Lord work out the change in his timing, in his way.

This morning I deliberately didn't goad the team into hurrying to get the vans packed on time. This morning I committed silently not to say, "Hey, c'mon, let's go!" I let all the team members move at their own pace. It was good for me to release myself from badgering them, and it was undoubtedly good for the team too.

Surprise: we left closer to our on-time mark than ever before.

We headed out over foggy roads, down the main pike for a while, then off on old Kentucky back roads, where we hit the hills. Matt had fresh legs and quickly proved a good climber. We passed mobile homes and another loose dog that sprinted alongside our bikes for a good two hundred yards, barking like a savage. He was big, mean-looking, some kind of rottweiler-Cujo mix. He darted in front of Caroline, nearly causing her to crash, dodged Wes completely, then spun around and zeroed in on my heel with his mouth open, his fangs razor sharp.

"Back off!" I shouted. The dog seemed to laugh and lunged closer. When his teeth touched my bicycling shoe, I grabbed my water bottle and doused his head. That cooled him off. He slunk away defeated.

At the top of the hill, the pavement changed. We entered a middle-class community with mowed lawns and a canopy of trees overhead. I didn't see any people outside. The houses ended before long, and we rode into a clearing. We pedaled another mile, and all traces of civilization disappeared except the road and power lines. The sun came out and we started to sweat. I kept my eyes peeled for someone to talk to, but I didn't spot a single person.

An hour passed as my mind wandered. I had been talking about faith, God, and church so much on this trip, I hoped I could meet people actually coming in or out of a church so I could talk to them. Many tiny churches dotted the backwoods Bible Belt landscape this morning. But 9:00 a.m. passed, the prime time for earlier church services, and we didn't see any open churches. Then 10:00 a.m. passed, and we pedaled by another couple of church buildings but didn't see any cars out front. Finally it was 11:00 a.m., the time when many churches hold their main services. We cycled by another church building but saw it also was closed.

I was just about to lament aloud about all the closed churches in the Bible Belt when we pedaled into Dorton, Kentucky, population 2,812, and saw a small church with the front door open. A number of people were hanging around outside, so we pulled over. I introduced myself and explained what we were doing.

The church people were friendly and smiling. A woman joked that everybody was welcome here, including us. It didn't matter what we were wearing or "even what you smell like," she said with a chuckle. I joked right back, apologizing for the sweat.

They introduced me to an older gentleman, their pastor. He was puffing nonchalantly on a cigarette, as is common in tobacco country. In Dallas that would have been taboo in many churches, particularly for a man of the cloth.

I grew super interested now. Pastor Davidson said hello and added it was time for church to start, but he would hold off for a few minutes while we talked. He lived two hours and ten minutes away, in Tennessee, and drove over to Dorton twice a week, Wednesdays and Sundays. He'd been doing that for the past nine years.

"The Lord sent me over here," Pastor Davidson explained with a gravelly voice. "I preach at a lot of churches around the area. They need a pastor, and I want to give them Jesus. He's the most important thing you can get."

He took a step back and checked his watch, being patient yet undoubtedly keeping an eye on the start time for the service. I hoped I could squeeze in another conversation or two before he made the call.

Two women stood nearby, and they instantly looked welcoming and warm and drew me in as an outsider. I learned that their names were Belinda and Esther, and I asked them to tell me a bit about their minister.

"He's awesome," Esther said. "A great shepherd."

"Dedicated," Belinda said. "Takes care of his congregation. We love him."

The pastor stepped forward again and explained that the church was close-knit, welcoming, and supportive of one another and the community. Although they were a small congregation, they had baptized five new believers in the past six months.

I met one of the new believers, Randy, an older man with a bushy white beard. He said he'd lived in the area all his life but had never gone to church or thought much about God. His older brother had attended church for years without making a commitment. Finally the older brother had decided he'd waited long enough, so he'd decided to follow Jesus. Then Randy had started coming to church too. He'd believed in Jesus shortly afterward.

A deacon poked his head out of the building and hollered that it was time to start the service. We all shook hands and said our good-byes. It felt good to know that people were being cared for in this little town in eastern Kentucky.

Two of our team members asked to use the restrooms inside the church. By the time they came back out, the church service was underway. The folks inside were singing one of the same songs that we sing at our church in Dallas.

We hopped on our bikes and rode for another hour and a half and stopped for Mexican food at the only restaurant for miles around. My stomach wasn't feeling great, but I downed a chicken enchilada anyway, and we kept riding. The road from there onward felt rough, and the grade turned steep immediately. We rode up and up, with Matt leading the charge, around switchbacks and up steep grades. The climb upward never seemed to end.

By midafternoon everyone except Matt felt out of fuel. We stopped at a convenience store for another restroom break. The enchilada was doing flips in my stomach, but for some reason I still felt hungry. Anything and everything looked good to eat. I wolfed down some beef jerky from the back of the van, then inhaled a sports drink and an ice cream bar from the store. We kept riding. Fortunately everything stayed inside of me.

Near dinnertime we pulled into the little town of St. Paul. We rode through the town square and around the block. A car came up behind us, and the driver motioned for us to pull over. Curious, we did. A big guy who looked to be in his midsixties climbed out, rushed over to us, and introduced himself as Jerry, the editor and publisher of the town newspaper. He asked a few questions about what we were doing. We told him about the trip, and he asked if he could write a story on us. I said sure. So when most of the team headed to our motel for the night, a few of us went over to Jerry's office.

We talked with Jerry for forty minutes. He was a hard-boiled small-town journalist with a degree in criminal justice who hated conjecture and loved facts. "When I'm on a story I don't go looking for moonlight and magnolias," he said. "I go looking for corruption and evil. People look at our town and see a river and trees, but they have no idea of the fortunes that were made and lost right in this area. You want to find corruption? Follow the money."

He asked us question after question about the road trip, which I'm sure he would verify later. Then he talked in great detail about the history of the town, dating back to 1890. He knew names and dates and explained how fortunes were made and lost in land speculation at the turn of the twentieth century. More recently coal mining had anchored the economy, but that had all gone bust in the late 1970s. He was concerned about the town nowadays because many young people were leaving.

"Nobody new has come here to live for the past fifty years," Jerry said. "We're hoping you'll send us some settlers. One of the things that's hard in this area is we're just lily-white. There's no diversity, and that's no good. It gets down to where you only have one point of view, and that can be very corrosive in a community. Hey, I'm not liberal. I'm not conservative. I'm a radical—probably the only one in this town."

He laughed, and I laughed along with him. Jerry told me he'd worked over the years to promote justice in various capacities. He was suspicious of small-town prosecutors, who tried only the most promising cases in an effort to make a buck from federal anticrime dollars. He detested the prison-for-profit system, and he'd worked to help expose the truth for falsely accused prisoners.

Our conversation turned to matters of faith and I asked him what he thought about Jesus. "Jesus was a radical," Jerry said. "They killed Jesus. They may kill me. I don't know. I saw Jesus once, at the lowest point of my life."

"Wow," I said. "You mind talking about that?"

He thought a long moment. "Actually, I would mind. Because if I start talking about it, I might begin to think it didn't actually happen. It was something that I didn't expect would ever happen to me. But it did. And it changed the way I looked at a lot of things. I'm not a believer in any organized religion because whenever I'm in a church I'm surrounded by people who pray for stuff, and every prayer begins with 'Please give me . . .' and then fill in the blank. I don't do that. I say, 'God, am I doing what you want me to do? I can't see the road signs. I'm watching for you. Do I need to reposition myself?' That's how I pray. I try to listen. I try to pay attention. Usually when I pray like that my eyes are opened."

He was speaking somewhat cryptically, but I liked where he was heading. I decided to press a little further and asked him to explain more of his beliefs.

"Much of the ministry of Jesus was about helping people," Jerry said.

"You serve God by serving people. We all have about the same amount of trouble in our lives, although a lot of people are carrying heavy loads. Sometimes it's hard to fully understand the loads others are carrying because we can hardly understand our own. I try to use the newspaper to remind people of the good they can find and warn them not to be misled by people who say they have all the answers. Writing can be a ministry, although I seldom tell people about it by using that word."

Jerry had a poetic way of talking and a marvelous mind. I wasn't sure I grasped all that he believed, and I doubted that he would ever tell me fully because he wasn't that type of person.

I couldn't help comparing this talk with the conversation I'd had at the small church earlier in the day. The church folks were more straightforward in their faith perhaps, more overt. They loved Jesus, testified about Jesus, baptized people in Jesus' name, and opened their arms to the community in Jesus' name. But Jerry fought for justice. He loved his community, too, and he served God by serving people—by asking questions and writing stories.

Thinking all that through caused me to have a better attitude by the end of the day. People were doing a lot of good in this part of the country.

We headed to the motel, joined the rest of the team, and ate a late dinner. The motel was clean and new, and I was asleep in two seconds. But ten minutes later the fire alarm clanged. All of us dragged ourselves outside in the dark and stood around for an hour.

There was no fire. Some guy, not from our group, had taken too hot a shower, and the mist had set off the fire alarm.

When the all-clear signal came, we shuffled back to bed. But now I couldn't sleep because the air-conditioning unit in our room was wonky. Whenever it turned on or off, it buzzed. There was no way to stop the buzzing sound.

I called the front desk, but there was no fix. So the AC buzzed on and off, on and off, all night long. I was very aware that another long ride was facing me in the morning. Somewhere around 3:00 a.m., I made a mental note to pray for a good attitude again before I started my day.

My last thoughts, as I slipped toward sleep, found me revisiting the various expressions of faith in Jesus I'd encountered the previous day. I'd heard Jerry's criticism about the church people, and I wondered how the church people saw him. Did either Jerry or the church folks realize the similarities between them—their shared values and goals? Were there assumptions on both sides that crowded out curiosity and blocked their view of each other? Maybe it was easier for me to spot their similarities as an outside observer.

That got me thinking about whether there were people in my world I'd made inaccurate assumptions about. People with whom, if I were listening more closely, I'd find something that surprised me. Commonalities to bond over. Distinctions to appreciate. Different experiences to acknowledge and respect. Was I as curious and observant with those who seemed familiar to me?

I made a mental note to pray about that too.

— 29 —

THIS. HERE. NOW.

I was in a dark, dark place. Last night had been rough. Thanks to the fire alarm and the buzzing air-conditioning unit, I'd barely slept. So I awoke on day twenty-nine tired all over. When I planned this trip, I had not considered the demands of rising each morning at 5:30 a.m., pushing hard for hours on end, and not stopping until 10:30 p.m., day in and day out. My stomach hurt as I crawled out of bed and stumbled into my clothes.

Once outside, I tried to say "Good morning" to the team like I meant it, but I wasn't fooling anybody. The day called for 104 miles and 7,000 feet of climbing. We were four days from the finish, and I wanted to encourage everybody to keep strong, to stay present in the moment, to make the most of each of these last days. But my smile was plastic.

If we rode with an easier pace, I felt sure I could handle the first 50 miles of the day. The last 50 miles I dreaded. I tried to suck it up—to accept the challenge ahead despite the condition of my collapsing body and spirit. I wanted to keep going strong and be up for those conversations we hoped to have today. Again, my whispered prayer was for divine appointments. I prayed that God would orchestrate this day exactly the way he wanted.

Flitting through my mind was a fragment of Scripture: "As your days, so shall your strength be."[1] I grabbed it like a life preserver. I'd been convinced that God wanted me to take this trip. Now I needed faith that he would give me the strength to finish.

At a breakfast joint I met a family of six, an elderly husband and wife and four grown-up kids, all around the table. The kids were related either by birth or marriage to the older folks. Everybody was smiling at first, but there was a choke in the daughter-in-law's voice, one I couldn't quite place. Her name was Mary, and she did most of the talking for the family. She said that she was a health-care professional and that family was so incredibly important to them. They all lived in the area, and Mary talked about how they valued being together as much as possible.

The conversation seemed to be progressing warmly, like most other conversations I'd had on this trip. We talked about the city and what each person did for work. John, the family patriarch, had been a coal miner. He had gray hair and a kind face. The conversation turned to faith, and John said they were all Christians with a strong trust in God. "Oh, I know he's the One," John said simply.

The woman sitting to my right wore a green T-shirt, and I didn't catch her name. She didn't say a word. From the corner of my eye I could see her profile. She looked like she'd been crying this morning, although no tears flowed now.

I asked what things had deepened their faith over the years. Mary told the story of how she'd been raised in church but had fallen away from her faith and didn't think about God much for several years. Then, thirteen years ago, she became pregnant. An ultrasound had been done at Vanderbilt University Medical Center, one of the finest hospitals in the country. The doctor had noted that the fetus had a ventricular septal defect

(VSD) and needed surgery immediately upon birth if it stood a chance of survival. An abortion was advised.

"I told the doctor, 'I'm keeping my baby,'" Mary said. "Then I started praying again. I went to church, and I was prayed for at church. Six weeks later I went back to Vanderbilt. The ultrasound lady put her hand on my arm. Tears came to her eyes and she said, 'It's a boy. He had us scared last time.' Then the doctor said, 'He's perfect. There's absolutely no sign of the VSD.'

"That's what brought me back to the Lord," Mary said. "God is always in our lives. He gives us what we ask for and what we need, although in his timing, not always in ours."

I rejoiced with Mary over this amazing answer to prayer. Then I turned to all the people around the table and asked what their dreams were. At last the woman in the green T-shirt spoke up. She motioned to John, the elderly man in the red shirt. "Only that the results of my dad's biopsy would come back okay." She began to cry, then stood and walked away to a far wall.

Suddenly it all clicked. On the outside they were trying to smile, but inside they were desperately battling the fear of the unknown. On my smaller scale, I knew how that felt today.

"We're headed to Kentucky today," Mary explained. "That's why we're all here together at breakfast this morning. For him." She motioned to John, her father-in-law. "He's had some trouble breathing. We're going with him to get the results today."

I turned to John. "How do you feel about that?"

"I don't think about it." John didn't sound ornery. Just matter-of-fact.

I offered to pray for the group, particularly for John, and they accepted. I asked John how he would like to be prayed for, and John said, "Just like you'd pray for anybody else."

Right there at the breakfast table at the diner we joined hands in a circle. I thanked God for the divine appointment of meeting this family today, for their hospitality, for their acceptance of me within their conversation. I prayed specifically for a good report today from the doctor. Then I prayed for each member of the family during this time—particularly John—that the peace of God, which surpasses all understanding, would guard their hearts and minds in Christ Jesus.[2] We all said amen together.

Peace filled the diner, a peace that didn't come from me. The woman in the green T-shirt joined us again. "Thank you for being here today," she whispered to me. "It was what we needed." The family and I shook hands and shared hugs all around.

Outside Wes, Caroline, Matt, and I climbed on our bikes, and I felt bolstered by the assurance that we were in the right place at the right time. God had arranged our appointment with that family to strengthen them through listening and prayer. Yet the morning's ride started out challenging. The roads rose in elevation right away. Despite the good conversation at breakfast, I felt more tempted than ever to put my bike on the rack and sit out the rest of the day in the van. Nothing felt good in my body. Every muscle ached.

We rode about ten miles, and I motioned for us to pull over. I needed to find a pit stop—fast. Normally I went to the restroom once a day for business's sake, but over the course of the last few days, I'd needed to go every time I stopped. This day felt worse than ever. My body was revolting against the exhaustion.

In the restroom I stared in the mirror as I washed my hands. My face looked hollow. Dark lines etched themselves underneath my eyes, and my cheeks looked drawn and thin. I was just about done for.

Could I go the distance?

Outside I climbed back on the bike and started turning the pedals. Again the road rose before us. We kept climbing, climbing, climbing. It seemed like hours on the hills. Finally we came to the tiny town of Lebanon, Virginia. A neighborhood was upon us, and as we passed a house, a woman spotted our bicycles and yelled to us with friendly enthu-siasm, "Hey! What are you doing around here?"

I welcomed another stop. The woman's husband walked around the side of the house from where he'd been working on a bicycle of his own. They introduced themselves as Cindy and Randy, both cyclists. Cindy explained that they knew of no other cyclists in their town, so they loved meeting other people who shared their passion. Randy described his love of riding and told us how the sport had helped him out of a hard spot. Six years earlier he'd been in poor health, smoking two packs a day. He'd known something needed to change. So he'd begun to ride, and his health had taken a turn for the better. Silently I wished I could say the same.

For the past two years, Randy had been the Virginia state mountain-biking champion for his age group. He said he was retired from the railroad but didn't look old enough to be retired. Cindy worked for the Virginia Department of Education.

My muscles recouped a bit while we stood and talked. It felt good just to be off my bike for a while. We talked about racing and safety during bike riding and some of the dangers we'd seen out on the road. We also talked about politics and the need for more and better jobs in the area. Two factories had been shut down but had recently been reopened, and everybody was happy about that. Cindy and Randy spoke carefully about various elected officials, and we talked about how cautious people need to be these days surrounding that whole subject. Then our conversation turned to faith.

"Well, we're in the Bible Belt," Cindy said. "We're Baptist, but we don't go to church anymore. I read my Bible every day, though."

There it was again.

Randy nodded. "I don't go because of all the hypocrisy. People act like they're living at the foot of the cross, but you see them Monday through Friday doing stuff they're not supposed to be doing. They look at me like,

'Why aren't you in church?' And I look at them like, 'Why are you cheating on your wife?'"

"We saw a prime example of hypocrisy in the church when our son was in high school," Cindy said. "They had this big celibacy poster they wanted all the kids to sign as a pledge for prom. My son said, 'I'm not signing that.' I said, 'You do what you want, but can you tell me why?' He said, 'Mom, half the kids who are signing that pledge have been sexually active for at least the past two years. That poster doesn't mean anything.'"

Randy nodded. "Or it's like folks who go to church who criticize abortion. They're against it until their daughter gets pregnant, then they push her to get an abortion. I appreciate honesty in people. You can't say one thing and then do another."

I nodded. I'd seen my share of hypocrisy. I knew what they were talking about. Every group has its portion of hypocrites.

Randy and Cindy offered us bottles of water, and the conversation turned to riding again. Matt's ears perked up when he heard that Randy held several KOMs in the area.

That term comes from an online app called Strava, which tracks cycling times for any rider connected to the app. You can ride different mapped routes in any area around the country, and the app measures who's fastest on certain hill climbs, crowning the fastest person "King of the Mountain"—or KOM.

The fact that Randy had multiple KOMs impressed Matt, who had been riding far faster and fresher today than Caroline, Wes, or especially me. He invited Randy to ride with us for a while. Randy grinned, suited up, grabbed his bike, and headed out on the road with us.

As we all pedaled to the top of a nearby hill, Randy really opened up about his thoughts on spirituality and Jesus. It probably helped that we were riding side by side instead of talking face-to-face.

Meanwhile, Wes's bike was having problems with the bottom bracket, and he struggled on the climb. When we stopped at the top, Wes wondered aloud if there was a bike shop in the area.

"The closest thing to a bike shop around here is back at my house," Randy said. Wes said that would be great. Glenn loaded Wes's and Randy's bikes up in the van, and they all headed back to Randy's house to work on Wes's bike. That spoke volumes to me. We had met Randy and Cindy less than an hour ago, but now they were caring for us. Their hospitality said much about true faith.

Caroline, Matt, and I kept riding. A few hours later we pulled over at a gas station so I could take another bathroom break. Wes had called to say that his bike was fixed and that he and Glenn were driving to meet us.

The restroom was grimy and worn. Grease smudges plastered the doors and sink. After I came out of the stall, I washed my hands, checked my phone, and found a text from Randy:

> Today was the most fun and enlightening day I've had in a long time. I know your goal was to promote religion, but there was no pressure or judgment from you. You guys are on the right track. For the first time in a long time, I've seriously thought about my spirituality. It was great meeting all of you.

Right there in the grimy gas station bathroom, I started to cry.

That text was a marker of exactly what we had hoped to do. We weren't out here on the road, beating our bodies, so we could argue with people. We weren't trying to convince anybody of anything. We weren't putting forward our own agenda. We were on this ride to sincerely listen to people. And by our listening, we hoped a work of profound depth would begin to take place in people's lives.

And right here was confirmation that it was happening.

— 30 —

KINDNESS

When I woke up at 5:30 a.m. on June 25, I felt horrible. Wes and Matt hadn't been getting along, and the whole team was on edge.

Matt had ridden faster than anyone yesterday, and we'd let him go ahead. Bicyclists do that when they're in groups. It's no big deal. He was fresh and strong, and he regularly rode all around Austin by himself. But yesterday he'd been separated from us for a couple of hours. A few of the team members had wondered if we should keep better tabs on him. Maybe we should go look for him. I shook my head. I knew he could find us again.

Wes was certainly one of those who wondered. And the previous night at dinner he had confronted Matt in front of everyone at his table. I wasn't there to witness it. But Matt was shaken by the talk, and later that night he came to our room to talk with Vela and me about what had transpired.

I knew Wes had only wanted to help. He was concerned about things running smoothly, especially when we were all so tired. In his heart, Wes was trying to protect me from any undue stress while we were on the road. Yet Matt hadn't been separated from us for so long on purpose. He'd taken a wrong turn, which caused a delay in rejoining the group. Now he wondered if he should head home.

Ugh, I thought when Matt explained all this to me. That kind of tension made my stomach churn. Having Matt go home was the last thing I wanted.

From my prone position in bed, I shook my head and half-shrugged at Matt. I didn't know what to do. I didn't want to solve this problem for him, and I knew he never wanted me to parent him, only to listen and give input if he asked. But I didn't have much steam to do either. We'd ridden more than 100 miles that day, and my tank was empty. But Matt and I talked a bit anyway, then he left to call his wife, my daughter. After that he went to talk to Wes to straighten things out, and they made peace.

When Matt came back into our room to sleep on a rollaway cot, it was well after 1:00 a.m. I heard him and wasn't able to fall back asleep afterward, still thinking about the tension of the day.

In the last year and a half, I could count the number of times on one hand I wasn't dead asleep by 1:00 a.m.

That morning in the parking lot, while I was getting my bike ready for the day's ride, I fell over. There was no real reason for it. I simply toppled over to one side, scraping my elbow. Maybe I was asleep on my feet.

My elbow started to bleed. A deep sigh escaped my lips. I just wanted to get on the road and finish this trip. I ignored the bleeding and hopped on my bike.

From Wytheville, Virginia, where we had spent the night, we started the ride toward Daleville, Virginia, with another 102 miles on the day's schedule and another 5,000 feet of elevation gain. The overcast sky cleared up quickly, but the fog in my head refused to clear. It seemed to take us forever just to get the first 30 miles in, and traffic backed up behind us on every curve or uphill stretch. I felt sick, and blood still trickled from my elbow. But I so wanted to go the distance.

We pulled off at a rest area for me to use the restroom. After I was finished and outside again, I looked around, found a shady spot, and struck up a conversation with Art and Lori, two likable young retirees traveling around in a motor home with a bike rack. Lori noticed at once that my elbow was still bloody from this morning's tumble. She asked if she could bandage it, but I drawled out a "Nah, I'll be okay." I don't know what I was thinking. I was a mess.

As the conversation progressed, I learned they were actually living in the vehicle. They had sold their house and given away most of their possessions, all with an aim of living simply. They'd been having a great time out on the road for the past thirteen months. This was a second marriage for both of them, and they hadn't been married to each other for very long.

We talked about the logistics of traveling for months at a time, things like how to get packages mailed to you out on the road, which we'd had experience with too. We talked about bike racing and how to keep training through winter months. They were passionate and peaceful people, strategically not in a hurry, open and conversant about many things. When it came to matters of faith, however, they seemed more reserved.

"Spirituality for us is focused more on nature, peace, and our family," Lori said. "I do yoga and love that type of meditating."

"We're not opposed to being churchgoing people," Art added. "Before we left on our trip, we talked about maybe finding a block of time on a Sunday morning when we're in a cool small town and dropping in on a church service, just to have the experience. We haven't yet gotten there, but it's something we're excited to do."

My gut still hurt. I was trying to be kind, but it's not as easy when you feel miserable. I remembered they'd said they'd been on the road for thirteen months. To me that sounded like ample time to find a cool small town with a church where they could drop in for a Sunday. But I bit my tongue instead of pointing that out. I genuinely liked this couple and didn't want to say anything to offend them.

"We both have traditional church backgrounds," Art continued. "We were baptized. I grew up Catholic. Lori grew up Southern Baptist. Separately, we were both Lutheran for a while. But it's a life-changing experience to go through a divorce. In a postdivorce life, you kind of come out the other side hoping for a rebirth. Our rebirth hasn't included church, even though our previous lives with our ex-spouses and kids did."

I asked them what they thought about Jesus. Lori didn't seem particularly happy to have been asked that question, although she said he was her Savior. Art said the definition wasn't static for him. "It's almost like the warm, fuzzy sensation of the house you grew up in—or the aunt and uncle who always loved you. I don't feel I need to have a specific sense of who Jesus is. But I'm thrilled to know there's a greater being out there."

Again I resisted the urge to jump in and willed myself to just keep listening.

Lori nodded. "We look at a lot of different religions and pick some of what we like from each. I know that sounds selfish. But there are a lot of religions that are great at any number of things, such as kindness and being positive toward the community."

Art described various kindnesses they'd encountered on the road. Once when it had been raining and the campgrounds were all full, they'd gone looking for a place to camp on a forest road. A stranger had let them park in his driveway. He'd found the perfect spot for them, helped them get settled, then returned thirty minutes later with fresh biscuits his wife had just baked. Art said that had really touched them.

The conversation was drawing to a close, but just before we said our good-byes, Lori offered to bandage my arm again. In a flash my mind weighed the story Art had just told and the many times Jesus had allowed people to care for him. It dawned on me that this was Lori's invitation of kindness to me. In many ways it was an act of faith.

This time I said yes.

Lori got out a first aid kit and cleaned and bandaged my arm. Her actions reflected true charity, and I saw at once that this divine appointment was not about me swooping into this couple's lives and doing a bunch of listening. It was about allowing them to minister to me. In receiving their gift, I was showing them respect.

Lori bandaging my arm was perhaps the most important part of our whole conversation. I wasn't called, even in my mind, to sort out where that gift of kindness came from. Perhaps it just came from the fact that they were made in God's image and reflected his character. All I knew was that I was called to accept the kindness. As Lori worked on my arm, I felt only gratitude and respect.

As I rode off, I battled with the question of whether I should have challenged them more. Yet I left with the peace that a second conversation could easily take place.

We rode another 20 miles, then stopped for lunch. By this time my stomach was a mishmash of hollowness and turbulence. It took us forever to be served, and I didn't feel much better after I had eaten. I tried to gut it out for another few miles after lunch, but nothing seemed to be working. Finally I stopped and asked the team to pray. They gathered around me and asked God to give me strength to keep going.

"Do you want to ride in the van?" Caroline asked when we were finished praying.

I looked around at the group. "I think I can ride another few miles," I said. We started riding again. After five miles, Caroline pulled next to me and asked how I was doing. I still didn't feel great, but I said, "Give me another five miles." She nodded.

That's how it went for a long while. Ride five miles. Check in. Five more miles. Check in. On and on this went. And slowly—very slowly—I started to feel better. Not conquer-the-world better. Just slightly better. Better enough to keep riding another stretch of five miles.

We kept going and going, and when we hit mile 80, I realized we only had 20 more miles to go. Maybe it was a mental trick. Maybe it was solely the power of prayer. Or maybe it was a combination of the two. But I knew then that I was going to finish the day's ride. I felt humbled by the kind support of the team.

We hit Daleville at the 100-mile mark and started riding through a neighborhood. There was only a mile or two left before we reached our motel. All of us looked exhausted. I was at the back of the line.

From the corner of my eye, I saw two women struggling to lift a couch off the back of a truck. One of them threw up her hands in frustration. It looked to me like they were not going to be able to get the couch off the truck and into the house.

I thought fast and shouted to the group ahead, "Hey guys, stop!"

We stopped. I offered to help them move their couch.

One of the women—I learned her name was Johnette—wore a baseball cap. Her hair was cropped closely above her ears. The other woman, Kelly, looked more traditionally feminine. They both had the same last name, and they introduced two beautiful little girls as their daughters.

Johnette looked suspicious at first and wondered aloud whether there was a catch to our offer to move their couch. We insisted there wasn't, and with their permission the team made short work of the job. I supervised. Standing around with my hands in my pockets was all I was good for by then.

Once the couch was in place, Johnette and Kelly offered us bottled water. I accepted, as did several of the team members. Then I asked if they would talk to me, and they agreed, although Johnette still appeared wary.

As I had guessed, they were a same-sex couple. Kelly was a nurse, and Johnette was a medical social worker. They had met at work. Both said that what mattered most to them was their daughters. The girls were biologically connected to Kelly, and they'd all been together as a family for the past three years.

"Just like you guys," Kelly said with a smile, motioning to the team, "I believe it's really important to take care of other people. I've been a nurse for over ten years, and my job is important to me in that respect, but there are other ways to help, like you guys helping move our couch. We're so appreciative of that."

Johnette nodded. Her demeanor remained somewhat hard, less trusting. "I've been at it for twenty-seven years, a medical social worker for my entire career. Wouldn't change a thing. I love what I do."

"Y'all are both caregivers," I said. "Thank you both for doing what you do."

After that moment of affirmation, I sensed more openness. The conversation shifted, and we talked about traveling and retirement. I wasn't there to make any judgments. I first wanted to be the ears of Jesus— listening to them, loving them.

Cautiously I brought up the matter of faith. "This is one of those things I've been deliberately asking people on this trip," I said, "knowing full well that it can sometimes be harder to talk about. But my goal is always to be curious, kind, and respectful. So I'm simply wondering what your thoughts are about faith and God, or however you might term it."

Kelly answered right away. "We both grew up in church, but in different denominations. Today we're not necessarily part of an organized religion. Yet we believe God can be with you anywhere. You can pray anywhere—in church or on the job. You can commune with God anywhere." She looked at their little girls. "We pray before our meals, and they say prayers before bedtime."

I smiled. "I'm curious—with growing up in church, was your experience good or not so good?"

"It was good," Kelly said. "At least, when I was younger."

Johnette's voice stayed edgy. "When church is the only thing you know, I guess it's a good experience. But then I went to college and started to meet different, you know, ethnic groups and stuff like that, that's when I made a firm decision that I didn't believe my parents' religion was suitable for me."

I nodded. "And if someone asked you today, 'What do you think about Jesus?' or 'Who is Jesus?' what would you say?"

Johnette spoke immediately. "Oh, I believe he exists."

"Definitely," Kelly added.

We talked a bit more about their experiences in church and what it was like to live as a same-sex couple in a small town. They said their community had been nothing but supportive. The more we talked, and the more I listened, the more the mood among us softened.

"Thank you so much for your help today with the couch," Kelly said as the conversation drew to a close. "I don't think there's enough gratitude and kindness in this world anymore."

"Yeah," Johnette said. "It was a genuine kindness that you stopped." Her voice sounded far softer than it had at the start of our conversation. She'd used that word, *kindness*, that had been in my mind all day in various forms.

"Well, thank y'all for having us here," I said, and looked at one of the little girls. She was sitting on the front porch steps and looking up at me with a big grin. Her eyes were shining. "It's really such a treat to meet you this evening at the end of our ride."

The little girl giggled. Kelly smiled. I looked at Johnette. This time she smiled too.

We took a few pictures. We said our good-byes. We all hugged. As we pedaled away I sensed within me a real joy in connecting with this couple. We could have our differences and still respect one another. I hoped they enjoyed being with me also.

As tired as I was, I also felt elated. I sensed a definite transition in the social landscape, a change to the American climate, albeit a small one. I hoped that change soon would soar.

I was truly living my dream, doing what I'd always hoped I could do—have deeper conversations in a divided culture. There was no anger in these conversations—not between the conversationalists anyway. There was no scorn or ridicule or name-calling. We were people from different backgrounds, with different ways of life, talking about Jesus.

Starting with love.

— 31 —

THE LISTENING ROAD

All that was left now was a quest to make it to the waters of the Atlantic, our finish line. Only three more days—but those three days would stretch our endurance even further. And today would be the hardest.

When I awoke on June 26 in Daleville, Virginia, a northern suburb of Roanoke, I felt depleted. As I lay still in bed, I whispered a prayer that came from the depths of weakness. It was the thirty-first day of the trip, and I felt too weary to approach one more person, too drained to focus on listening well. Yet if God wanted me to talk to people, I was still willing.

My specific prayer was that today any initiative for talking would come from strangers, not from me. That God would bring to me the exact people he wanted me to talk to. And that I wouldn't even need to approach people—that they would approach me.

Even after I prayed, I found it hard to release this request fully to the Lord. Old habits die hard. Our motel was only a few minutes from the Appalachian Trail, and the night before I'd seen some hikers in the lobby. I'd noticed one young man, laden with a rucksack, who'd had his foot in a black walking cast. When I saw him the next morning, I couldn't help but ask about his foot. And so the conversation started.

Evan was twenty-five, quiet in demeanor, reserved in conversational style. He'd been hiking the trail for fifty days, he explained, but an old running injury had come back to haunt him. So he'd seen a doctor, who'd set his foot in a cast.

"Everybody hurts," Evan said when I asked him how he was coping. He was talking about more than the physical. I heard an unmistakable pain in his voice, the wistfulness of unmet desires. He'd wanted his trip along the Appalachians to go one way, but now it was going another.

Evan indicated that he was rethinking much about his life, struggling with questions of pain and suffering. When you hope for one thing and life turns out differently, how do you process it? What does it all mean?

I started to open my mouth but stopped. I wanted to talk about the hope that's found in Jesus, a hope that does not disappoint, even when events and circumstances don't turn out as we plan. Yet I sensed that Evan and I weren't at that level of depth yet. I needed to listen more. So I asked, "Is there anything you need?"

Evan looked at me steadily for a long moment. His mind seemed to be going a thousand miles a minute. Tentatively he said, "I'd appreciate prayer."

That said everything. I prayed with Evan carefully, earnestly. I prayed for his foot to heal. I prayed that he would get to complete his dream of hiking the Appalachian Trail. And I prayed that through all of this he would move closer to Jesus.

We promised to stay in touch.

I spoke with one other person before we left for the day. Yuan had come to the United States from China in 2005, when he was sixteen. He'd started working in restaurants, had always dreamed of owning his own restaurant someday. And he had finally fulfilled his dream. The night before we'd actually eaten in his restaurant.

This morning Yuan and I talked about faith. He said he had none. But he'd been to a Christian church with friends, and he was open to reading religious texts. Christine, one of our support staff, spoke Chinese. She got Yuan's address and promised to send him a Chinese Bible after she got home.

Caroline, Wes, and I started riding—just the three of us today. Matt had returned home, and he'd left on friendly terms with everybody, including Wes. That was good. I so longed that we would all finish the trip well as a team. There was no question that we loved and respected one another. But the logistics of working together in close confines and being exhausted beyond what we had ever imagined had definitely stirred some tensions.

My second specific prayer of the day, sent up from my pedaling position as we rolled out, was for one good moment that united our team members before the trip ended. One particularly memorable moment that we could share in spirit. I didn't know what that moment might look like. Yet I wanted us to be able to look back on this trip when it was finished and say, "That encapsulated true togetherness."

I said amen as we finished the first five miles. Everything about my body felt rough. My legs churned out one stroke at a time. I couldn't seem to warm up, no matter what I did.

I glanced at Caroline. Her breathing was thick, yet she looked determined. She didn't feel great today, she'd told us earlier. I glanced at Wes. His chin was resolute, all energies focused on forward momentum.

Nobody wasted a breath. We rode another five miles. My back hurt. My legs ached. I felt so crummy, I wanted to quit for the day. But something kept me moving.

Today's route called for a ride through the Shenandoah Valley and the

Blue Ridge Mountains—only 75 miles total, but very hilly. We would be pedaling through the mountains much of the time, and toward the day's end we'd encounter the steepest grade of the entire trip—ten miles of sheer climbing with gradients of up to 17 percent. A 6 percent grade was considered steep.[1] I wasn't sure if anybody could go the distance today, much less me.

All morning we rode in the presence of pain and tiredness, with me checking in with Wes and Caroline every five miles. *Five miles at a time.* *Five miles at a time.* I continually willed myself to keep going. Everybody rode sluggishly, at times as if in slow motion.

At 1:00 p.m. we stopped in Lexington, Virginia, a town of about 7,000. Glenn parked the van in front of a restaurant. The sun beat down on us as we walked inside. I immediately looked for a chair, feeling my legs might collapse.

The hostess seated us outside on the balcony. As I sat in the shade of the awning, I glanced around, feeling tempted to look for people to talk with. But then I remembered my first prayer this morning—that God would bring people to me. I decided to shut up and eat.

The food arrived quickly. A delectable-looking club-style sandwich was plunked in front of me: ham, salami, swiss cheese, and three layers of fresh bread. For some time all I did was eat. As I finished up the last of my french fries, I heard a low sound. Somebody familiar was talking. But I glanced around the table and everybody was eating in silence.

I closed my eyes and listened more closely. There it was again. Nothing audible, yet I sensed a familiar nudging in my soul.

Do you truly believe that I am for you and not against you?[2] the Voice asked.

You know I do, Lord, I whispered in my mind.

Look for answers to your prayers today, God said. *Not to one prayer, but to both prayers.*

Both?

Both.

Our waitress stood at the table, asking about dessert. I opened my eyes.

"Nothing more, thanks," I said. "Just the check."

We finished up and walked outside. And my jaw dropped.

A group of people stood around the van, an entire crowd of strangers. They were looking at the wording on the side: "Conversations Coast to Coast." Pointing. Gesturing. Murmuring among themselves. The team gathered behind me just as a woman walked up with her young son, a quizzical look in her eye.

"What's this all about?" she asked us. "You're traveling around just talking to people? Will you talk with me?" Several others in the crowd looked our direction and nodded.

People were actually asking to talk.

The team and I fanned out and went to work. I started talking with the woman and her son. Out of the corner of my eye, I saw Caroline and Wes each talking to somebody else. Glenn had another conversation going, and Vela and Judy were talking to yet another person.

The sign on the van had acted like a magnet. These weren't bystanders whom I'd approached. Each person had a stake in the initiating.

Amanda talked to me about her mom's suicide and how her entire family was still reeling. Jesus' words came to my mind and mouth, and I told her that he'd come for the lost and the broken. That the Bible says those who are well don't need a physician, but those who are in need of healing and restoration do.[3]

Randall, a young Inuit man from Alaska, said he had his life charted out in a series of stepping-stones. He was a cook now, in school, with plans to become first a base welder, then an underwater welder. He wanted to retire at age fifty, then buy a motorcycle and travel around the United States. He described himself as spiritual but not religious. "I've become more of a thinker than a believer," he said. "But I'm very open to discovery." I encouraged him to read the stories of Jesus from the Bible. He said he would.

Wes talked with a young woman named Kayla for a long time. Her parents were divorced, she'd recently lost a close friend, and she struggled with depression. She hadn't been able to afford college, but out of the blue someone had given her a generous gift, enough for school. There she'd connected with strong Christians who helped her look for answers and eventually start walking the road to faith. Kayla asked Wes lots of questions about who God was and what he was all about.

Conversation after conversation played out in front of that restaurant. As soon as I finished talking with one person, another person was waiting. We heard about passion and adventure and loss and heartache. We heard from people who had strong faith and from those who had none. We heard from people somewhere in between. And because the people in this crowd had initiated the conversations, I felt more freedom to ask follow-up questions, to dig deeper, to communicate more freely about the person and work of Christ.

At last, after more than an hour outside the restaurant in Lexington, the conversations finished up. People drifted away, and Wes, Caroline, and I prepped our bikes to keep riding.

There it was again. The familiar sound. I listened closely.

That's the answer to your first prayer, I sensed God saying. *But I'm not done yet. Do you truly believe that I am for you and not against you?*

I grinned, nodded, and kept riding.

The road climbed gradually for many hours. Then late in the afternoon we passed mile 50, and the road started to climb in earnest.

At first it didn't seem so hard. Five miles went by. Ten miles. We stayed together.

Ten more miles to go, and the grade took off like a rocket ship. The road narrowed. The trees closed in above us. The track before us shot almost straight up.

This was it. The hardest part of the entire trip.

Caroline began struggling immediately. We pulled over and checked in with her. She'd thrown up an hour earlier and still wasn't feeling great.

She insisted we go on ahead. Riders will do that on a hill. You're all in a group on the flats. You stay close together to draft. But on the steepest of hills, each rider faces an individual battle.

Wes and I nodded and started pedaling again. I glanced backward and saw Caroline waiting for the van that Glenn was driving. (He, Judy, and Vela had gone to buy ice.) The other support vehicle followed Wes and me.

Sweat soon soaked me. These were the steepest hills we'd tackled on this entire trip. Wes felt it too; his breathing came out rough. Wes led for a while. Each stroke of our pedals was a major effort. We cranked and cranked.

I saw Wes toss his loaded water bottle to the side of the road, knowing a team member would pick it up later. A water bottle doesn't weigh much, but riders will toss anything in an effort to shed weight.

Every muscle ached. Every car that came down the hill smelled like burning brakes. Wes slowed, and I passed him.

Ten minutes went by.

Twenty minutes.

Thirty minutes.

We kept climbing straight up.

At the thirty-five-minute mark, I could just make out a campground ahead—our destination for the night. I saw cabins and a store and a tiny lake with a split rail fence around it.

Wes and I rode to the crest of the hill and into a clearing. The terrain leveled out at last. We pulled over by the store, stopped, and let out a long whoop. After thirty-five minutes of absolute agony, we had made it.

"Man, we are flatlanders for sure," Wes said with a wry chuckle.

"I know what you mean." I patted him on the shoulder and wheeled my bike into the shade.

So many emotions rushed at me. Elation. Relief. Gratitude. Pride. We'd finished the hardest day of the trip. Yet there was a twinge of sorrow, too, that Caroline wasn't there to taste this last victory with us. She had been such a trooper.

My hunger reared its head again and nearly eclipsed my concern about Caroline. An ice cream bar sounded good to me, and this little store would surely stock them.

When I emerged from the store, I sat on a bench to enjoy my snack. Wes was checking his bike thirty yards away, where he'd wheeled it underneath the lakeside trees. Both of us were quiet, lost in our milieu of emotions.

I almost didn't see her when she first crested the hill, small against the far line of trees. Then I rubbed my eyes in disbelief as she drew closer. Caroline had ridden her bike up the steepest portion of the route. Wes and I had thought she'd stopped for good when we'd last seen her. But she'd only paused to catch her breath—and to tell herself to keep going no matter the cost.

Caroline rode into the clearing. From my vantage point on the bench, I witnessed the entire scene unfold before me.

She saw Wes first. He was shaking his head with sheer admiration. She came to a stop near him and stayed on her bike but slid off her seat, her feet firmly planted on the top of the hill. Wes took a few steps forward and enfolded her in a warm embrace. Caroline burst into tears and wrapped her arms around his back. I found my bearings and started jogging toward them.

"Hoo, man—who's not an athlete?" Wes exclaimed. "Do you have any idea how steep that was? I'm so proud of you! So proud. You didn't quit."

Caroline sobbed in his arms. Wes cried too. For a moment I stopped and watched them, tears flowing down my face. I simply drank in this moment of glory. We were athletes, warriors, travelers, conversationalists. All three of us had made it to the top and had listened on this road. The challenges and difficulties we faced had propelled us forward. We had succeeded—and succeeded in unity.

Wes and Caroline let go and straightened up, dried their tears, and started to chuckle. Caroline reached behind her to her pack and pulled out Wes's water bottle.

"I thought you could use this," she said.

Wes laughed. "You picked it up and carried it?"

"It gave me purpose," Caroline said with a shrug. She hadn't even emptied out the bottle. It was still full.

Now it was my turn to hug Caroline and congratulate her. I hugged Wes, too, and he hugged me back. We all let out a whoop. A nearby bench beckoned, and the three of us walked over and sat by the cool of the lake. I was still holding the wrapper to my snack.

"You had ice cream without us?" Caroline gave me a playful splash from her water bottle.

"Well, um, I didn't know if you liked that flavor," I said with a grin as the van drove up near us and parked. Glenn, Judy, and Vela had followed Caroline the last ten miles.

"Glenn," I called. "Hey, would you get us three more ice creams, please?" I showed him the wrapper I was holding. I knew very well that Caroline liked that flavor.

Glenn laughed. A few moments later he emerged from the store, ice creams in hand, and brought them over. Wes, Caroline, and I slid off the wrappers in unison and bit into the bars, the act as triumphant as popping a cork and spraying champagne into the air. The entire team had worked so hard. Each person had sacrificed something to take this trip. The whole team shared this victory.

God is always for us, I thought, as we stared at the lake in contented exhaustion. *Every sunset. Every steep mountain climb. Every long stretch of majestic flatland. He is for us, not against us. He blankets each day with an invitation to goodness. Everybody receives this invitation, and all are welcome to feast at his table.*

"We will always remember this moment," Wes said.

"It's already my favorite memory," Caroline murmured.

There was the low sound again. I inclined my ear. One good moment that the team could share in spirit.

Amen, said the Voice.

— 32 —

DESPERATE
DEPENDENCE, AGAIN

It would take two more days of hard riding before we reached the ocean. Today, June 27, we would ride about 100 miles from our cabins at the top of the steep hill near Montebello, Virginia, to the town of Fredericksburg. And the final day, June 28, we'd go 88 miles from Fredericksburg to Annapolis, Maryland.

I rose early and began the morning by giving thanks to God for everything he'd done on this trip. I knew we would not be where we were without him. But it was a short prayer time because even my attention span felt depleted. In spite of all the triumphs we'd experienced lately, I was running on fumes. It seemed like I was nearing closure—in the miles, in my strength, in my emotions. Even my spirit was tying things up.

The team had come together well. I'd had plenty of conversations. I just wanted the next two days to be incident free. But I had a gnawing sensation in my gut. If I'd learned anything on this trip, it was that nothing happens according to plan when you're riding cross-country on a bike.

We didn't have any food with us for breakfast, so we drove down the mountain and along the Blue Ridge Parkway to the nearest town. The scenery was crazy beautiful outside the van window, although I felt trapped inside. I so wanted to be out on my bike.

We found nowhere to eat in that town, so we drove to the next one, where we found a pancake house. I was hungry and already a bit grumpy. The service was slow. The restaurant's air conditioner must have been stuck on "freezing," because it was about fifty degrees inside. Our poor waitress wore a sweater. Her nose was red.

We didn't leave the restaurant and get on our bikes until 10:00 a.m. That was half our morning's ride—shot.

The road was scenic for the first bit, with lots of rolling hills and blue mountain vistas in the distance. But soon enough we went from shady roads to boiling sun. The temperature heated up and didn't stop climbing until it hit one hundred degrees. An hour later we stopped at the entrance to Lake Anna State Park to get water. We soaked cloths and placed them under our helmets to help cool down.

In the afternoon, as we rode through a neighborhood, I spotted a Black woman sitting on the front porch of her house with a dog. Out of reflex I stopped, introduced myself, and asked if she wanted to talk.

She shook her head at first. Too busy. Then she started chatting, and I started chatting, and pretty soon Tamika was telling me stories about her travels and career.

She said she had a master's degree in social work and a job at a school for special-needs kids. Her boss was a White female, and during a season of conflict Tamika had felt unsupported and discriminated against. Her voice rose as she told me the story.

"Wow, I'm feeling some heat here," I said, just to acknowledge her feelings. But what I meant apparently didn't come across to her because she retorted, "How would you feel if you experienced racism like that?!" And boom, we were in it.

I took a breath and tried to own that corporate sin. "Tamika," I said,

"I'm so sorry you experienced that from someone like me. Please for-give me."

She paused, took a breath, and said in a voice that had lost its edge, "Yes, I will." The heat dialed down, and she poured out more of her story.

We talked for a good ten minutes, and it sounded like things were coming to a close. Then Tamika, who'd been too busy to talk at first, asked, "Do you have time for one more story?" I nodded, and she talked another fifteen minutes.

I couldn't help but chuckle to myself. This was something I'd seen more than once on this trip. People were sometimes reluctant to talk. But once they sensed we truly wanted to listen, they could talk all day. We ended with smiles and a high five.

Caroline, Wes, and I kept riding, pedaling at a good pace on a two-lane road with a steep ditch beside it. We rode single file with Wes in front, Caroline next, and me bringing up the rear.

Just a few minutes down the road, Wes slowed slightly. When Wes slowed, Caroline slowed too. But I wasn't paying attention and clipped the back of Caroline's wheel with my front tire. She stayed upright, fortu-nately, but I wasn't so lucky. The contact caused me to swerve slightly, and my front tire left the pavement. I lurched into the ditch, my bike picking up speed.

My front tire hit a rut and stopped fast. The rest of the bike—with me on it—careened end over end. I hit the ground, tucked and rolled, and landed with my face in the weeds.

A driver stopped his car and shouted, "Hey! Do you need an ambu-lance?" That's how bad it looked.

Slowly I stood up. I shook myself, stared at the driver, and managed a wan smile. "No thanks," I said. "That's a little trick I do all the time."

The line didn't come out as funny as I'd hoped. He shook his head and drove off.

The team gathered around me and dusted me off. My right wrist shouted with pain. My left shoulder hurt, too, and would soon bruise up. That shoulder still ached from my crash before the start of the trip.

At first I wondered if my bike would be rideable. Then I saw that the frame had been scraped, but the bike seemed otherwise okay. I climbed back on and started to ride, only to find that I couldn't use my right gear shifter because of my injured wrist. Any movement of the fingers on that hand sent bolts of pain up my arm.

We kept riding anyway. The day's relentless heat and the stream of setbacks weighed on us, and the pace slowed even further. We were thirsty and hot, and it seemed like we could never drink enough. My head and shoulder both throbbed. My wrist screamed. All I wanted was for the day to be over.

Finally we reached our motel in Fredericksburg. We went out for dinner. Back in my motel room, I tried to process the day as I soaked my wrist and shoulder in Epsom salts.

The last leg of the trip was set for tomorrow. The end was so close, and my feelings were so mixed. I had loved taking this trip so much. It was the culmination of a dream, the trip of a lifetime. But as I turned in for the night, I admitted to myself that I was desperate for it to be completed. Could I actually make it through the final ride tomorrow, all the way to the finish line?

At 6:40 a.m. on June 28 the entire team was actually up, showered, dressed, and ready to leave on time. It was amazing. Even the vans were packed. And a McDonald's sat right across from our motel, so we wouldn't have to go anywhere for breakfast. But when we walked across the street and tried the front door, we found it was locked. It turned out the manager hadn't shown up to work that morning.

We tried to laugh about it and walked a block down the street to a diner. Service was slow there, and the dialogue sounded tense between our server and another server. After we had eaten and paid, I said to our server, "Hey, we're going to leave now, but before we do, how can we pray for you?"

She choked up, and I could see mist coming to her eyes. She talked about struggling with finances and about an upcoming court appointment. We gave her a generous tip, promised to pray for her, and were on our way. It was another good reminder that everybody has a story, everybody needs a listening ear.

Wes, Caroline, and I climbed on our bikes. This last ride of the trip immediately proved to be difficult. We took a number of wrong turns. I ached all over. The day was hot, and sweat poured off us. Wes had a flat. Lunch took forever. Daylight was burning. Then after lunch we took a bike path that separated us from the vans, and it took thirty minutes for us to find one another again.

When we reached the outskirts of Washington, DC, the traffic became epic. We rode into the city and passed the Pentagon. One of our support vehicles got pulled over because they were filming out of the window. They had no idea they couldn't film in that area.

I knew this ride would be a battle to the very end. But today it felt like absolutely nothing was coming together.

We rode on toward Annapolis and hit more traffic. Motorists honked at us and made obscene gestures. At one point we had to ride down a six-lane highway.

We hit a blighted urban area and rode through a neighborhood that looked really rough. We passed two men in an argument, their faces six inches away from each other, shouting, ready to fight. I briefly considered calling 911 but kept going.

We pedaled on, and the sky clouded over. Wes's flat tire had been fixed, but he kept having mechanical problems with his hub, the central part of a wheel. With 40 miles to go, his back wheel locked up completely and wouldn't turn. Our forward progress ground to a halt. Thankfully, Wes was able to swap out his back wheel, and we kept going.

By late afternoon it took all my effort to concentrate on the road ahead. We seemed so close to our finish, yet still so far away. The roads narrowed to two lanes in each direction, then to one. My wrist, shoulder, and stomach ached. I needed a restroom.

We stopped at a strip mall and downed some Mexican food for a snack. I went to the bathroom and looked in the mirror. My face looked like a piece of driftwood. I couldn't focus. I couldn't think. I just wanted to lie down. There was no way I could effectively engage anyone in another conversation.

Outside the restroom Judy was talking with someone, and she beckoned me over, but I shook my head. I just couldn't do it. That was a lesson for me right there. Sometimes conversations need to be put off until a better time.

Outside the restaurant I climbed back on my bike by sheer force of will. Wes looked haggard. Caroline wasn't saying anything. We started pedaling.

The air became misty and gray. A storm was rolling in. Then we started to hit hills. One right after another. Constant hills. Nothing but hills.

With 30 miles to go, my right hamstring cramped up. We'd been riding for thirty-three days, and my legs hadn't cramped at all until today. My cycling cleats were clipped into my pedals, so I unclipped my right foot and started pedaling with only my left leg. I went over a few hills that way, and that helped the pain a bit, so I clipped back in.

We hit another hill. And another. And another. My hamstring cramped up again, and I tried to sit far up toward the front of my seat, hoping I could use the force of my quadriceps instead of my hamstrings to turn the cranks. Then a large hill loomed in front of us. I shook my head and slowed.

Wes rode up next to me. "You okay?"

I couldn't utter a word. I was completely out of gas—physically, mentally, emotionally, even spiritually. There was no way I could get up this hill.

Wes discerned what was going on right away. "Maybe," he said, "God wants to make sure you cross the finish line knowing who's God."

I nodded and slowed even more.

"And it's not me either." Wes's voice was raspy. He was beat tired himself. "But c'mon, let's get you to the top."

He put his hand on my lower back, the both of us still on our bikes, and began to push me along. I sputtered a sound something like a sob and pushed down weakly on a pedal. Wes had been a strong, loyal teammate throughout this grueling trip, even with the occasional tension between us. And now, at the end, he was still there for me. He had one final reserve of power, and he was using it to help me go forward.

I broke down and started to weep. Wes kept pushing. We both kept pedaling. He pushed me over the final two hills.

The smell of salt lay in the air. We were so close to the sea. But then the wind whipped up, and the rain began. With five miles to go, we stopped, donned rain gear, and kept pedaling.

I counted down the miles on my trip computer. Four miles to go. Three miles. Two miles. One.

I'd had this image of us all riding to the ocean in triumph. But as we rode toward the marina that would be our final destination, nothing I saw was as I'd imagined. With 100 yards to go we passed a restaurant, and I spotted some familiar faces outside—then a few more ahead, down by the water. Friends and folks from our church had come to cheer us on our last push. Caroline's parents were there, and other dear people who wanted to celebrate our arrival.

We pedaled onto the pier. Boats and yachts spread out before us. Seagulls flew overhead.

Everybody clapped for us on the last fifty yards. Twenty-five. Ten. Five. One.

I put on my brakes. Wes, Caroline, and I rolled to a stop. We had done it. The trip was over.

And I felt miserable.

We managed to smile for a picture or two, but peace hovered somewhere far from me. We stood near the pier pilings and dipped our hands into the Atlantic Ocean. People gathered around with their umbrellas as the rain continued to fall.

I tried to make a bit of a speech. I'm not sure what I said. Wes stood on my right, and Caroline stood on my left. On behalf of the team, I thanked everybody for being there, for helping to make this possible, and then I shut up. That seemed the most sensible thing to do, considering how I felt.

I knew God wanted us to trust him every minute of every day, and I remembered how at our church we talked about "the joy of desperate dependence." I was definitely feeling desperate. And dependent. But I didn't feel much joy—not yet anyway.

I hugged Caroline and Wes. I hugged the rest of the team members. Vela and I kissed. The wind blew. The rain fell on us. Our long ride was finished at last.

After we'd packed the bikes on the van at the pier, Caroline's parents took us to a nearby boat, where they'd set up a dinner for us. Fresh grilled salmon. Delicious shrimp tacos. Delectable crab cakes. It was a real feast. Yet all in all, the day hadn't felt very triumphant to me.

As I pushed back from my dinner plate and looked out across the boats in the harbor, I knew we had just one more day together as a team. Tomorrow we'd be packing the vans, mailing packages of equipment home, heading to the airport. No riding. Just going home.

One final prayer slid silently from my soul.

Lord God, thank you for seeing us through to the end. I feel so utterly and desperately dependent on you. Please, now, if I can make one final request: let me sense your joy.

— 33 —

SPACES OF GRACE

Vela and I spent the night at the home of the man who'd led me to the Lord. We washed clothes, took hot showers, and lay down in a good bed by the grace of God. I had finished the ride feeling so low, but I was still hanging on to the words of Jesus: "My strength is made perfect in weakness."[1]

The next morning I got up early as usual. I puttered around for fifteen minutes or so, then I went back to bed and slept for another hour. It was Saturday, June 29. Tomorrow was Sunday, and I was scheduled to preach at our church back in Dallas. I didn't know what I was going to say, but I figured I could study on the plane. I had so many thoughts surging within me.

The plan was for Glenn and Judy to drive the van back home to Texas, making a detour to Colorado on the way to visit their kids. Wes and Jeff would drive the other support vehicle home. The rest of the team would fly.

After breakfast we packed and stuffed and stowed and boxed up things for mailing. With a few hours to spare before our flight, Vela and I drove into downtown Washington, DC, and stopped at the National Mall, the huge landscaped park that houses the Lincoln Memorial, the Washington Monument, and the United States Capitol grounds. Surrounding the mall are any number of museums, art galleries, memorials, sculptures, and statues.

As I strolled the sidewalks of the National Mall, I thought back over the trip and considered what we'd just accomplished.

We had logged nearly 3,000 miles on our bikes, all the way from the Santa Monica Pier in California to the Annapolis Pier in Maryland. We had made it all across America. Coast to coast.

We had also recorded at least 116 conversations with people from all walks of life: mechanics, young families, seniors, truckers, college students, fishermen, bikers, Native Americans, African Americans, a bartender, a retired admiral, a couple from Armenia, a hotel owner, a descendant of Daniel Boone, restaurant managers, farmers, a sheriff's deputy, men at a Bible study, Amish farmers, hikers, single moms, a cake decorator, a ferry owner, a family selling puppies, pastors, a newspaperman, cowboys, a same-sex couple, and so many more.

The people we had talked with came from every persuasion imaginable: Republicans, Democrats, independent thinkers, Christians, Jews, Muslims, Sikhs, Buddhists, atheists, agnostics, seekers, dreamers, hopers. We had talked courteously, kindly, and respectfully—without arguing—about things that are often so divisive. Politics. Passions. Race. Hopes. Faith. Jesus.

We had stayed in thirty-one different places, including historic Route 66 motels, state parks, a wigwam motel, a Shaker village, a railway car, KOA cabins, B&Bs, camps, a lake house, a ranch house, inexpensive chain hotels, and an Indian lodge.

We had ridden through deserts, mountains, flooded riverbanks, cities, farmland, and many small towns.

We had seen some crazy things along the road: turtles, old recliners, a town swarming with wild donkeys. We had dodged deer. Explored caves.

Patched tires. Received gifts. And then there was that day we had counted all the people who waved at us—245 in a single day. It would take a while before any of us could process all we had seen and felt.

I noticed a man and his children walking in the shadow of the Washington Monument. As I got closer I could hear him describing to his two young children the advantages of this country, and I couldn't help myself. I walked up, introduced myself, and struck up a conversation. He had emigrated from India, and even with all the messy stuff going on in America, he enthused about how much he loved this country. The conversation slipped into matters of faith, and once again I found myself in a surprisingly deep conversation. Although we didn't agree on all things, I simply listened, allowing spaces of grace to form around his words.

After the man and his children said their good-byes, I watched them for a moment. This final conversation had felt like the answer to my prayers, a high point to end on, and suddenly I found my soul lifting.

The conversations aren't going to stop, I thought. *This is what we came on this trip to do. And this is what we're going to keep doing once we get home.*

As exhausted as I was, I felt deep satisfaction in completing the dream that had gripped me for eighteen years. We had done it. We had taken the trip and dived into deep conversations with strangers from coast to coast.

We had listened.

And the conversations were just beginning.

ACKNOWLEDGMENTS

Northwest Bible Church—I want to thank you for embracing a really big vision of having thousands of surprisingly easy-to-start conversations about Jesus all over our city. Your willingness to embrace this vision challenged me to make this eighteen-year dream a reality.

Vela, my wife—I can't thank you enough for braving these crazy adventures with me.

Reese and Katie—Thank you for the amazing way you bring out the best in others.

Wes and Caroline—Thank you for riding across the country with me, even on days when all of us were on the edge, relationally, emotionally, and spiritually.

Sheree, my daughter—Thank you for coaching and training me.

The Conversations Coast to Coast team—This would not have happened apart from you. Thank you for investing your time, energy, and resources. Paul, Jeff, Jon, Judy, Glen, Muna, Sarah, Joy, Christine, James, John, Kris, Melissa, and all the people who joined me for parts of the ride along the way.

My supporters—Thank you for investing financially in Conversations Coast to Coast.

And final thanks to my writing partner, Marcus Brotherton; agent, Rick Richter at Aevitas Creative Management; and Jessica Wong and the team at Thomas Nelson.

NOTES

Chapter 4: Riding with Pain
  1. Luke 15:11–32.

Chapter 5: A Listening Presence
  1. John 11:33, 38 NIV.
  2. John 11:35.

Chapter 6: Friendship Despite Differences
  1. John 14:6.
  2. Mike wasn't entirely correct about this statistic, but I left his words the
     way he said them. According to recent Pew Research Center reports,
     about 26 percent of the American population now identify as irreligious,
     meaning without a religious affiliation, and this trend is on the rise. This
     may have been the statistic Mike was thinking of. Yet the percentage
     of Americans who identify specifically as atheist, meaning they don't
     believe in God whatsoever, is much lower, only about 4 percent of the US
     population. About 5 percent of Americans claim to be agnostic, meaning
     they don't know if there is a God. And 17 percent describe their religion
     as "nothing in particular." The stats on atheism and agnosticism have
     remained relatively flat for the past two decades. For more information
     about the Pew study, see "In U.S., Decline of Christianity Continues
     at Rapid Pace," Pew Research Center: Religion and Public Life,

October 17, 2019, https://www.pewforum.org/2019/10/17/in-u-s
-decline-of-christianity-continues-at-rapid-pace/. For a broader
overview and information on other studies, visit Wikipedia, s.v.
"Irreligion in the United States," last modified November 26, 2020,
https://en.wikipedia.org/wiki/Irreligion_in_the_United
_States and Wikipedia, s.v. "Atheism in the United States," last modified
September 14, 2020, https://en.wikipedia.org/wiki
/Atheism_in_the_United_States.

Chapter 8: Pursuing Truth and Beauty

1. Matthew 4:19.
2. I found it intriguing that Sasha, who professed not to have any faith, was
   alluding to Matthew 10:30 and Luke 12:7.
3. John 8:32.
4. Leon Wall and William Morgan, *Navajo-English Dictionary* (Window Rock,
   AZ: Navajo Agency Branch of Education, 1958), s.v. "bilagáana," https://
   digscholarship.unco.edu/cgi/viewcontent.cgi?article=1000&context
   =navajo.

Chapter 9: Sparking a New Dialogue

1. Ephesians 2:8–10.

Chapter 10: Gentleness and Respect

1. Matthew 5:3.
2. Ephesians 2:8–9.
3. 1 Peter 3:15.

Chapter 12: The Greater Win

1. Amy Bleuel, *Project Semicolon: Your Story Isn't Over* (New York:
   HarperCollins, 2017).

Chapter 13: Openness and Hope

1. Jim was technically correct about this statistic as a reflection of average
   lifespan. Yet according to journalist and author Amanda Ruggeri, an
   authority on ancient Rome, this statistic should be contextualized alongside
   the high infant mortality rates. Up to half of all children in ancient Rome died
   before age ten. If you lived beyond that, you could expect to live into your
   forties and fifties and, in rarer instances, into your sixties and seventies. So

it's not that people typically died at age thirty-five. See Amanda Ruggeri, "Correct Your Tour Guide: Two Major Myths About Ancient Romans," *Revealed Rome* (blog), June 21, 2012, https://revealedrome.com/2012/06 /ancient-rome-daily-life-women-age/.

Chapter 15: Going the Distance

1. A number of colorful variations of this story exist. See Clay Coppedge, "A Bald-Headed Whiskey Town," Letters from Central Texas, *Texas Escapes* (online magazine), January 3, 2017, http://www.texasescapes.com /ClayCoppedge/Bald-Headed-Whiskey-Town.htm.

Chapter 20: Day by Day

1. Galatians 5:22.
2. Ephesians 3:19 ESV.
3. Ted Loder, *Guerillas of Grace: Prayers for the Battle*, 20th anniversary ed. (Minneapolis, MN: Augsberg Fortress, 2005), 76.
4. Lamentations 3:22–23.

Chapter 21: The Value of Every Interaction

1. Psalm 131:1–2 ESV.
2. John 14:6.

Chapter 22: Expect the Unexpected

1. John 14:6.

Chapter 23: Meeting People Where They Are

1. Zack is entitled to his beliefs of course, yet regarding proof of the existence of God, any number of today's top researchers disagree. For instance, many faith-based thinkers, professors, and philosophers have done extensive research into the existence of God. They conclude that there is strong philosophic and scientific—not to mention theological—evidence for believing in what they describe as a personality-based "primary first cause" of the universe—that is, God. For starters, see the works of Dr. William Lane Craig (*Does God Exist?*) or Dr. J. P. Moreland (*Scaling the Secular City*). The field of secular research into the existence of God is equally fascinating. Leading neuroscientist Dr. Jay Lombard, who is not a Christian, argues from a scientific perspective for the existence of God in his book *The Mind of God: Neuroscience, Faith, and a Search for the Soul* (New York: Harmony Books, 2017).

Chapter 25: Simple, Clear Priorities

1. Bucksnort was actually the original name of the town of Sonora, Kentucky, current population 475. It was a railroad town, and apparently some folks thought those early locomotives sounded like the sound of a deer snorting. The name was changed to Sonora in 1859. See Robert M. Rennick, *Kentucky Place Names* (Lexington, KY: University Press of Kentucky, 1984), s.v. "Sonora."

2. Matthew 6:34.

Chapter 29: This. Here. Now.

1. Deuteronomy 33:25 ESV.

2. Philippians 4:7 ESV, paraphrased.

Chapter 31: The Listening Road

1. *A Policy on Geometric Design of Highways and Streets*, 4th ed. (Washington, DC: American Association of State Highway and Transportation Officials, 2001), 507, 510, 556, https://law.resource.org/pub/us/cfr/ibr/001/aashto.green.2001.pdf#page=556.

2. Isaiah 41:10; Romans 8:31.

3. Matthew 9:12; Mark 2:17.

Chapter 33: Spaces of Grace

1. 2 Corinthians 12:9 NKJV.

ABOUT THE AUTHOR

NEIL TOMBA is a graduate of Dallas Theological Seminary and the senior pastor of Northwest Bible Church in Dallas, Texas, a position he's held since 2001. He and his wife, Vela, have three daughters, two sons-in-law, and two grandchildren. This is his first book.

NeilTomba.com